THE DAY TRADERS

THE DAY TRADERS

The Untold Story of the Extreme Investors and How They Changed Wall Street Forever

Gregory J. Millman

TIMES BUSINESS

RANDOM HOUSE

For James S. Millman
"Par nobile fratrum" (Horace)

All rights reserved under International and Pan-American Copyright Conventions.
Published in the United States by Times Books, a division of Random House, Inc.,
New York, and simultaneously in Canada by Random House of Canada Limited, Toronto.

Library of Congress Cataloging-in-Publication Data

Millman, Gregory J.
    The day traders : the untold story of the extreme investors and how they changed
Wall Street forever / Gregory J. Millman. — 1st ed.
        p.   cm.
    ISBN 0-8129-3186-6
    1. Electronic trading of securities.   2. Stocks—Data processing.
I. Title.
HG4515.95.M55   1999
332.64′0285—dc21   99-16466

Random House website address: www.randomhouse.com

Printed in the United States of America on acid-free paper

98765432

First Edition

Book design by H. Roberts Design

Contents

Introduction

T his book is about making money the old-fashioned way: by exploiting the disintegration of an old order. The old order is the system of regulations, agreements, and understandings that has governed the world's capital markets since the 1930s. The designers of that system had hoped to tame the animal spirits of market speculation that they blamed for the crash of 1929 by establishing what amounted to a government-sponsored information cartel. Now, new technology is breaking the cartel, and the animal spirits are running wild again. The old order isn't going down without a fight. But it is going down. And there is money to be made in its collapse.

Day traders, a.k.a. Extreme Investors, try to outsmart and outmaneuver professionals at the biggest Wall Street, Frankfurt, London, and Tokyo financial institutions by placing smarter, faster bets on second-to-second changes in stock, futures, and derivative prices. The professionals are typically equipped with advanced degrees in financial economics, hundreds of millions of dollars' worth of computer hardware and software, and privileged access to information about the flow of orders through the market. By contrast, many people joining the day-trading gold rush know little about how the financial system works; they have spent their lives playing video games, arranging flowers, cutting hair, racing cars, selling insurance, nursing, lawyering, accounting—whatever—and turn to trading for a change. Most know from the outset that the odds against success are high. But playing this tough game against these tough odds beats the ho-hum humdrum of ordinary jobs and lives—and there's always a chance that if they do everything right, they can beat the odds. This is the message repeatedly reinforced in day-trading training courses, how-to books, and Internet chat rooms. The prosperity of the business depends on people believing that they can pit themselves against the best professional traders at the biggest Wall Street houses—and win.

Sometimes they can. Professors Jeffrey H. Harris and Paul H. Schultz of Notre Dame studied the performance of day traders and found that "unusually fast or skillful traders" can beat the pros. But successful day trading demands intense focus and discipline, a keen mind, fast reflexes, and capital. And day-trading firms rarely turn away anyone who lacks these requirements. The game is open to everyone. If aspiring day traders don't have enough capital, brokers often suggest that they borrow it.

It remains to be seen whether a new regulation requiring firms to screen prospective day traders will make any practical difference in who is allowed to trade. The day-trading firms have a powerful economic incentive to keep the game as open as possible, because they make their money charging commissions on trades. Attorneys for Momentum Securities, one of the leading day-trading brokerages, claimed in court papers that many of the firm's customers traded from one to three hundred times per day, and that because Momentum charged fifteen dollars commission for each trade, a single customer could generate forty-five hundred dollars in commission revenues each day. This is not out of line with other day-trading firms.

Trading this frequently does not allow much time for analysis and reflection, but day trading is not about analysis and reflection.

Most day traders but not all are young; most but not all are male. Some seek in the Extreme Investor's game a unique opportunity to prove themselves as men. Testing for old male virtues of strength, speed, and courage used to be a part of every boy's passage into manhood. But in a world without lions and battles, where even wars are fought by remote control, how does a boy prove himself a man? Those who try themselves against the market confront adrenaline-pumping challenges that sometimes prove fatal—literally, not just in financial terms. Training programs teach aspiring day traders to react instinctively, because thinking interferes with success—when the market is moving, thinking means missing opportunities. People who trade a hundred times a day without thinking may be expected to lose money, and neophyte day traders are told to expect losses as part of the learning curve.

But one psychologist who treats many day traders says that the game is pathologically addictive. Training programs suggest it will take three to six months of losing before traders come up the learning curve and begin to win. By then, many are hooked. They trade as long as their money holds out, and when the money goes, hope often goes, too. Sometimes the consequences are fatal.

In August 1999, a day trader in Atlanta wrote a note promising to kill "people who greedily sought my destruction," launched a shooting spree in two day-trading brokerage firms where he had reportedly lost over a hundred thousand dollars, then killed himself. Mark O. Barton's case was uniquely horrible. But in a year of reporting and writing this book, I learned of other suicides by day traders.

Universal access to real-time market information and powerful trading technology mean that day trading cannot be stopped. Indeed, there are sound economic reasons why it should not be. Day trading has made markets more efficient and changed Wall Street forever by giving rise to new, online exchanges. More efficient markets have in turn made successful day trading even more difficult. It is an extreme financial sport, offering danger to all who try it, and limitless rewards to the few who succeed.

This book is divided into six major parts.

Part One, "The Gold Rush," introduces the patriarchs and prophets of modern day trading and then takes readers behind the scenes—into the training programs and onto the trading floors where novices learn to read the market, recognize where prices are going, and make trades that make money. It presents the bluff and parry of a high-stakes game that pits Wall Street professionals against a motley crowd of mere wannabes and, through first-person accounts of traders who have made it and traders who have failed, shows why it is so tough for traders to do what they know is right, and what it takes to succeed.

Part Two, "Raising Livermore's Ghost," puts the contemporary gold rush in historical context, with a backward glance at the first day-trading master, Jesse Livermore, the bucket-shop wizard of the Gilded Age, whose penetrating reminiscences have the force of scripture for many traders. He died a year before the bombs fell on Pearl Harbor, but in the 1980s, a strange confluence of technology and scandal brought bucket shops to cyberspace and raised Livermore's ghost again. This part of the book tells the story of the market-mutating electronic communications networks, of the people and the technologies that made them possible, of Wall Street crimes and misdemeanors so egregious that they led market regulators to open the markets to the masses again.

Part One shows where day trading is today. Part Two explains how it got there. Part Three, "The Global Trading Pit," shows where it is going. Europeans and Asians are just beginning to enter the Extreme Investing game. Informed sources say that the day-trading wave now breaking in America is just beginning to rise in Germany, Italy, France, Japan, and the United Kingdom. The technology of the Internet has made national borders all but irrelevant. In June 1999, the National Association of Securities Dealers arranged a joint venture with the Japanese venture capital firm Softbank to build Nasdaq-Japan, a new exchange to allow trading of Nasdaq stocks during the Japanese market day. So, markets everywhere are becoming accessible to traders everywhere. This section shows how that has happened and what it means, not only to traders, but also to regulators and major institutional money managers, some of whom are drawing on cold-war military technology to cope with the threat posed by day traders.

Part Four, "Bandit Boot Camp," presents a day-by-day account of fledgling traders learning the game at the first, and still the most intensive, day-trading training program in the country, a month-long total immersion in the markets and technology of Extreme Investing.

Part Five, "The Bad and the Ugly," focuses on the courtrooms and regulatory agencies where some of the most interesting, and lucrative, market action is taking place. Here the reader will find the story of the "unsuccessful" trader who sued the party from whom he had borrowed money with which to trade and walked away from court with an award of approximately $3.5 million. Less salubriously, a coil of suits and countersuits in the Texas courts has pried the lid off some of the day-trading brokerage industry's best-kept secrets—including alleged money laundering, corporate espionage, racketeering, and several varieties of fraud.

The last part, "The Extreme Investor's Manual of Online Day Trading," presents concisely some useful information for aspiring day traders. It includes a checklist to consider before starting, a primer summarizing the essential how-to information presented in training courses and the broad trading literature, advice on legal recourse for people who believe they've been cheated by a day-trading broker, and a short list of Websites for more information. There is also a comprehensive glossary of trading terminology that readers unfamiliar with market jargon may find especially helpful.

Part One

THE
GOLD
RUSH

Chapter 1

Cut to the Chase

*Life and Death in
the Trading Rooms*

Harvey Houtkin sits straight up in his chair, cocks his head slightly to the left, starts talking, and keeps right on, fast and loud and uninterruptible, smashing through rules of grammar and syntax like a tank through a rail fence, crushing courtesies and politeness and prudent reserve like frail wildflowers beneath the unrelenting earth-grappling treads of Brooklynese.

"They called us bandits! Bandits!" he explodes, his hands flying into the air, round cheeks trembling, chin shaking with rage behind the fat man's goatee. "Look at them! The top regulators all come from the industry, and the lawyers and economists they hire for staff go to work from the first day with their lips pursed to kiss all the industry ass they can so they can get a job in the industry after a few years. I'd rather deal with the mafia. At least with the mafia you know where you stand—you borrow money and don't pay it back, they break your leg—but these guys!"

The hands go into the air, and the eyes glint with the zeal of the reformer, and the head shakes as if to say wordlessly, that's how they kept their criminal, collusive game going, and that's why they fought

Harvey, a self-described "Brooklyn Jew boy" from the projects who wouldn't go away, wouldn't roll over, kept fighting back and fighting back, and finally beat them. But why say something wordlessly when you can say it in so many words? So he says it again.

Just when you're about to write him off as another loud-mouthed, self-interested, self-promoting operator from the under-belly of Wall Street, you remember that he's right. The regulators were in bed with the industry; and they did try to crush him with arbitrary rules, restrictions, lawsuits, and general harassment; and he did fight them almost single-handedly; and he did win; and he does deserve the title "King of the Bandits," though he doesn't claim to be a king. He just calls himself the "Original SOES Bandit" and occasionally poses for pictures, as he did for *Fortune* magazine, in a Zorro mask.

Harvey Houtkin started it all. He's the man. He's the reason why thousands of people across the whole United States, the world even, can sit down in front of blinking computer screens and buy and sell stocks without phoning a broker, directly, in seconds, for exactly the price of the bid and offer on the screen. He's the reason why they can even look at a screen and know what the price is, the real price, not some sham price like the prices you used to see when you looked at the Nasdaq, but a price you can really buy and sell at. He's the reason why they can step ahead of the Wall Street houses, eat the big boys' lunch, bidding a teeny more or asking a fraction less to catch markets on the move—up or down, it doesn't matter. He's the reason why.

Harvey's the man, large and in charge, bad haircut notwith-standing, his round, well-upholstered presence settled in a tall, well-upholstered chair beside the screens his fight made possible, in a soft, fully carpeted building where all the men seem to be round like Harvey, and all the women blond and slim—except for the brunette in the picture frame on his bookshelf, in a bare bikini straddle on a Malibu beach, whose name sounds like "Kaireena," who's a fitness instructor with a program on a national all-sports cable channel, and who wrote across her photo a long, tender, per-sonal note expressing her deep gratitude for all he taught her about trading and offering to come back here to his headquarters in Montvale, New Jersey, anytime he feels the need for a fitness instructor around the place.

"She came here with her fiancé. He's her husband now, I think, a good-looking guy too," Harvey says. "They were sitting in the training class, and she couldn't figure out how to buy, so she asked me, How do you buy a stock? I said, here, Why don't you buy CSCO? and I helped her with the mouse, and she did, and I walked around to do something else and forgot about it. A few seconds later I notice CSCO is up a half a point, so I said, Why don't you offer that out for sale? and she did, and bang! She made half a point, on a thousand shares—you know, that's like five hundred dollars—and she's just looking at me with these big eyes and says, 'Ooh, you can just make money whenever you want to! Do it again!' And me, What did I know? I just got lucky. I shrugged and said, Sorry, just once a day."

The man.

Thanks to Harvey, there are sixty or seventy mostly middle-aged career changers and fortune hunters trading here, behind colorful screens in a quiet upstairs room, and there are other smaller rooms full of computer programmers and back-office types, and a school on-site where new aspiring traders come to learn the game. And across the country are thousands more, some trading at the twenty or so branches of Harvey's firm, All-Tech, some trading at branches of the competing firms that also owe their existence to Harvey's victories in the courts, some trading from their own homes, with software and information they could never have gotten if it weren't for Harvey, not professional traders necessarily, just people from all walks of life who want to buy and sell stocks this way and couldn't if it hadn't been for him.

For Harvey, it's all a dream coming true. He always said that the markets ought to be open to everyone, not just people from the right schools who made the right connections and kiss-assed their way into a soft job with a big brokerage firm, but everyone. Why should anybody pay more to buy a stock than they have to—just to support the collusive, sweetheart deals, the featherbedding, back-scratching, and logrolling of market insiders? One of his biggest fights was the Timpinaro case, back in 1993, in which the National Association of Securities Dealers tried to prevent a plumber Harvey had trained from using the then state-of-the-art Small Order Execution System (SOES). Harvey won. But he's still boiling mad about it.

He's steaming with the wrath of the righteous. It's World Series Week, and the Yankees are three games ahead, and the online brokerage E*Trade is running ads with a voice-over that goes "Your investments paid for this dream house . . . unfortunately it belongs to your broker" as a well-dressed, WASPy-looking couple enter a mansion, turn briefly to smirk at all you suckers who paid for their new house, and close the door in your face.

"Who paid for their advertising budget!" Harvey shouts. "Do you know what it costs to buy thirty seconds in the fourth game of the World Series! The fourth game!? Half a million dollars! Where does that money come from? Not from the $14.95 they say they charge you to trade. They sell customers' trades to a market maker! They're supposed to have a fiduciary duty to the customer, but they're selling the orders! It's commercial bribery!"

What difference does it make to save money on a brokerage commission if you pay more to buy a stock or get less from selling a stock because your broker is selling the right to execute your order to someone who gets the money to buy that right by charging you a higher price or paying you a lower price than you could get doing it yourself directly? Shouldn't the broker be looking out for your interests, buying at the cheapest price for you, selling at the highest price for you? In any other industry, this would be called a kickback, it would be illegal, but the Securities and Exchange Commission has allowed it to go on for so long that they are afraid to stamp it out now because that would disrupt the structure of the market, outraged Harvey fulminates.

And again, just when you think he's over the top, you remember he's just saying what everyone in the securities industry knows is true and accepts as a matter of course, so much so that if you check the prospectus for any broker, online or off, you'll likely find some dense disclosure language buried in a screed of unintelligible legalese advising that the broker "may" sell someone the right to execute your buy and sell orders, no matter how bizarre it seems to anyone whose vision of economics, law, or morality is unblurred by the light of Wall Street.

One day, Harvey got mad as hell and decided he wasn't going to take it anymore.

* * *

He wasn't always a bandit and a rebel.

In fact, he must have been a rather quiet and studious youth because he graduated from Brooklyn Tech, one of the three most competitive public high schools in New York City, and he loves to talk about the workload there almost as much as he loves to talk about the markets. Sputnik had just been launched and the space race was on, and Brooklyn Tech was a critical nursery for mathematical, engineering, and physics talent. The school was so tough that it had special permission not to give students the New York State Regents exam taken by all the other high school students in New York because the exam was too easy for the Brooklyn Tech kids, Harvey says. He says when he graduated and went to the Baruch College school of business at the City University of New York, it was so easy he had leisure for a full-time job working as an assistant to an investment manager on Wall Street. "I planned to be a dentist, but when I saw how much money he was making—and it wasn't that hard—I said, This is for me!"

After he graduated, he got a job with a small firm. Because he hadn't gone to a big Ivy League school, he couldn't get a job with a big, classy firm. He sat next to Carl Icahn, and they did arbitrage together. In fact, Harvey modestly claims credit for teaching Carl Icahn what arbitrage was all about and helping him get the idea. Later they both went on to get revenge on the white-shoe set that had spurned them, though in different ways, Carl by greenmail and corporate raiding in the 1980s, Harvey by SOES Banditry in the nineties.

By the early eighties, Harvey had his own small firm and some clients, and he was doing well until the crash of 1987 wiped him out. The big market makers in the National Association of Securities Dealers had all posted prices at which they were supposed to be willing to buy and sell stocks. Under the Firm Quote Rule—always capitalized when people on Wall Street use the phrase because it's part of their sacred trust—firms had to honor the prices they had posted. But the big NASD market makers were understandably reluctant to buy stocks in the midst of a crash, so they just ignored their ringing phones.

"That's when I found out that nobody on Wall Street gives a rat's ass about anybody else," Harvey growls bitterly. "Carl Icahn used to say if you want a friend on Wall Street, buy a dog. They didn't give a rat's ass about me. What did they care about a fuckin' Jew boy from Brooklyn?" Harvey's firm went bust. About the same time, his father died after three months in the hospital with cancer. "I was totally drained of all emotion. I just said, Fuck them then."

Back in 1984, the National Association of Securities Dealers had introduced an automated, computerized trading network called the Small Order Execution System (SOES). In principle, this system was intended to give small investors instant access to the market on equal terms with big brokerage firms and market makers. In principle, anyone with a computer could buy and sell stocks automatically, directly, for the prices indicated on the screen. In practice, market makers (the firms and individuals that stand ready both to buy and to sell stocks for stated bid and offer prices) could withdraw from SOES at a moment's notice. During the 1987 crash, in addition to not answering their phones, they also withdrew from SOES. It was difficult during the crash to get trades executed on the New York Stock Exchange and in the Chicago futures pits, but it was impossible to get trades executed on the Nasdaq.

After the crash, a blue-ribbon panel led by Treasury Secretary Nicholas Brady recommended that participation in SOES be mandatory, and even the industry and its regulators were unable to resist the pressure. Under the original rules governing SOES, a market-making firm had to honor its price for orders of up to one thousand shares and it had to be good for five such orders before it could take a breather and perhaps adjust the price.

The catch was, as Harvey knew, the prices publicly quoted on the Nasdaq (National Association of Securities Dealers Automated Quotations) system were not really the prices at which big firms did business among themselves. The industry had developed a scandalous culture of collusion. Brokers took orders to market makers, who paid what in another industry would be called a kickback. The profits of the market makers depended on the difference between the bid and the offer prices—the bigger the difference (the wider the spread), the more money they made. As two then-obscure academic researchers demonstrated during the early 1990s, market makers did their best to keep these spreads as wide as possible when they dealt with the public. For example, they never quoted prices in odd eighths. A stock on the move jumped from, say, 10 to 10¼, to 10½, to 10¾, to 11, skipping right past 10⅛, 10⅜, 10⅝, and 10⅞ on its way up. There was a good, sound reason for this—market makers had agreed they could all make more money this way. When one of them slipped up and quoted a price in odd eighths on the Nasdaq, the phone rang and the voice on the other end muttered "Moo goo gai pan" in a fake Chinese accent, a reminder that posting unconventional prices was called "making a Chinese market" and was cause for ostracism or worse.

Harvey didn't mind the prospect of ostracism. The people who refused to answer their phones during the 1987 crash had already put him out of business once. And since they had grown accustomed to a collusive, club-like way of doing business, the market makers were a big fat target. Like small, quick mammals stealing eggs from the nests of dinosaurs, Harvey and his little band of outsiders took advantage of SOES to score easy profits at the expense of the market makers. The Nasdaq publicity machine dubbed the outsiders "SOES Bandits," and they wore the name with pride.

*   *   *

Harvey blew a giant hole in the gates that separate privileged insiders from the mass of outsiders. Now, a full-scale gold rush is underway, and anyone with a computer can join.

In September 1998, in an office at 50 Broad Street, just a few feet from the site of the legendary buttonwood tree under which, in 1792, a band of waterfront hustlers ducked a law against public sale of stocks by founding a private company to be called the New York Stock Exchange, a balding, soft-spoken, middle-aged man watched quotes flicker on his screen.

Downsized out of his controller's job in the sticks of Pennsylvania a year before, he couldn't find another job, so he decided to try trading stocks online for a living. His target: to earn a thousand dollars a day.

After all, what's a thousand dollars a day, when the T-shirted Gen X-ers trading at the next row of desks are making a hundred times that in a morning?

Broadway Trading, the company in whose office he trades, is one of scores of electronic trading brokerage firms that have opened since Harvey and his original SOES Bandits broke open the gates of Market City to any barbarian with a modem.

Upstairs, fifty hopefuls filled a small conference room. They came from everywhere, they had done almost anything for a living, and they all dreamed of grabbing a fortune from under the noses of Wall Street's best and brightest. They had paid $1,500 a head for an introductory course in how to be a SOES Bandit.

The founders of Broadway Trading used to teach neophytes to trade as professionals on the floor of the American Stock Exchange. So there's reason to believe them when they say that they can teach anyone to trade successfully. Plenty of people take them at their word.

The company used to offer the course free, but then the number of applicants exploded. Even though Broadway Trading cofounders Marc Friedfertig and George West have written a best-selling book on their course, the $1,500 fee is less than a third of what competitors charge for similar introductory courses. So it could be argued that the hopeful traders attending the seminar are getting quite a bargain.

Marc Friedfertig views the tuition less as a source of revenue than as a filter to help make sure that the people taking up space in the seminar room are at least somewhat serious in their intentions. Broadway Trading makes its real money by charging traders two cents a share commission on their trades after they graduate from the course. People who make money trade more and trade longer than traders who lose, but making money at this game takes a certain seriousness of purpose. So it makes sense to screen for seriousness.

In this session, the fifty who made the cut include an intensive-care nurse from Long Island who used to rely on professionals to manage her savings, until she noticed them losing more than they made for her. So she decided to manage her savings herself. She read a lot of books on the market and opened an account with an Internet brokerage and began to "position-trade," moving in and out of stocks every couple of days. She's been so successful that now she wants to quit her day job and trade full-time. "I have patience," she says. "I can sit in front of the screen all day."

A pilot named Jim used to work with Eastern Airlines but lost his job when that carrier went bankrupt. He managed to find a job with a Taiwanese air cargo company, but now he's had it with long flights back and forth over the Pacific. Sipping Arizona green tea from a brightly colored bottle, a gold chain glinting behind the open top button of his expat shirt, Jim says he's here because he's looking for something to do in his retirement, which he hopes will come soon. He went to Broadway Trading's Boca Raton office during a layover and made a little money trading there. So he thinks he'd like to do it full-time.

Betty is a green-eyed immigration lawyer from Miami; her boyfriend, David, is an apartment manager there. They are here at the seminar to improve their investment skills.

They got their introduction to the market a few months ago, when Betty inherited some money from her father. She and David invested it together, picking a few stocks to buy in June 1998, when the Dow hit a historic high.

Having bought at the top, they lost a lot of money as the Dow went down. Despite that experience, Betty wants to trade full-time because the law is a slavish, time-consuming occupation that **11** keeps her at the mercy of client demands and court schedules. Trading looks like freedom by comparison, especially this kind of trading. "You can take a day off if you want," she says with a far-away look in her eye. And David will be a good partner, she says, because unlike her, he knows something about the markets. In fact, he sometimes gets up at 5:00 A.M. to sit in front of the television watching CNBC all day, until it changes over to the *Geraldo* show in the evening.

Arthur is an insurance man. He says he made a bundle on stocks, but then lost it all. He is here to learn what he needs to know to be a winner. That seems to be a pretty tall order. During one of the introductory lectures, Arthur demonstrates a remarkable ingenuousness about the markets.

The speaker is talking about how the price of a stock moves up when there are more people trying to buy than sell and down when there are more people trying to sell than buy.

The furrows on Arthur's forehead shift up toward his thinning, sandy-gray hair as he raises a slow and tentative hand.

"You talk about this like it's just a game between buyers and sellers," he stammers.

"Right. It's just a game," the speaker blurts.

"But what about when you read in the papers that the market moved because of something in Japan or something Clinton did? Do you mean to say that's not true?" Arthur moans, with the incredulous dismay of a child who has seen a department store Santa take off his beard.

The speaker looks at Arthur strangely and shrugs.

Not all of the attendees are so out of touch. Scott, a big guy in a white knit golf shirt, has just quit his job as a trader with a securities firm in New Jersey. Scott's brother is an options specialist on the floor of the American Stock Exchange, and Broadway Trading's president used to trade options there too. That's how Scott found out about this new way of playing the markets. In his previous job, he earned a salary and a bonus that amounted to half of his trading profits, and during the great bull market of the 1990s, that was nothing to sneeze at. Yet the money to be made trading this new way is potentially much, much better. Scott is cautiously optimistic. "I was talking to Marc, and he told me that professional traders often don't do as well at this as people from backgrounds unrelated to the market," he says. The reason seems to be that professionals often think that they understand the markets. That can be a problem. The markets are changing so radically that many old rules no longer apply. Pros who are unwilling to listen, to be humble, to accept that they can no longer trust what they know, simply get rolled over by the market action.

That is especially painful when someone like Serge Milman is hunched over a keyboard in a modified fetal position at the next desk, his feet propped on a blue plastic milk crate, a Cyndi Lauper CD blasting from a yellow Walkman into his ears. Milman became the pinup boy for the new breed of market renegades when his hungry grin graced the cover of *Forbes* in April 1998. He had emigrated from Russia with his parents at age five, in 1978, and graduated from New York University with a degree in computers and finance in 1995.

Serge wanted to be a trader, but every bank and broker in New York turned him down when he applied for a job. Maybe the interviewers could sense that what he really wanted to do was play video games.

Serge grew up playing video games. Even now, when he's not trading, he's apt to be surfing the Internet, looking for a game. So when he stumbled on Broadway Trading and discovered that he could actually make money playing a video game he was, like, way cool!

Every day from 9:30 to 4:00, he sits in front of a screen at 50 Broad Street, looking for opportunities in the over-the-counter market. As bids and offers flicker on and off, he hits the bids and takes the offers and reverses within seconds, buying and selling hundreds of thousands of shares of stock of companies about which he knows nothing except that the price is moving. He doesn't research their business, doesn't care about their prospects tomorrow. All that matters is the quarter-, eighth-, and sixteenth-point moves in the price. A spread of three-eighths of a point is found money. By the end of the day, he's usually out of the market. "It's just like Nintendo," says Noah, the manager of Broadway's Boca Raton office, come to New York for the seminar. Noah boasts that he helped train Serge, not that Serge needed a lot of help. Serge's skill on the keyboard and his devotion to the screen made him a natural. Unlike Noah himself.

It took extraordinary measures to make a trader out of Noah. A professional, albeit minor league, baseball player, Noah had already laid down his bat and glove for an easy, aimless life of fishing, photography, and hanging out in Florida when he happened to meet Marc Friedfertig during a morning jog. They became friends, Marc told him about the money to be made twisting the tails of the lions of Wall Street, and Noah agreed to give it a try. Trading soon brought him to a sort of higher wisdom. He realized at last why he had never made it to the major leagues. "Every year in spring training, I'd be the last one cut," he said, "But I'd be cut. I know why now. I didn't have the focus and discipline." That problem popped up again when he started trading. Noah's attention wandered. He had a tendency to walk away from his screen to use the bathroom or get a cup of coffee, and that meant missed opportunities.

This was a disappointment to Marc, who really wanted his friend to succeed. So one day, as Noah showed signs of getting a bit distracted and leaned back in his chair to stretch, the traders on either side pinned his arms and Marc chained him to the chair.

*   *   *

About a third of the people in the seminar room are over forty, another third under thirty, the rest scattered between. Three of the fifty are women. Two are Chinese, one African American. They've all read the *Forbes* article about Serge Milman, so the moderator opens by telling them that later in the session they'll have a chance to ask Serge questions directly and also to meet some of the other "top guns" from the trading floor. A thrill goes through the crowd, a stir of side conversations in excited voices.

But first, they have to be prepared. The kind of trading that goes on here is nothing like what most people have been taught to think of as prudent investing. It has its own language, a curt shorthand unintelligible to the untrained, code phrases like "he lifts," "down off the bid," "back away," "hit me," "SPooze," spoken at a yell to the rhythm of fingers clattering on keyboards and the flicker of refreshing screens.

Forget about studying companies, they're told, or even knowing what they make or do, or what their price was yesterday. This is only about what's happening right now, in the market on the screen. It's the markets on a subatomic level, where science contradicts itself curiously and everything you know is wrong. This is Extreme Investing.

At the front of the room, next to a vast screen, a bodybuilder stands in jeans and a golf shirt. Jay is Marc Friedfertig's brother-in-law, a relationship to which he owes his presence in the firm, though he never mentions it. He prefers to talk about his black belt in a special form of martial art that attacks acupuncture points for "one-touch knockouts." Or about his puckish online pranks, like using the electronic trading systems to buy just one share from someone trying to sell a thousand "just to annoy them."

On the lunch break, Jay entertains an elevator full of students with the story of how he first got into trading. He and a buddy had accumulated a bunch of mailings from discount credit card companies, so they got the cash advances and bought commodity futures. "In the morning, we were up $175,000, and I was shouting into the phone, 'Buy ten more! Buy ten more!'" he guffaws. "By the afternoon we were down $368,000. I was worried, until my partner said, What can they do to us? We're twenty-one-year-old kids with discount credit cards. What can they take?"

Jay shifts from leg to muscle-bound leg in the front of the room, gesturing at the multicolored screen that every trader here watches constantly. A red banner at the top presents selected data in real time: the Dow industrials, the semiconductor index, the Standard & Poor's futures, the spread between cash and futures, and the Nasdaq composite. Beneath, the screen splits into six fields. A nonstop scroll of white letters on a blue field in the upper left lists every single change in bid and asked prices for every stock on the Nasdaq, logged to the second so traders can identify which stocks are moving, how fast, and when. On the upper right, a customized ticker spotlights market maker actions that affect stocks the trader wants to keep a close eye on, identifying the stock, the direction and intensity of price movement, the number of market makers lining up with bids to buy or offers to sell, and a brief description of the current action: MASH up off ask, WEED joins bid, ISLD high bid, etc. Underneath these, a broad position window spans the screen with a constant scroll of similarly comprehensive news and information about stocks the trader owns or has shorted (borrowed and sold with the intention of buying them back later when the price falls). Beneath, three quote windows open on stocks the trader plans to buy and sell, listing every market maker with a bid or offer pending.

In fast markets, the windows are a blur. Eyes have to be trained, hands have to be fast on the keys. No wonder skill at Quake has turned out to be a key to riches for Serge. No wonder research, information, fundamentals, charts don't matter at all. There's no time to think about that stuff. There's just time to see and react. "Use your first instinct. Usually your first instinct is the best," Jay barks at a bewildered questioner wondering how to keep track of it all.

He tells them they'll have to learn how to play both sides of the market, long and short, how to make money when stocks rip up and when they plunge down. They'll have to learn how to discern the true intentions of market makers while concealing their own. They'll have to know when and when not to trade. For example, the first fifteen or twenty minutes after the opening bell are treacherous, because a surge of orders at the open creates false moves, undertows, and riptides in the flow of prices. The most important rule is the hardest to live by: take small losses and get out when you can, not when you have to.

"Why do people keep doing this when they've already made a million?" someone wonders aloud.

"It's addictive. When you make one, you want two." Jay pumps a fist.

Later, Marc Friedfertig comes into the room to give a brief welcome. It stretches into an hour-and-a-half discourse on the principles of "trading like a market maker." Marc Friedfertig has the slightly disheveled mien and approachable manner of a devoted young rabbi. He's a man on a mission. For him, trading is spiritual combat. He works hard to puncture the ballooning dreams of fast money. "Trading is humbling! This is not easy! We say it's probably six months before people make money, and they lose money learning!"

From the looks on the faces in the seminar room, though, the dream balloons are puncture-resistant. Someone asks if it's possible to get through this bad patch by paper trading—not actually buying and selling, but merely pretending to, and keeping a record of how it goes. The answer is *no*, emphatically! Paper trading creates unrealistic expectations! You miss the feel of the market, the all-important feel! "If a stock is hard to buy, it's going higher; if it's easier to buy, it's going lower!" he says, to a room full of bewilderment.

He tells them that the best days are the ones where the market opens down. The worst are often the ones that start with the market up. Today, the market opened high. At the close, even Serge had done badly—by his standards—merely breaking even after trading seven hundred thousand shares.

Some of the people in the room want to trade remotely, logging in from their homes. It's one of the big appeals of the trader's life, part of the dream of independence—no more fighting traffic, no more commute, set your own hours. Marc cocks an eyebrow. It's *possible,* of course, but . . . a lot of people on the *West Coast* (he almost sneers it) have this idea that they can get up early in the morning, take advantage of the time difference to trade the open in New York, break to go to their jobs, and log on at lunch to trade the close. And make money, good money, ten, twenty, a hundred thousand a day. In their spare time.

Right. As if. This market isn't some laid-back California kind of thing.

This is Extreme Investing! Every dollar you take out of this market is a dollar you have to take away from someone else who **17** wants it badly. Someone bigger than you, *who doesn't like you and doesn't like what you're doing and wants to screw you if he can, whether it makes money for him or not.*

"Market makers don't like us! We're taking money out of their pockets! So they play games with us!" he shouts. What kind of games?

Maybe Goldman Sachs has been trying to unload XYZ stock in a weak market. No one's buying. So Goldman switches over to the buy side, flashing a very public bid on the screen. John Q. Sucker sees Goldman move in as a buyer on the stock, figures what's good enough for Goldman is good enough for him, and starts to buy too. A few more John Q.s join the action, and Goldman manages to unload its shares in the false momentum. After that the price falls back again, and everything is just as it was before except that the suckers are poorer. Tip: Don't buy when the first market maker moves in on a stock; it might be a decoy. Always wait until at least two other market makers have joined the feeding frenzy before you do.

Discipline and timing are everything! It doesn't matter whether a stock is going up or down; as long as it's moving, there's a trade. But the more obvious it is that a stock is a buy, the closer it is to the end of its move—the likelier it is to fall back.

Focus! Every stock has its own pattern of movement. The patterns change from day to day. This isn't about price, it's about motion. And a stock's motion isn't really measured by price; it's measured by what Friedfertig calls "levels."

The market is an auction. Levels are about the pace of the auction, how fast the price moves up or down, in what increments, whether in whole dollars or fractions thereof—halves, quarters, eighths, sixteenths, sometimes even thirty-seconds and sixty-fourths. Big stocks like Microsoft have paper-thin spreads, and the bid and offer levels look like tall stacks of colorful pancakes on the screen, with prices rising or falling teeny by teeny. Small, high-risk stocks sometimes move in whole-dollar increments as a matter of course. Their bid and offer levels look like a thin crust atop a deep purplish blue band. The thin crust is the national best bid and offer, or inside market price; the deep blue band contains all of the other, faraway bids and offers.

So when Microsoft jumps an eighth, or a quarter, or a half, it's a much bigger move than some FlyByNight jumping or falling a dollar or two. Not in absolute price, of course, but in all-important *levels.* Because the unimportant FlyByNight auction always moves at least in dollar increments—but widely traded Microsoft is ripping through multiple levels. This trading is all about motion.

The screen shows who is lining up on the buy and on the sell side for each stock. It shows the upticks and downticks in price. It shows the surge of demand and supply. But the trader has to figure out what all of that means, what the levels are today (because they do change from day to day), and whether this all adds up to a play now or not.

The trader has to figure this out in a second or two. And act on it before anyone else in the market acts, because the race is to the swift.

All while somebody much bigger than you who doesn't like you is trying to smoke you. A big firm buying heavily, say, then bidding the highest price on the screen. Looks like a heavy buyer. Looks like this stock's a buy. Caution! Caution! This may just be a short squeeze, a clever scheme engineered to force traders who have sold borrowed stock in anticipation of a price fall to buy the stock back. It's a trap for the unwary.

This is not to say that the big market makers spend all of their time thinking of ways to squash small traders just for the fun of squashing them. After all, they do have businesses to run. They have the VWAP to think about.

VWAP is the yardstick big pension funds and institutions use to measure the performance of their brokers. Stock prices are moving up and down continuously through the day, and big institutional investors like to know that their brokers bought at the best prices available. The VWAP, or value-weighted average price, tells them, on average, what the price was during the day. If a brokerage firm fills the institution's order for a price higher than the VWAP or executes a sale at a price below the VWAP, there may not be another order from that customer anytime soon.

19

So, gulling small traders isn't just a sadistic amusement. It's a sound business practice too. Brokerage firms and market makers who successfully decoy traders into running the prices up and down for them can beat the VWAP handily.

Thus, the traps for traders can be part of a complicated, multi-layered strategy. It helps to know therefore how various market makers usually think and act in order to interpret what they are up to today. Every market maker has its own strategies, trading styles, and priorities. They leave tracks on the ticker when they move in and out of stocks, much as large carnivores leave tracks around watering holes. Anyone who plans to hunt in this jungle had better learn to recognize those tracks well enough to know what is normal and what is not. It is a matter of survival.

Age and wisdom are not prerequisites to understanding this.

Serge Milman and his buddy Landon come into the seminar room after the market closes, dressed as if they just left their skateboards in the hall. Serge wears shorts, sneakers, and a T shirt; Landon wears shorts and a tails-out Banana Republic–type shirt. Serge looks athletic, oddly enough, though he spends his entire day hunched over a keyboard in screen-worshipper position. He has close-cropped hair, a square face, intense eyes behind glasses. Landon is tall, skinny, youthfully ungainly, his face mainly a shock of wild red hair and a long aquiline nose flanked by bird-bright eyes.

Serge shifts from foot to foot, popping a loose fist into an open hand.

Someone asks him if he knows anything about the companies he trades. Sure, he says, he knows something about some of them. He trades Intel; he knows Intel makes semiconductor chips. And he trades Amazon; he knows they sell books. But he doesn't know much more about them, and he knows a lot less about a lot of the stocks he trades. "It's not important to know what they do," he says.

The only information about the company that's important is the information that appears on the screen: its stock symbol (unless there's some news, in which case half a headline might scroll across a window). But that's OK, because the quintessence of a company's identity has nothing to do with what it makes, who it employs, how it is managed, where it is based. Those details may matter somewhere, in some far-off part of the economic universe, but they don't matter on this starship. Here, a company is just a stock symbol and a shifting array of bids and offers.

Serge's eye is always on the ticker, the portion of the screen that alerts him to changes in stocks he wants to watch. He had to train himself to absorb it all, he says, and even with his background in video games, it still took time. When he started out, he kept 5 stocks in the ticker. A year ago, he had 120 there. Now he keeps an eye on 40—simultaneously.

He shifts from foot to foot.

Any tips for newbies?

Keep a diary, he recommends, keep a diary every day. Landon nods.

They talk over each other. The idea is to cut losses and let profits run, they say. Cut losses—that means taking a loss, admitting you were wrong. It means admitting you were *wrong;* that's what makes it so difficult. Asked what mistakes he still makes, after making over a million dollars last year and who knows how much this year—because it's only September after all, and the market's in violent, volatile upheaval, beautiful conditions for day trading—Serge doesn't hesitate. "Stubborn, too stubborn," he says.

He's boyish, awkward even.

Landon looks cool by comparison. Landon is not famous anywhere but here. But here he's known as Serge's equal, or very close. He made a fortune today, trading just one stock, TLAB. Selling on the dips—buying on the upticks. Over and over. He made six figures. Just today.

No one would have expected that of him a year or two ago. His roommate, a dark-haired, slender girl, works as Broadway Trading's director of educational services. Gliding gracefully to and from her desk in a long, black, sheath-like dress, she told someone earlier in the day that Landon had been more or less aimless before he started trading. In fact, he'd been working in a flower shop for two years. His father—it takes little imagination to figure out why—offered to put up the $70,000 that Broadway Trading re- **21** quires of all of its new traders to open an account, the money to cover trading capital, margin calls, and so forth.

Daddy has bragging rights now.

Landon sits in the row where the very best, top-gun traders sit, right next to Serge, and plays the market the same way as Serge, like a video game, only lately, he plays a little better than Serge, it seems.

Asked again what matters in a stock (somehow the people in the room can't get out of their mind the idea that revenues and expenses and management somehow matter), Landon says, "Are there more sellers than buyers, or more buyers than sellers?! We're here to day-trade! Not to buy a company because it has a good product or good management! We're here trying to be the first in when we think a stock is going up *right now!*"

Extreme Investing.

Get the point?

Not everyone does. Along the sides of the room, middle-aged baby boomers in golf shirts lean against the walls, here and there an arm arcs limp, tentative with a question. It's all so different, so strange. Maybe it's a generational thing. And yet . . . and yet . . . wouldn't it be great if only . . .

*   *   *

Greg D. took the introductory course almost two years before. New York has not yet eradicated the broad Plains drawl of this Nebraska native. A quiet man, forty-three years old, with thinning, gray-brown hair, he speaks slowly and gives the impression that he has chosen each word after considering several alternatives. Yet he talks about the long apprenticeship he has served here in deeply spiritual language, as though it were a kind of Pilgrim's Progress from benighted ignorance to the Heavenly City.

Until 1995, he'd been married to a very attractive woman, a buyer for a chain of department stores. She drove a Porsche. He drove a red Dodge Stealth. Greg still gets misty-eyed about the car. "All the gadgets, it was top of the line, beautiful. The Dodge Stealth is basically the same car as the Mitsubishi 3000. In fact, Mitsubishi makes it," he says, with nostalgic pride.

Ever since his junior year in high school, Greg had been fascinated with the markets. They were the lodestar of his life. He chose to study accounting and become a CPA, mainly because he thought that if he learned to read and understand financial statements, he'd be able to make money in the stock market. His wife would probably blame the markets for their divorce, he says. He spent all of his time away from work reading *The Wall Street Journal,* scanning *Investors Business Daily,* charting prices, working on trades. Like a man with a coy mistress, he didn't often get what he wanted from the market. But the more the market played hard to get, the more he concentrated on how to get. Meanwhile, he and his wife grew apart.

At the time of the divorce, Greg was controller for a small company based in Harrisburg, Pennsylvania, that was involved in trade with Russia. In 1996, a year after the divorce, he was downsized out.

He was middle-aged, and when he took inventory of his life, it added up to his clothes, his stereo, and his TV. He looked for a job in Pennsylvania, but his age counted against him, and he thinks that a background working with small companies instead of big ones probably hurt too.

As he was sending out résumés and accumulating rejection letters, he happened to notice an ad that Broadway Trading had placed in *Investors Business Daily.* It was one of several ads from SOES trading firms. What made Broadway most interesting was that there was, at that time, no charge to take its training course. Other firms charged around $5,000 for training.

Greg came to New York and paid an extended visit to an eighty-five-year-old aunt who lived in a rowhouse in a deteriorating neighborhood in Queens. He took a bus to the subway and then rode the subway to the Wall Street area for an hour-and-a-half commute to Broadway's training course. In those days, Broadway Trading allowed new traders to open an account with as little as $40,000. With the total dedication of a mystic entering a monastery, Greg sold what he owned. He cashed in his life savings and barely man- **23** aged to come up with the money to open his account. For the first few months, he was still getting a check from the unemployment agency in Pennsylvania. (He hastens to say that he continued to look for work during this period and adds, "I've got the rejection letters to prove it.") He used the unemployment money to rent a seat at Broadway Trading for $400 a month. The seat fee gave him access not only to a seat, but to a keyboard, screen, and, most importantly, ongoing coaching and support from other traders in the trading room. Greg didn't expect to stick around long. His idea was to take the training course, work at Broadway long enough to get the hang of trading, and then move back to Pennsylvania, where the cost of living was lower, and trade from home there.

Getting the hang of trading turned out to be much harder than he'd expected. Within his first eight months as a trader, he lost $32,000, almost everything he had.

He borrowed more. His brother loaned him $20,000 at the stiff interest rate of 15 percent. He raised $5,000 on his credit card and got another $5,000 "signature loan" from a direct mail solicitation by a bank.

"I didn't want to give up," he explains. "There was a feeling of, What could I do if it didn't work? Where could I look for a job— New York? Pennsylvania? Nebraska, where my parents are? I knew how hard it was to find a job at my age."

Yet he knew that his age was also making it much harder for him to get the hang of these markets. "It's harder for an older person to learn. You have to be adaptable, flexible, willing to change. That's easier for a younger person."

In May of 1997, the prospect of having to admit failure and quit finally focused his attention on doing what he had to do. He started to cut his losses, and then he started to make a little money. He was still deeply in the hole, but he had a feeling that he might be able to climb out. So the summer went well. Then in September, he lost another $8,000.

He kept a diary. In fact he kept two diaries, one at home and one at the office. He noticed a pattern. The more he thought, the more he analyzed, the more he exercised his powers of deduction, the worse he did. "When I'm doing good, I'm just in the flow, just buying and selling," he explains. He had read all of the books about trading on Broadway Trading's recommended reading list, and a lot of others besides. But the books didn't teach the most important principle, how to "divorce yourself from your ego, from the voice that says, 'I know I'm right.' "

He noticed that the voice seemed to get stronger after he had winning days, winning months. Success led to pride, and pride led to failure. His big loss in September 1997 had come after a good summer and a very good August.

A year later, he was still struggling against that voice. But his track record showed steady progress. In May of 1998, he made $8,000. In June, he made $6,600. In July, he made more than $15,400. In August, the month when worries about Russia and Asia and Monica Lewinsky torpedoed the Dow, Greg made $29,000.

After nearly two years as a trader, he had not only passed the breakeven point and won back the money he had lost while learning, but he was also well on his way to achieving his goal of making a thousand dollars a day. He was also achieving a certain wisdom, a Zen-like sense of his own insignificance in the face of the market.

"Yesterday, I lost three thousand dollars," he said, quietly and calmly. "My fault was, I got stubborn. I thought I knew more than the market. TLAB was buying CIEN, I was playing the arb spread. The spread widened. I had a feeling. I knew this was a good trade; I knew how to play it. The market was saying no, people were disgusted with the deal, but I got stubborn. That's unusual for me now. I had some relearning to do."

Despite the loss, he was up $12,000 for the week.

Greg D. had experienced a remarkable conversion. All his life, he had been thinking that successful trading was about beating the market. Now, he saw that it was more about beating himself.

He'd never really felt that he needed other people. In fact, when he started trading, he planned to stay around the trading room no longer than he had to. Then he would go back to his own place and trade alone. He no longer believed he could go it alone. **25**

"In the room, there are more people watching more stocks. Yesterday, somebody shouted that SANM had gapped down. I don't know what they do—contract manufacturers I think—but I bought the stock. Then all day it went up."

A big-screen TV tuned to CNBC is always running in the trading room. Before a station break, the announcer typically says something like "When we return, we'll talk about a company down 4 points this morning that builds computer parts" or "When we return, we'll talk about a company up 2 that has a new osteoporosis drug." In a roomful of people watching hundreds, thousands of stocks, someone probably has been watching both of these and will shout the name, and the traders in the room will buy, because they know that when the news report runs a few minutes later the crowd is apt to follow.

Most importantly, though, Greg had learned humility. He'd learned to love admitting he was wrong. He knew his career had gone up a notch when he lost $500 in thirty seconds and felt good about it. "I bought something on news," he relates, "A company called CHRZ that does something to do with the year 2000 problem. It used to be a hot stock, but not that day. I lost five hundred dollars in half a minute, and if I'd waited for the stock to turn, I would have lost a thousand. Nothing else to do but sell the position. I did what I could to protect myself. The mistake was in the purchase, but since I made the mistake, I had to sell, and I did. Accepting that I made a mistake and losing five hundred dollars was the best outcome I could expect under the circumstances."

A screen catches his eye. Around Broadway Trading, the action on the screens of some top traders is fed to monitors for anyone to watch. Greg notices some unusual action on the screen of George West, a cofounder of the firm. The screen shows that George has made a lot of trades that morning, but hasn't made much money on them. Until now, he has been short. Suddenly, he reverses. Greg exclaims, "What the hell is going on!? George is buying the world! Futures must have rallied! I'm going to go in the other room and trade."

With a polite but hurried "Excuse me," he's through the door.

*   *   *

Greg D. is a survivor. Not everyone makes it. This is Extreme Investing. The psychological stress of the learning curve is severe. Sometimes it drives aspiring traders to suicide.

A race car driver from Canada, nicknamed Frenchie, he'd lined up some backers and come to New York to day-trade at Broadway, and he couldn't make this final curve. No one knew how badly he was taking it; few knew him well enough to remember his full name. The losses pushed him to the wall for the last time, and when he didn't show up for work, someone learned his body had been found hanged in a rented room.

After that happened, Marc Friedfertig made a special arrangement with a psychotherapy clinic called the Village Institute. Any trader who feels that the stress is getting too heavy can set up a session with Dr. Frederic Wolverton, a specialist in addictive conditions. Broadway Trading pays the bill.

Why a specialist in addictions? Among the addictive conditions that Dr. Wolverton treats is gambling addiction. The trading that goes on here is so close to gambling that traders can easily slip over the line into the pathology of addiction. Perhaps it's remarkable that more don't. "One of the features of addictions is that fantasy and wishes prevail over judgments and the ability to accurately assess reality and act accordingly," Dr. Wolverton explains. But in order to trade successfully, the way Serge Milman and George West and, on a smaller scale, even Greg D. trade, a trader has to put aside facts, data, analysis, and deduction and develop an intuitive feel for where the markets are going. Putting aside objective intellectual analysis is risky. Relying on feeling instead of data, the trader sails into heavy emotional weather without the compass of reason.

"This is an unusual kind of trading," Dr. Wolverton explains. "These people are trading stocks in companies they know absolutely nothing about." As Greg D. discovered, success depends on getting into a flow of the market, somehow becoming one with all that is happening, and acting on instinct. **27**

Paradoxically, says Dr. Wolverton, acting on instinct can also be fatal. Sometimes the instincts that take over are coming from a dangerous place in the trader's personality. "They can arise from personal ambition, or the desire to look good in front of the group or to feel empowered by a successful day of trading, or just plain and simple greed," he says. Such ambitions and desires drag traders away from the rules that, when followed religiously, enable them to trade successfully.

For example, "Cut losses" is one of the fundamental rules, probably the most fundamental of them all, and as Greg D. discovered, it is also the hardest to live by. Cutting losses means admitting that a decision was wrong, and sometimes admitting that means turning loose of an entire set of fantasies and wishes built on the belief that the decision was right.

In his practice with traders from Broadway and elsewhere, Dr. Wolverton has found a common denominator. "They don't feel that they've been adequately loved, reinforced, or built up by fathers they respect," he says. "These guys have a lot of trouble with their fathers." One of the jobs of a father is to help a son develop the confidence to meet challenges. The fathers of traders who have come to him for counseling tend to have been either authoritarian or uninvolved. "I think that these people are drawn to trading because they erroneously look at it as a way of building themselves up. Something about trading holds out the illusory promise that success can come quickly and easily, so it holds particular appeal." A trade is not just a trade, but the last best hope of proving to themselves and the world that they are real men, wealthy, powerful, and confident. Turning loose of a bad trade, cutting the loss, means abandoning that fantasy and facing the terrifying insecurity of their condition.

All of the traders at Broadway are male, as are most attendants at the seminar. It seems reasonable to suppose that any psychological quirks and anomalies that they may have are likely to flourish in the weird hothouse of the trading room. Even when there are fifty or a hundred other traders in the room, each works in virtual solitude, in one dimension. To say it is a superficial life exaggerates its depth. Reality is as shallow and transitory as the shifting electron field that creates the image on the screen. Companionship means hearing the shouts that come from unseen faces behind other screens across the room.

"Trading is incredibly intense and incredibly isolating," Dr. Wolverton says. "It can suck you in. At the end of the day, you feel good or bad about yourself as a person based on whether you've made or lost money. It's a thin life that lacks values, people, intimacy, and a sense of the world having in it things far more important and deeper than the job itself."

Success in trading is not the same thing as success at life. People who have no life beyond trading do not want to be reminded that it isn't the most important thing in the world. But unless the trader can put the markets in proper perspective, psychic hungers will eventually force themselves to the front and take control.

"One of the symptoms we look for is when they can't stop themselves in the middle of a losing streak. When they can't stop themselves, they've probably crossed the line from trading to gambling," Dr. Wolverton says.

At this point, emotions and feelings demand satisfaction. The trader loses his grip on reality and clings to fantasies of almost hallucinogenic intensity.

In order to shift the balance of psychological power back toward sound sense, Dr. Wolverton prescribes a regimen designed to curtail emotional attachment to the outcome of trades. Often, the program involves cutting the volume of trades back drastically, to a level so small that losses and wins hardly matter financially, so that fear and greed are removed. The trader then has to relearn the basics, trade strictly in accordance with rules and methodology. Once sound trading habits are reestablished, the size of trades is gradually increased. So far, Dr. Wolverton says, every trader who has come through the program has been able to recover control and trade successfully.

One of them was Mark A.

He says that this program of therapy saved him from self-destruction.

* * *

They call him "Dr. Mark" here, the way they might call a punch-drunk boxer "Champ." He really is a doctor, or almost was. After dropping out of college in the eighties, he spent a couple of years truckin' behind the fat old Grateful Dead band, selling tie-dyed T shirts to provide himself with the simple necessities of the Dead-head's mellow life. Once he'd gotten the truckin' out of his system, he joined Outward Bound and spent a couple of years leading mountain survival expeditions in the Sierras, then went on to earn a degree in outdoor activities from a college in Arizona. That led somehow to a special pre-med program for nonmedical undergraduates and acceptance by a good medical school, where he was a star student.

Dr. Mark was in the fourth year of med school—"the easy year" he calls it—when he tried trading for the first time. He happened to catch the trend just right and made $50,000 dollars in his first month. It was truly easy money, and it proved to him that by applying solid scientific methods, he could make a fortune in his spare time. He graduated from medical school and went on to residency in one of New York's best private hospitals.

He faltered there. After his outstanding success as a med student, he was shocked to receive poor performance reviews from his superiors at the hospital. Meanwhile, he was on the way to losing about three times what he had made in the markets, using the same charts and patterns and scientific trading disciplines that had seemed to bring him early success.

In hindsight, he now reflects that his initial $50,000 score had nothing to do with know-how and everything to do with having had the luck to step at precisely the right time into the biggest bull run in American market history. But with everything else in his life falling apart (his girlfriend dumped him too), he couldn't admit that then. He spent his days in his apartment, charting stocks, lying on the floor with the phone nearby so he could make trades. When he went out, he carried a Quote-Trac, a little box about the size of a beeper that gave him the latest market quotes at the touch of a button.

"I had become to all intents and purposes a compulsive gambler," he now says. He was fed up with medicine. He wanted a life of no bosses, freedom, and all the things that money could buy—the life of the trader as he fancied it. He found out about SOES trading through some ads in *Investors Business Daily* and visited three firms.

The first two were basically one-room operations, a single senior trader surrounded by kids in baseball hats shouting "Shit, man, I think I'll buy that. It's going up . . . oh, fuck! oh, shit!" Nobody could tell him who, if anyone, was making money.

Broadway Trading seemed a cut above. Here, the trading room chatter sounded cool and professional, the firm's founders wandered around offering advice and encouragement to traders, and everyone's profit and loss performance was clearly displayed on the screens, so he could tell that a lot of people were making money. He took the training seminar and started trading in July 1997.

He was prepared to lose money for a while. The training seminar had made it clear that all new traders have to lose for a while before they start to win. He gave himself six months, until January 1998, and said if he was not making money by then, he would quit.

January came and he was still losing, but he couldn't quit. The problem wasn't that he never won. The problem was that he sometimes won. He would lose money for three weeks, then win for two, then lose for four, then win for one. Success always seemed to be just around the corner, just a week or two away.

Day to day, it went like this: "I would be trading in the flow, calm, cool. Then I'd see a trade I really believed in. The sector goes up, and the futures go up, but my trade goes down. That's not supposed to happen! I hold. It goes down farther. Fuck! I can't believe I'm wrong! I sell. Then the futures go up. Quick! The surge is on! I was right! I buy! Whack it out! I've taken a small loss. I'm angry, upset, disappointed. I tell myself I should stop. I get up. I almost leave. I see a flash of green on the screen! I sit down again. I trade more, I lose twice as much. To get even, I buy Amazon, one of the riskiest stocks there is! I knew enough to tell myself I was out of control, but I placed bigger bets and lost more. I was a gambler. Gamblers get big- **31** ger when they're losing. They overtrade; they don't face reality. The gambler cannot stop in the face of reality and facts. Someone said the definition of insanity is doing the same thing over and over and expecting a different outcome. I kept losing, but told myself that some day I would get it, and if I'd do well for a week, I told myself, I've got it!"

Sitting at a sidewalk table at a corner coffee shop on Broad Street, on a beautiful, sunny late-summer day, he says it does him good, now, to talk about it. He says he's always at risk of going down the same road, always at risk of slipping into gambling again. He talks in the jargon of the twelve-step program. He says he finally hit bottom and admitted he needed help. He went to the Village Institute and met with Dr. Wolverton, who recommended that he join Gamblers Anonymous. He did, but there was a problem.

Gamblers Anonymous requires that members abstain from all forms of gambling, including buying and selling stock. That was impossible for a man who had to make his living as a trader. Dr. Mark wasn't going to go back to medicine. Even if he tried, there was no particular reason to believe he'd be more successful at it now than he'd been the year before.

He takes a sheaf of papers out of his backpack. They are scrupulously detailed schedules of how he will spend his time, what he will eat, when and where he will exercise, who he will socialize with, minutely and inflexibly planned, day after day after day for weeks in advance.

This is his higher power. The first step in a twelve-step program is to admit that one has hit bottom. The second is to come to believe that a higher power can offer healing. "I must rely on a higher power," he says, sipping a latte. "My rules are a higher power. If I follow my rules, God (in a sense) will bestow on me gifts."

Among the rules are commandments that govern his conduct on the trading floor—rules that tell him how he must think about a trade, when he is allowed to enter, when he is required to close out, no matter how good the underlying idea seems or how much he may still believe in it. Among the rules are restrictions on how much he can trade. When pressures begin to build and he feels the compulsion to gamble again, he picks up the phone and calls an alcoholic trader at a major brokerage house, his mentor, a man familiar with the twelve-step routine who listens to what Dr. Mark has to say and helps him focus on what he has to do.

He no longer talks much about freedom. He says he must continue to follow the rules, or else he will certainly slide back into the self-destructive patterns from which he has only recently escaped.

Two months into his program of therapy, the rules were working. Dr. Mark pointed with cautious pride to a string of winning weeks. "That's unheard of for me!" he exulted. "I don't have any new fundamental knowledge. It's just the psychological, spiritual change in my head." Whether the change could endure, only time would tell.

*   *   *

Anyone can learn this infectious game. That article of faith or credulity is the key to its epidemiology. Traders are discovered like starlets in old Hollywood, plucked from humdrum grinds and shot before they know it into lives full of promise, with glamour and wealth just a few keystrokes, maybe a mere mouse click, away.

At Harvey Houtkin's All-Tech headquarters, the star trader is a former manager of a Harley-Davidson dealership. "I'm trying to make trading mainstream," says Harvey. A self-test for trading aptitude he prepared merely asks variants of these questions: "Are you tired of your job? Do you want to be your own boss? Would you like to make more money?"

Who isn't? Who wouldn't?

At Broadway Trading, across the room from Dr. Mark's station, behind where the dynamic duo of Serge and Landon sit, a tall, skinny kid in a bill-back baseball cap tips rearward on two legs of a folding chair. He was a waiter in a restaurant on Long Island when one of the Broadway Trading principals happened by with a large party. The kid took everyone's order in his head, without using a notepad, and delivered the dishes with flawless recollection. The principal decided the kid had the stuff to be a player. **33**

All he needed was capital. A backer was found, and now there the boy sits, testing the proposition that anyone who can remember fifteen or twenty drink orders, salad dressings, entrees, and desserts can probably keep in mind the last four or five levels that six or eight stocks have jumped and anyone who can juggle five bowls of soup simultaneously can manage to hit the right keys when it counts.

But market regulators worry that trading may be getting more mainstream than it ought to be. They've been saying this loudly and often, and backing their words with actions.

In the fall of 1998, long-armed Massachusetts state securities lawmen reached all the way to Houston, Texas, to finger the flamboyant founders of Block Trading for making the game a little too easy for just anyone to play. It wasn't the first time Block co-founders Jeff Burke and Chris Block had gotten their names in the papers. A year earlier they'd made the cover of *Inc.*, even rated a spread in *Details,* two young men in matching black Ferraris who had come so far, so fast, from humble origins as cold-calling stock pushers for Lehman Brothers, where they started each day with a list of stocks and several hundred phone numbers to work the *Glengarry Glen Ross* hard way. Half the targets wouldn't answer, half of the remaining had the mother wit to hang up fast, some of the rest just wasted their time, and ultimately of the hundreds and hundreds maybe just ten talked long enough to qualify for the prime name list—the elite corps of mental cripples and greedy stragglers in the financial race for survival that these wolfish young brokers called back just a little while later with a-genuinely-exciting-new-opportunity-I-thought-of-you-right-away-when-I-saw-it-now-listen pitch. Moving to the close, Chris hopped on his desk and panted his patter into the headset while his feet did a victory dance on the blotter pad. Jeff also got physical—when prospects demurred—by hitting the floor in push-up position and pumping out fifty, sixty, seventy until he finally wore the suckers down.

One day, Harvey Houtkin's name turned up on the cold-call list. "You guys are like mushrooms! They keep you in the dark and feed you crap!" he roared back at them. They were trying to play with

The Player himself. By the time Harvey was finished with them, Chris and Jeff had both signed up for his training course to learn the SOES Bandit game, and after trading at All-Tech for a while, they peeled off to set up their own brokerage firm.

They grew rapidly—by 7,900 percent in the 1994–1996 period alone, according to the *Houston Chronicle*. Their brochures touted "the unlimited earning potential of day trading"; borrowing a page from Harvey Houtkin, they allied themselves with the little guy, claimed they helped individual investors profit from small movements in stocks, crowed that "the day is coming when the New York Stock Exchange, foreign exchanges, indeed all ostensibly free and open markets, will be unable to parcel information to the privileged few." They recommended that investors start with at least fifty thousand dollars in capital, preferably double that, but the Massachusetts securities regulators said that Block would arrange loans for customers who didn't have that much money.

Block didn't mention that service in its publicity materials. According to the regulators, Block didn't mention it in its filings to the Commonwealth of Massachusetts Office of the Secretary of State, Securities Division, either. According to Docket No. R-98-53, Administrative Complaint, in which the securities regulators moved to revoke Block's registration in the state and sought cease-and-desist orders against its principals, forty-four of the sixty-eight accounts in Block Trading's Boston office were trading with money borrowed from customers or other third parties. Yet Block Trading had told the regulators in writing that it did not "facilitate loan activity."

The regulators took a dim view of this. They also raised eyebrows at the fact that nowhere in Block's publicity material was there any statement that investors were more likely to lose money than make money while trading through the firm, even though, according to the allegations in the complaint, all but one of the sixty-eight accounts at the firm did indeed lose money.

The Massachusetts action in the fall of 1998 was the first shot fired by consumer protection regulators in what looked likely to be a long campaign against the day traders.

There was no doubt that day traders and day-trading firms were conducting business with less than extreme sensitivity to the concerns of regulators. Marc Friedfertig, cofounder of New York's Broadway Trading, had exulted in print that electronic day trading gave individual investors access to an investment opportunity that had disappeared approximately seventy years before—the bucket shop. In fact, he strongly recommended that all new candidates for Broadway Trading's training seminar first read the scriptures according to Jesse Livermore, the bucket shop wizard whom the jazz-age tabloids tagged "Boy Plunger of Wall Street," to whose story we now turn.

Part Two

RAISING LIVERMORE'S GHOST

Chapter 2

Jesse's Way

The First Day-Trading Master

Jesse Livermore was a hyphenated man: hard-headed, half-educated, self-made. He was both resolute and mutable, but not credulous, fanciful, or enthusiastic, and he was wholly unsentimental about the market. He always said that a trader should have no allegiances to either the bull or the bear side, and whenever he chose a side, he put everything he had on it. Yet he switched from bull to bear or bear to bull with no more attachment to his previous opinion than a weather vane when the wind changed.

Jesse Livermore wasn't a great trader because of the money he made, though he made an astonishing amount of money. He was a great trader because he made a lot of mistakes, learned from them, and talked articulately to a good reporter about what he learned, so his lessons were preserved for posterity.

Jesse Livermore was right about the markets often enough to make several fortunes, but he was wrong often enough to lose them.

He said that success meant "guessing right sixty percent of the **39** time," but there was more to it than that, because sometimes he managed to lose money even when he guessed right. Usually he lost by acting too soon, or waiting too long, or letting someone else talk him out of what he knew was right.

When he lost, he examined himself disinterestedly, starting from the obvious premise that he had done something wrong and proceeding to analyze exactly what that was. He never blamed the market for doing the wrong thing, and if he took bad advice, he held himself responsible for having taken it; he did not blame the person who gave it.

His lessons are easy to summarize. They are so obvious that they hardly seem worth stating, but that is always true of hard, profound lessons. Jesse Livermore learned these lessons from repeated painful experience, from merciless self-examination, from long and ruthless reflection. He spent most of his too-short life trying to practice them, and sometimes he succeeded; but eventually he broke, the way fighters do.

He learned that the only sure thing in the market is whatever the market is doing—not what data or analysis or tips or opinions suggest it ought to do or probably will do. He learned that the only way to know what the market is doing is to look at the tape, the prices at which stocks are actually being bought and sold. He learned that the overall trend of the market is more important than the news on any individual stock, because all boats move up or down with the tide. He learned that success at speculation consists of finding the direction in which the market is really moving, the "line of least resistance," and moving that way as soon as it is clear.

The markets in Livermore's day were murky, corrupt, and frequently manipulated, but he learned that even all of the Robber Barons working together to prop up a stock could not keep it up when it had to go down. He learned that the market moves by fits and starts, and that a trader who is right about the overall direction can still lose if his timing is off.

On November 28, 1940, at 5:35 P.M., an attendant making his hourly rounds at New York's Sherry Netherland Hotel noticed a man slumped in a chair near the door of the ground-floor men's room. He looked ill. The attendant went for help. The assistant manager of the hotel came and recognized the man immediately as Mr. Jesse Livermore.

Mr. Livermore's name, and his nickname, "The Boy Plunger," had once been notorious across the whole country. His habit of being on the right side of panics had started in the great panic of 1907, the market cataclysm that forced President Teddy "the Trust Buster" Roosevelt to ask his archnemesis J. P. Morgan to save the country from total financial meltdown by acting as the banking system's lender of last resort. Jesse Livermore had been merely thirty years old then, but he was so well-prepared for the crisis that the events of a single day propelled him into the millionaire's club three times over.

About twenty years later, people said that Jesse Livermore had shorted the market in another notorious bear raid and blamed him for the great crash of 1929, "which he watched from his Fifth Avenue office, while boys chalked up blackboard quotations for his eyes alone, and where thirty telephone lines linked him with an imposing array of brokerage houses and with a private corps of statisticians." After that, there were death threats, and he hired a bodyguard with a gun, but he kept speculating.

There was nothing else to do. Born on a Massachusetts farm in 1877, Livermore had worked the stingy soil between the rocks until he was old enough to leave, at age sixteen. He went to Boston and got a job marking prices on a chalkboard at a local brokerage, Paine Webber & Co. He had always been good at mental arithmetic, and the price changes fascinated him. Five hours every weekday—two hours on Saturday—all he had to think about was the prices changing. He paid attention and remembered. When a big run happened, up or down, he could recall exactly how the prices had moved the day before. On a Monday afternoon, when the market had closed, he would think about what the prices had done that day and write down in his notebook a forecast of how they would move on Tuesday, Wednesday, and Thursday.

One day a fellow clerk came to him with a proposition. The **41** clerk had gotten a tip on a railroad stock. Jesse Livermore didn't care about the tip, but he took out his notebook, looked at the price action on the stock, and decided to take the ten dollars he had saved out of his wages and pool with the clerk to buy Chicago, Burlington & Quincy Railroad stock on margin. The stock went up, and Jesse made $3.12 on his investment. His employer objected to such speculation by a clerk, so Jesse Livermore quit his job and began a new career as a bucket shop gambler.

In the stock-mad Gay Nineties, the high-class end of the market was beyond the reach of the average investor. Most got their taste of market action in these quasi brokerages. Although some of the bucket shops were seedy holes in the wall where sawdust and cigar butts littered the floor and spittoons were less frequently polished than one might prefer, many tried to look respectable. Like legitimate brokerage firms, the bucket shops all had big boards where boys marked up the latest prices quoted by telegraph from the New York, Chicago, and sometimes even the foreign markets. Many had ticker tape machines. In some, the telegraph wires went no farther than the wall, and the ticker tape merely unwound from a box where the proprietor had placed a day's worth of phony market action the night before. But there was no need for bucket shop operators to resort to such blatant fraud. It was easy enough to make money more or less honestly at this game, once the men were in the door. So, to get them in the door, many bucket shops imitated established brokerages by offering free lunch, free cigars, and private back rooms decorated with pictures of what was then commonly agreed to be the fair sex, portrayed in the unadorned glory of Eden.

The bucket shops differed from established, legitimate brokerages in one respect. "Buying" and "selling" in the bucket shop was just a shorthand for the direction of a bet—"buyers" won if prices rose, "sellers" if prices fell. The terms didn't really imply a transfer of ownership, as they did in a legitimate brokerage. This distinction between the bucket shops and the established brokerages was, for some, a mere technicality and, for others, an important argument in favor of bucket shops.

In those days, the stock market game was wide open. There were almost no rules at all, and what rules existed were made to be broken. Financial statements couldn't be trusted. Manipulation and outright fraud were too common to be considered scandalous. Whenever a wave of buying or selling hit a particular stock, the immediate question was which of the Robber Barons was sallying against what rival's fief. Tip sheets and touts made good money purporting to answer that recurring question. Rumors and tips counted for a great deal, both in the brokerage firms and the bucket shops; the opportunity to trade on inside information was the aspiration of even the lowliest bucket shop punter.

But Jesse Livermore traded in a unique, disturbing way. He ignored the tips and rumors that other traders sought. He concentrated instead on the minute-to-minute fluctuations in prices. He didn't particularly care why they changed. All that mattered were the changes themselves. When that fellow clerk at the Paine Webber office had asked him to go in on the Chicago, Burlington & Quincy Railroad trade, Jesse checked his notes on the stock first. The pattern of changes told him the price was going up, so he put some money on it, to test his reading of the price changes.

Jesse Livermore was inventing what is now called technical analysis, but he never called it that. He just called it "speculating," and he kept doing it because it kept working. Not long after that first trade, he brought a thousand dollars home and spread it out on the kitchen table in front of his mother. She said that she still disapproved of gambling. Jesse protested that he wasn't a gambler, he was a "speculator." Years later, long after his mother was dead, Jesse Livermore would protest to journalists that there was a big difference between gambling and speculating, as if he were still trying to convince her. Or himself.

The first time his name appeared in the papers was 1901, when his wife came back from Europe with twelve thousand dollars' worth of jewelry in her handbag and customs officials held the gems overnight. The papers reported that Livermore paid over seven thousand dollars in customs duties to release them the next day. **43**

He made his money in bucket shops. He played bucket shops all over the East Coast, then moved on to Chicago, St. Louis, and even Denver, trading in disguise, under assumed names, because eventually most of the bucket shops in the country barred Jesse Livermore for the same reason that casinos bar card counters—he won.

Livermore's market acumen was sometimes preternatural. In 1906, on vacation in Atlantic City, he happened to stop at a brokerage office to check the market. Looking at the ticker, he got a "queer feeling" about Union Pacific Railroad shares. He decided to short the stock. Then he shorted more, and then more, until he had sold enough to satisfy the "queer feeling." The next day, news of the San Francisco earthquake broke. The market did not react immediately. Livermore took advantage of the delay to add to his short position, and when the big slide finally came several days later, he was short over ten thousand shares. He made a quarter of a million dollars on that trade, his first big win.

But if his success depended on clairvoyance, Jesse Livermore would be just another oddity in the crowd of mildly interesting eccentrics who add an occasional spot of color to the gray tedium of Wall Street. Jesse Livermore never claimed clairvoyance. He didn't allege that he saw the San Francisco earthquake coming. He just said that he noticed something on the ticker tape that he could not describe, had a queer feeling that he ought to short Union Pacific, did, and stuck with the position even when the market seemed to shrug off the earthquake, then added to it. So he made in just a few days a fortune respectable by our contemporary standards, but fat city in 1906 dollars.

As a bucket shop punter, Jesse Livermore always knew that the exact price at which he could place a buy or sell bet was the most recent price to come across the ticker tape. This gave him a big advantage over the customer of the legitimate, established brokerage, for whom the most recent price on the ticker was mere history. The brokerage customer could not buy or sell for the price on the tape, because in order to buy or sell, the brokerage customer had to send an order to the brokerage office, where someone heard it and wrote it down and then sent it, by telegraph or phone, to the stock exchange floor, where the clerk wrote the order down and took it to the broker who took it to the specialist post, where the price might be higher or lower than the most recent price on the ticker, depending on what else had been happening in the market while the order was sauntering along.

When Jesse Livermore could no longer trade in the bucket shops because they had barred him, he tried to trade through legitimate brokerages, and he lost. After he had lost his first fortune by playing the market through the legitimate brokers, he recognized that he had to overcome the problem of tardy information, so he learned how to test the timeliness of what the tape was saying by sending small, exploratory buy and sell orders down to the exchange floor. The speed with which they were executed, or the slowness, told him the truth about the market. The truth was always in the price.

Jesse Livermore listened for the truth in the price the way Old Testament prophets listened for the voice of God. He would drop everything and go wherever he thought the price was directing him. After he had made a quarter of a million dollars by shorting a California railroad during the San Francisco earthquake, Jesse Livermore took a fishing vacation in Florida. While he was fishing, some friends pulled up alongside his boat. One of them had a newspaper. Jesse Livermore glanced at it and saw that the stock market had rallied, even though money was tight and interest rates were headed up, so there was no fundamental reason why it should rally. In fact, it should be headed down. So he put away his fishing rod and climbed into his friend's boat and went ashore to find a brokerage office in order to sell stocks short.

When he got to the brokerage office, he noticed that Anaconda Copper was on the point of breaking through the 300 mark. Although Jesse Livermore had come ashore to sell stocks short, he knew from years of watching prices move that when stock prices break through levels like 100, 200, 300, they usually shoot up much higher before falling back. He figured that if Anaconda Copper crossed 300, it would go all the way to 340 in no time. So instead of selling the market short, he bought Anaconda Copper, thirty-two thousand shares.

Then a storm knocked out the telegraph wires. The next day, only one price report came back, and it said that Anaconda Copper traded at 292. Livermore had lost a lot of money. He couldn't do anything with the telegraph down, so he waited. The stock opened the next day at 298, rose a little, then fell back to 301. The truth was always in the price, and the price was telling him that it had been a mistake to buy. He gave the clerk an order to sell all he owned. He got back a report that said five thousand shares had been sold for 299¾, the next two thousand for 299⅝, and so on, each lot selling for progressively less, with the last sold at 298¾. The truth in the price was loud and clear.

The prices at which his sell order had been executed told him the market was going down, so Jesse Livermore returned to New York to do what he had left the fishing boat for—sell everything short. He spent three or four months selling the market short and then took a vacation in Europe. When he saw a news report that the market had rallied in New York, he came back and resumed his short selling. Money was tight, he said, the prices couldn't keep rising. On October 24, 1907, the Great Panic came, and Jesse Livermore made three million dollars that day.

He tried to tell the newspaper reporters that it wasn't luck and it wasn't easy. "It sounds very easy to say that all you have to do is to watch the tape, establish your resistance points and be ready to trade along the line of least resistance as soon as you have determined it," he said. "But in actual practice a man has to guard against many things, and most of all against himself—that is, against human nature." Fear and greed were the biggest threats. Jesse Livermore called them the "enemies that bore from within." His battle went back and forth.

In 1908, he lost almost a million dollars trying to corner the cotton market, and went broke. Then he won it all back in a few days. But in 1915, he was broke again and declared bankruptcy. His debts totaled two million dollars, and he had no assets. By 1917, he had repaid all of his creditors in full. Despite his bankruptcy, he had been able to borrow a stake and play the war boom for all it was worth. After the war, he switched to the bear side and made another fortune during the recession. In 1924–25, Jesse Livermore bought wheat in five-million-bushel lots in a rising Chicago grain market, turned bear at the top, sold what he'd bought, shorted fifty million bushels more, and made more than a dollar a bushel by some estimates in what others called the "Black Friday" wheat market crash. Incidentally, he dabbled in stock price manipulation, fronting for the Sinclair pool and others. He engineered a short squeeze when he cornered the stock of the famous Piggly-Wiggly chain stores. The squeeze was so severe that the stock exchange suspended its ordinary rules to give the short sellers five days to cover, and Piggly-Wiggly founder Clarence Saunders lost his fortune.

When Jesse Livermore was flush, he lived large: yachts, private railroad cars, a big Long Island estate. He married three times and declared four bankruptcies. Every time but the last, he paid all of his creditors back in full.

He declared bankruptcy for the last time in 1934. He had debts of approximately 2.5 million dollars and assets of only eighty-four thousand. Despite the Great Depression, he soon made enough from speculating in wheat, cotton, and corn to pay the state and federal authorities eight hundred thousand dollars in back taxes. In 1939, he opened a financial advisory business, selling an investment system he called the Livermore Market Key. The system used certain stock groups as indicators of the market's direction, an approach now generally used by technical analysts, but then strikingly novel. Jesse Livermore had been a financial advisor once before, during an earlier bankruptcy. "For my services, I received a percentage of the profits—when there were any," he told a reporter, derisively. "That is how I lived. Well, say that is how I sustained life."

On November 28, 1940, he came to the Sherry Netherland Hotel for lunch. He had lived at the hotel for five years. Though he was now living on Park Avenue, his office was only three blocks away, so he often came by for lunch. He arrived about 12:30, ate **47** lightly, had one drink, and spent two hours scribbling furiously in a small notebook attached to his wallet. He seemed nervous and excitable, but there was nothing unusual about that, lately. He left the hotel bar around 2:30, but returned at 4:30, looking upset. He didn't speak with anyone in the bar, but had two more drinks before going to the washroom at 5:25. On the way, he passed the hotel manager, Eugene Volt, who said, "He looked normal and cheerful enough to me."

At 5:35, hotel attendant Patrick Murray saw him slumped in a chair in the men's room and called the assistant manager, Vincent Murphy, who came and recognized Mr. Livermore immediately. Mr. Livermore still looked normal, except for the blood trickling from his head and the .32-caliber Colt automatic revolver at his feet.

On a scratch pad attached to his wallet, the police found an eight-page note addressed "Dear Nina," a pet name for his wife. "Tired of fighting," it said, and "my life has been a failure" and "couldn't carry on any longer" and "everything is in a bad way." It mentioned "trouble" several times, but said many endearing things about Mrs. Livermore and expressed contrition for what he was planning to do, according to *The New York Times*. It was signed "Laurie" short for "Lauriston," Jesse Livermore's middle name.

Inspector Patrick J. Kenny notified Mrs. Livermore, who became hysterical and could not go to the scene. Mr. Livermore's son Jesse, who much resembled his father in the distant Boy Plunger days, arrived very shaken to make the formal identification. The medical examiner dispensed with an autopsy and accepted the police verdict of suicide.

Chapter 3

The Billion-Dollar Brewski

A Story of Scandal

The historical memory of the 1929 Crash would keep most Americans from investing in the stock market for decades after Jesse Livermore's death, and the post–World War II bias toward highly regulated markets made his old, bucket-shop-style game unplayable by all but a few professionals. Then, at the end of the twentieth century, powerful new technology brought the extinct bucket shops back in a new avatar: electronic communications networks (ECNs). It is impossible to put Extreme Investing in context without understanding the quirks of financial history that brought these powerful new alternative markets to their present position of market dominance and raised Livermore's ghost again.

Bill Lupien, a specialist on the Pacific Stock Exchange, began to build the first ECN in 1983. Called Instinet, because it originally served only institutions, Lupien's creature remains a major force in the market, though it lost the first prize for size to the day trader's favorite, upstart ECN Island, late in 1998.

Lupien did not invent Instinet, any more than Thomas Edison

invented the lightbulb. But, as Edison did with the lightbulb, Lupien perfected and commercialized an invention someone else had pioneered, so he deserves more credit for what the invention became than the inventor himself.

Unlike Jesse Livermore, Lupien never put too fine a point on the distinction between speculation and gambling. As a boy, he had put himself through San Diego State University by successfully betting on horse races. He was a reasonably good handicapper, did his homework with the *Racing Form,* and picked his share of winners. In his spare time, he played a lot of poker. In 1965, he found that his experience with horses and cards had been excellent preparation for his first job with the California-based brokerage firm Mitchum, Jones & Templeton, Inc. "It's like playing cards or any game. If you get enough clues you ought to be able to figure out what's going on," he says.

As a specialist, Lupien enjoyed a big advantage over the other players at the gaming table of the stock market. The specialist's job is to make a market in the stocks assigned to him, to buy when others want to sell and sell when others want to buy. Lupien stood ready to buy and sell his assigned stocks at every moment, as long as the market was open, and every order placed on the Pacific Stock Exchange to buy or sell those stocks had to come through him. He kept a record of all bids and offers as they came in, and this record, or "book," gave him information that no one else could see—the pattern of limit orders above and below the current market price. The book was a weather vane that told him which way the market wind was blowing. Since specialists make their money on the difference between the price they pay and the price they receive when they buy and sell stocks, the "book" was more than an important tool. It gave Lupien an information monopoly. Like a card player with a marked deck, he could read every hand at the table while keeping his own cards secret.

Sometimes, the pattern of bids and offers revealed more than the direction in which prices were likely to move. It showed how the really big buyers and sellers were positioning themselves, even though they were trying to keep their plans secret. Lupien often saw the market moving because of information that was unavailable to most traders and that wasn't supposed to be available to him. So when he acted on what he saw, brokers began to suspect him of having some inside pipeline or secret intelligence source. But he says he was "just counting cards."

His knack for surmising what the big boys were up to became more important with the debut of institutional investors whose appetite for stocks was unprecedented. Historically, banks, insurance companies, foundations, and other major institutions had equated safety with bonds and shunned stocks because of their risk. But in the late 1960s and early 1970s, inflation was eroding the value of bond portfolios. Meanwhile, upstart scholars in a new field that would eventually be tagged "financial economics" were convincing managers of big financial institutions that the stock market could indeed be a safe, sane, and eminently reasonable place to invest.

Institutional investors didn't deal in small numbers, and their orders were coveted by specialists on the various regional exchanges in United States. But Lupien noticed that the institutions often took their business to the New York Stock Exchange even when the Pacific Exchange specialists offered better prices. At the time, there was no consolidated, national ticker tape system; only the New York Stock Exchange prices got reported in the national press, and the institutions were leery of dealing at the less liquid regional exchanges for fear the prices there might not be as good as the closing prices reported from New York.

Lupien attacked this problem on two fronts. He pushed the Pacific Exchange to automate, hoping that superior technology could help bring the institutional business West, and he also got himself appointed to an advisory committee to make recommendations to the SEC on how to develop a truly national market system. It was at a meeting of this committee held in 1971 that Lupien first saw Instinet demonstrated.

Instinet's inventor was a quixotic aerospace analyst driven by a personal dream of eliminating the brokerage industry and the stock exchanges. He claimed that his fully computerized exchange would allow institutional investors to trade directly among them- **51** selves, without any middlemen. He already had about seventy very satisfied institutional subscribers, because although the technology was risibly rudimentary by today's standards, it did a badly needed job better than any other available mechanism. Instinet's dumb terminals displayed the prices at which subscribers were willing to buy (bid) and sell (offer) stock, and any subscriber could hit the bid or take the offer simply by typing a few simple commands on a keyboard connected via phone lines to a mainframe computer in New York. Transactions happened automatically and instantaneously at the prices displayed.

Lupien saw Instinet both for what it was and what it could be: a totally computerized, fully interactive, virtual stock exchange that could eliminate many of the delays and disadvantages of the cumbersome system in which he worked and had so far managed to prosper. He doubted that the system of specialists, brokers, runners, clerks, and cascading paperwork would be able to service the demanding new institutional investors. In fact, he had already run into problems trying to service them. The big problem was the same one that had vexed Jesse Livermore on his first foray out of the bucket shops and into the legitimate brokerage sector: time delay.

As Lupien watched the Instinet demonstration, he had a galling memory fresh in his mind. Not long before, he'd put out a large bid to buy a stock. An institutional trader on the other coast found out about this bid and decided to hit it. The trader sent a sell order for fifty thousand shares to Lupien's post, and the order moved across the country just as orders had moved in Jesse Livermore's day, relayed from hand to phone-dialing, paper-shuffling hand until it reached Lupien on the Pacific Exchange floor. Meanwhile, someone else hit the bid. So when the broker representing the institutional trader came to the post with the sell order, Lupien told him the price had changed. The broker relayed the new price to the trader, and Lupien got an angry phone call from the trader, who threatened never to use the Pacific Exchange again because the specialists there didn't honor their posted prices.

Instinet could solve that problem because it eliminated all of the intermediaries between buyers and sellers and allowed traders to hit bids and take offers electronically, instantaneously, at the touch of a button. But because it eliminated paperwork and middlemen, it threatened to eliminate jobs, so it was a hard sell at the Pacific Exchange. "They didn't want us to have this. It was like cavorting with the enemy. It was this fourth market, electronic black box. They didn't understand it, but they didn't want it," Lupien says.

After long negotiation, he managed to get clearance to install it, and one day, the loudspeaker on the exchange floor reported an eighty-thousand-share trade in one of Lupien's stocks. The other specialists looked over to see which broker had been responsible for the trade, but no one was standing in front of his post. After a long pause, one of the other specialists came up to ask Lupien where that big order had come from.

"Off the black box," Lupien said.

"I didn't know you could do that on there. How do I get one?" the specialist asked. Before long, every specialist on the exchange had a connection to Instinet.

The system performed so well that Lupien decided to buy the company—a big chunk of it, anyway. He put in a million dollars and went to his friends in the securities industry to line up more investors. But Lupien's vision for Instinet differed dramatically from its inventor's. The quixotic aerospace analyst had seen Instinet as a way to eliminate middlemen and bring institutions together directly. Lupien, by contrast, saw Instinet as the best friend middlemen ever had. Instinet lowered costs and increased speed on stock market transactions—and nobody did more stock market transactions than specialists, brokers, market makers, and similar intermediaries.

The new investors Lupien lined up appreciated his vision and pressed him to take executive command of Instinet in 1983. Meanwhile, the founder was promoted to chairman and cashed out a few years later.

Lupien opened Instinet to all kinds of users—brokers, specialists, market makers, money managers, institutions, almost anyone **53** with an interest in buying or selling stocks, except individual investors. "Not because I was opposed to individuals," he says, "but because I didn't understand how to deal with the regulatory issues, and frankly I'm not sure it could have been done then economically. The cost of providing the connectivity and the infrastructure would have been too high."

In 1983, when Lupien came on as Instinet's president, the highest quality modems were 300 baud and long-distance telephone calls were so expensive that he told his sales force that one new subscriber in a virgin market wouldn't be enough to cover the telecommunications costs. It took at least three banks, brokerage firms, or institutions to open a new market. "One of the trends I rode hard was the dropping of telecommunications costs. Every time they dropped, I'd expand the market," Lupien recalls.

Despite this constraint, the market grew, and subscribers discovered that Instinet provided advantages much greater than the mere ability to buy and sell automatically, as impressive as that was. It gave every user unprecedented access to information about the supply and demand for stocks. This information was particularly useful to participants in the Nasdaq market because the Nasdaq wasn't like other exchanges.

The acronym *Nasdaq* stands for "National Association of Securities Dealers Automated Quotations." As the name implies, the prices posted on the Nasdaq were just quotes. They weren't actually the prices at which dealers bought and sold stocks. Anyone interested in those bids and offers had to call the firm that had posted them in order to execute a trade. Not too surprisingly, perhaps, people who called to buy often found that the price had gone up in the time it took them to dial the phone—and people calling to sell found the price had gone down in the same interval.

By contrast, Instinet created a genuine market in which posted prices really meant something.

When Lupien joined the company, flickering green lines of text and numbers would display, in the lower left-hand corner of monochrome green screens, each stock's Inside Market as well as a list of the bids and offers of the Nasdaq market makers in that stock.

The bids and offers were time-stamped and dynamic, moving as market makers changed their quotes. But at first, users couldn't automatically hit or lift these bids and offers. That was the first thing Lupien changed. "Starting in September of 1983, we began to automate the Nasdaq execution process. We brought in brokers. They were in here with institutions, one big happy family, trading with each other," Lupien says.

Like a specialist on the floor of the exchange, every Instinet subscriber had access to the whole order book. But the Instinet subscriber had even more. Across the top of the Instinet screen scrolled a ticker unlike any other ticker available at the time. Customized to the user, it not only showed every trade in the stocks selected, it also displayed every update in every market maker's quotes for the stock and even displayed all of the incoming bids and offers from other Instinet customers active in the stock.

Plus, there was not one, but two ways to buy or sell. The first and most straightforward was to line up a cursor on a bid or offer and hit a key for an automatic, confidential execution. Alternatively, a user who wanted to haggle could send a message to open a confidential negotiation with a bid or offer party.

Instinet also provided a useful bit of information in the form of the "interest count" and the "present count" for each stock. The interest count showed the number of people who had put any given stock into their customized tickers. The present count showed how many of those had the stock in the execution field of their screens *now*. A subscriber could track numerous stocks in the ticker but could only focus on a few at a time. Whenever a subscriber decided to focus on the bids and offers in a particular stock, Instinet kicked up the present count by one.

A subscriber could see how big the potential market for a stock was by looking at the interest count and could watch the present count to gauge the intensity of that interest. "Say I just sent out a bid," Lupien explains. "I watch the present count. Suppose it's fifteen when I send my bid, and then it races up to three fifty. Suppose all three fifty look at it, and they don't sell to me. Do you think I got some information from that? You bet I did. I'll tell you what I got. I ran an advertisement that three hundred and fifty people looked at, but nobody offered me stock. What are they doing? They're either buyers, or they're just curious. How do I know they're buyers? Because I showed them a terrific bid. If they were sellers, they'd have hit it!"

In effect, this feature allowed Instinet traders to send out the same kind of market-testing "scout" orders that Jesse Livermore had used.

Bill Lupien left Instinet in 1988, shortly after Reuters made a tender offer to buy the company. He estimates that during his tenure and for a while after his departure, Instinet's business grew at a compounded average annual rate of 75 percent. Instinet functioned so efficiently and so well that it replaced the broad public market as the most important venue for price discovery in Nasdaq stocks. That was not entirely a good thing.

When, in 1991, two young college professors attending a conference in Jackson Hole, Wyoming, got together for a beer during a break in the proceedings, they paid their own tab, but their beer ultimately cost the New York financial establishment well over a billion dollars. This get-together led to a research program that pried open a Pandora's box of sleaze and collusion in the Nasdaq market. Ironically enough, the regulatory response to these discoveries brought bucket shops to the masses again, live and online, through clones of Instinet.

The professors, William Christie and Paul Schultz, had been doctoral students together in the late 1980s at the University of Chicago, the lakeshore Rome whose economic catechism teaches that people are, above all, rational economic animals acting in their own self-interest. If the Chicago School had a patron saint, it would probably be Blaise Pascal, the eighteenth-century French mathematician and philosopher who subjected the question of the existence of God to quantitative risk analysis, calculated that a bet in favor of God had a higher expected payoff than a bet against, and hooked up with the austere Jansenist sect to do penance for years before dying in the odor of sanctity with—it is no doubt safe to presume—reasonable expectations.

Economics students at the University of Chicago learn endless variations of the basic truth that people generally take care of number one first. They cut their teeth on questions like, how will laws that require seat belts in cars affect pedestrians? The answer: More pedestrians will be killed by drivers wearing seat belts who take more risks because they feel safer. Tossing around questions like that isn't just a way to pass time while waiting for the city to plow the snow during the long Chicago winters. It's a way to win Nobel Prizes, as a long roster of Chicago School Nobel laureates proves. In fact, if there were a market in Nobel laureates, the price at the University of Chicago would probably be low because the supply is so great there.

In 1776, Adam Smith wrote of an "invisible hand." Had better hallucinogens been available then, *The Wealth of Nations* might have shown more of the spirit of the Chicago School: folks there can see it. Christie had studied under Merton Miller, who won his Nobel Prize for figuring out that it doesn't really matter whether corporations raise capital by issuing stock or by borrowing, and that as long as interest payments are tax deductible, but dividends aren't, it makes a whole lot of sense for executives to borrow, borrow, borrow. Viewed in this light, the junk bond boom of the 1980s was quite rational, actually. Small wonder Merton Miller often found himself at odds with hacks in high places. When the derivatives disasters of the mid-1990s exploded into the headlines, journalists and Congress folk went crusading forth in search of something to regulate, but Miller stood firm against the tide, defying uninformed opinion and defending the proposition that rational self-interest was the best medicine for the derivative market, as it is for every market. Miller's dedication to free markets would pit him against his own protégé in the scandal that tore open the Nasdaq.

Christie and Schultz, washed in the blood, born again in the spirit, true believers in the Chicago School market creed, had hands laid on them by their advisors and received their University of Chicago Ph.D.s within a year of each other and went their separate ways, Christie to teach the market gospel at Vanderbilt Uni-   **57** versity, Schultz to evangelize the buckeyes at Ohio State. They didn't keep in touch, and they obviously missed that old Chicago feeling. In 1991, they happened to run into each other at the Western Finance Association conference in Jackson Hole. "We got together for a beer one night and decided it might be fun to work together," Christie recalls. "So we chatted about data sets."

At Ohio State, Paul Schultz had access to the Bridge Quotation System, a service that provided Level II Nasdaq data in real time. At Vanderbilt, Bill Christie had found data compiled by the Institute for the Study of Securities Markets that gave every single intraday revision in the inside market quotes for years back.

They decided to start their collaboration by downloading daily data from the Bridge Quotation System. One of the days they happened to download was November 15, 1991, a day when the market fell by 4.1 percent. That was the biggest slide since the October 1987 crash, and it gave the young professors an idea.

There had been a lot of talk about how market makers had acted in their rational self-interest during the 1987 crash. In order to avoid having to buy stocks, they had stopped answering phones and thrown a wrench into the SOES system by entering prices that locked or crossed the market. Regulators had responded to public outrage by forcing market makers to keep SOES operational even when quotes are crossed, and the two young professors wondered what the market makers had done during the subsequent mini-crash four years later, on November 15, 1991.

They assumed that market makers would behave rationally, and widen their price spreads, or the difference between what they are willing to buy for and what they are willing to sell at. When markets get volatile, it is rational to demand more reward for taking more risk. Because they were good Chicago School economists, Christie and Schultz decided to look for evidence that the market makers had done the reasonable thing. They began by trying to classify stocks by width of spread, starting with ⅛, then ¼, ⅜, ½, and so forth.

They ran into a problem right off the bat. "We were looking at thirty-five of the biggest Nasdaq stocks, and we couldn't find any

one-eighth spreads." Christie says. "We found this surprising, because these were among the largest and most active Nasdaq
stocks. We assumed the inside market would have narrowed to the
minimum tick size of one-eighth on occasion." How could it be that
market makers eager to bail out of a crashing market would never
have quoted the minimum possible price increment?

Christie assumed a mistake had been made when they down-
loaded the quotes from the Bridge system, so he decided to check
the results against his historical data from the Institute for the
Study of Securities Markets. When he did, he found good news and
bad news.

The good news was that they apparently had not made a mistake downloading the Bridge data. The bad news was that the
anomaly they had discovered looked even gnarlier now. Not only
could they not find any ⅛ spreads, they also could not find any ⅜,
⅝, or ⅞ spreads. As a rule, Nasdaq market maker spreads started at
¼, moved to ½, then to ¾, then on to the next dollar.

It looked as if market makers had found a way to guarantee
themselves a minimum spread of at least a quarter on every Nasdaq stock, no matter what the supply and demand conditions
might be. This implied that the Nasdaq was not a market, but
rather a cartel. And these professors were University of Chicago
types—they really didn't believe that cartels could exist very long,
because sooner or later the cartel members would break the rules,
to act in their individual interest. So Christie and Schultz went on
to collect every inside quote revision that occurred during 1991 for
one hundred of the biggest Nasdaq stocks. They found that the
pattern they had discovered in a small sample was repeated in the
large. "Our bottom-line conclusion was that market makers were
working in concert to make abnormally high profits on spread revenues," says Christie.

Being academics, of course, they didn't say it anywhere near so
frankly and clearly in the paper they wrote to summarize their research. Their original title was "The Frequency of Odd Eighth
Quotes on Nasdaq." They each presented the work at their own
universities, Schutz at Ohio State and Christie at Vanderbilt, and **59**

they planned to present it again at a conference at the University of California, Los Angeles, in March 1994. Meanwhile, they submitted the paper to the prestigious *Journal of Finance.* The editor told them they needed a better title. "By the time we got to the conference, the paper was titled 'Why Do Nasdaq Market Makers Collude to Maintain Wide Spreads?' The chief economist of the NASD was our discussant on the paper. He got up and said, 'You're totally wrong; no way there's collusion; couldn't happen.' But he never gave a good explanation for why we observed the pattern. After the conference, someone came up and introduced himself as someone working in the securities industry, and he said, 'You aren't even close when you think that market makers are colluding—you're exactly right,'" Christie recalls. He got the same kind of comment from other people familiar with the market.

The *Journal of Finance* accepted their paper in May. A few days later, Paul Schultz was having lunch with a colleague who mentioned that the two universities could probably get "a couple of days of press out of this." Schultz phoned Christie, who went to the director of Vanderbilt's M.B.A. program, told him the story, and asked if Vanderbilt's public relations department might be interested in doing a press release.

He asked, "Do you really want to do this?"

Christie was perplexed. "I didn't see any downside. We issued the press release on May 24, 1994, and the only person to call was Scott Paltrow of the *Los Angeles Times.* He called me on Wednesday and asked me to fax him a copy of the paper, called back later, asked me some questions, and ran an article in the business section of the *Los Angeles Times* on Thursday, May 26. Although we'd had total control over the paper and its results until then, starting Thursday we'd set a ball in motion there was no way we could stop."

The Paltrow article quoted Richard Ketchum, then chief operating officer of the NASD, who didn't dispute the findings that the top seventy stocks never traded at spreads narrower than ¼ but said there was a "legitimate reason" and that the study "is irresponsible and in fact we believe it is slanderous."

Christie got back to his office after lunch and found a phone message from a conference call of lawyers in San Diego, Los Angeles, and New York asking "to talk to you about this Nasdaq matter immediately." He feared that they were lawyers for the exchange, calling to demand that he either retract the paper or face a lawsuit. But when he returned the call, he found that they were in fact working on a class-action suit against the market makers. "I said, 'You can't possibly be thinking of doing this on the basis of our work,' and they responded, 'No, no, we've been working on this for years.' Whether they had or not, within the next month they had indeed filed litigation against the biggest market-making firms."

In October, a spokesman for the Justice Department acknowledged to a reporter that it was investigating the Nasdaq, and in November, the SEC launched its own probe.

Under attack now on all legal and regulatory fronts, the NASD vowed to appoint a group of "outside experts" to review the performance of market makers. Apparently, they had a little trouble finding enough outsiders to do the job because the panel they came up with was dominated by executives of Nasdaq trading firms and current or former NASD officials, as *The Wall Street Journal* noted.

But the securities dealers made up in quality for what they lacked in quantity of outsiders when they hired Merton Miller, the Nobel laureate from the University of Chicago, and Christie's former advisor, to rebut the Christie and Schultz paper in a conference on financial market reform held at Vanderbilt in the spring of 1995.

The very idea that market makers, who were engaged in the cutthroat competition of the stock market, could do what Christie and Schultz were accusing them of doing defied the most basic principle of Chicago School economics. Cartels only work if everyone does business by the rules. But sooner or later, an opportunity comes up to profit by breaking the rules. Rational animals acting in their own self-interest will invariably seize those opportunities. It didn't make sense to suppose that market makers who wanted to bail out of stocks that were tanking, would refuse to sell for less **61** than a quarter-point spread, cartel or no. Wall Street traders who live and die by their short-term profits would hardly pass up opportunities to undersell their competition now and then.

There had to be another explanation. Merton Miller was sure he had found it. He said that the suspicious-looking price patterns on the Nasdaq were merely examples of a well-known statistical phenomenon called "clustering," and said, "It is absolutely not necessary to have collusion to reach these results. It happens spontaneously."

But a few months later, the Justice Department stumbled on another cluster—a cluster of documents showing that the NASD had known for years that its members were colluding and applying "peer pressure" to keep prices high. And the SEC found a cluster of tapes. Most if not all telephone conversations between traders were taped. But traders tended to forget that after a while. The tapes included traders agreeing to engineer run-ups in stock prices so that they could unload their shares on an unsuspecting public at high prices. It caught traders phoning dealers who quoted odd-eighth spreads to accuse them of making a "Chinese market." Sometimes, the dealers who narrowed spreads answered their ringing phones to hear a phony Chinese accent ordering chop suey, moo goo gai pan, or other Chinese foods. Message delivered. Click.

Oddly, on May 27, the day after the *Los Angeles Times* published the first article about the Christie and Schultz paper, market makers cut in half the spreads on some of the Nasdaq's biggest stocks. On average, in one day, spreads on the ten most active Nasdaq stocks declined by 40 percent. What happened? Had the market makers suddenly decided to quote in odd eighths?

Not at all. In fact, the market makers had been quoting prices in odd eighths all along—they just hadn't been quoting them to the public. On the really important market, the market where the big insiders traded among themselves, there had never been collusion or price fixing. But that market was private, closed to the public, available only to Instinet subscribers.

Thanks to Instinet, the Nasdaq market had become a sort of Jekyll-Hyde affair, a market with a dual personality. One personality worked by classic Chicago School rules—in this market, rational traders motivated by short-term profits competed with razor-thin spreads to beat the other guy's price. This was the Instinet market. The other personality was the Nasdaq, a strange, dark place whose secrets had been exposed by Christie and Schultz, by the Justice Department, and by the SEC investigators.

The market makers had discovered that it was in their short-term self-interest to keep spreads artificially high on the Nasdaq, the public market where John Q. Public bought and sold. As long as the market makers maintained a disciplined, united front, they could make a minimum quarter of a point per share whenever they bought from and sold to the public. Nasdaq wasn't really a market at all, if the word "market" is understood to imply competition. All the competition occurred away from the public's eye, on Instinet—the only real market for Nasdaq stocks.

The SEC decided to treat the Nasdaq's disorder with a radical form of shock therapy. In August 1996, the securities market watchdog announced new order-handling rules. The new rules required that the best prices available on Instinet, SelectNet, and similar systems be displayed publicly on the Nasdaq. It also required market makers to display all investor limit orders—orders to buy or sell for prices above or below the current market. The investigators had discovered that Nasdaq market makers had habitually ignored limit orders they didn't like—for example, if the market maker was offering a stock for ¼ and a customer sent in an order to sell at ⅛. Now, the market makers had three choices: execute the limit order, send it to another market maker, or send it to an ECN.

The order-handling rules cut market maker profits (spreads) by approximately a third across the board, *and* in 1997 the market makers agreed to settle the class action lawsuit for a record-breaking $1 billion, of which lawyers for the plaintiffs got a wallet-busting $144 million. But the true cost to market-making firms was much greater. The order-handling rules opened the market gates to upstart competitors, new, Instinet-like ECNs. The first out of the gate was Island.

Chapter 4

Islands, Archipelagos, and Electronic Bucket Shops

T he word "island" is rich with connotations, suggesting a place where palm trees sway in gentle breezes as the surf whispers against the strand and smiling beauties out of Gauguin, adorning the thornless bushes with their smocks, bathe among the misty cascades. A paradise wherever the eye can see.

Built, often enough, on a foundation of guano. Some of the most idyllic South Pacific hideaways began as barren slabs of rock, millennia ago. Discovered by migrating birds, who annually returned, always leaving during their brief stops more than they took away, the rocks grew and grew, as the thick, rich guano provided a fertile base on which wind-borne or bird-borne seeds germinated, took root, and burgeoned into the green and blossom-brightened forests of now happy isles.

The casual visitor knows nothing of these islands' genesis, and probably would not care to think about the malodorous foundation of such bliss. There is also, in cyberspace, such an Island.

A subsidiary of Internet brokerage Datek Online, the ECN Island is indisputably an all-American success story. Started in 1992 by two kids, one a trader and the other a computer genius, it succeeded hugely by offering day traders a combination of speed, liquidity, and convenience more alluring in its way than all the houris of Oceania.

So idyllic is this Island, so congenial to traders, that hardly anyone gave more than a shrug when *The New York Times* reported that investigators from the Manhattan district attorney's office and the Securities and Exchange Commission had dug deep beneath the halcyon surface into murky and malodorous depths to find "a record of aggressive, and sometimes illegal, trading activity, of fines, censures, and suspensions, and of shadowy deals involving offshore accounts."

Island's story began when Sheldon Maschler joined a tiny Brooklyn-based securities firm, called Datek, in 1987. Maschler had learned the SOES Bandit game from Harvey Houtkin, a former partner, and he set up a trading operation at Datek. But Maschler had a cavalier attitude toward the rules of the game. "Under him, Datek always operated in the bowels of the industry," Houtkin says. People still talk about the press conference at which Maschler got into a shouting match with the president of the Nasdaq, threatened to punch him in the nose, and got "escorted" out by security guards. Fines, suspensions, citations for hundreds of infractions of trading rules decorate the biography of this flamboyant trader. The old adage says that a man can be known by the company he keeps. Maschler kept company with Robert Brennan, the penny stock promoter behind First Jersey Securities, barred for life from the brokerage industry because of massive fraud. Another member of Maschler's merry fellowship was Howard Citron, an old friend from Brooklyn with a record wide enough to embrace both stock fraud and drug dealing, according to *The New York Times*.

The smartest thing Sheldon Maschler ever did was to hire Howard's son, Jeffrey Citron, as an office clerk in 1988. Jeffrey had just graduated from high school. Before he was twenty, Jeffrey would be a millionaire.

A lot of the credit for that sudden prosperity goes to a high **65** school dropout named Joshua Levine. Self-effacing Levine modestly attributes his skill with computers to all the time he spent programming because he couldn't attract a girlfriend. Others call him a genius who, before he joined Datek, had built systems for global hedge fund powerhouse Tiger Management.

Levine and Citron became buddies and pooled their talents to automate Datek's operations. Speed was everything to the early SOES Bandits. Their success depended on their ability to spot and seize profit opportunities before the big market makers noticed they were there. Levine's computer savvy helped in small ways and big ones. He split the wires on a Nasdaq monitor and attached other monitors to it, so Datek got several monitors for the price of one. He wrote a DOS-based program called The Watcher, licensed by several day-trading brokerage firms, including Broadway Trading, and seen in action in the first chapter of this book. He enhanced it with a program called The Monster Key, which let Watcher traders cut ahead of everybody else in the market to get their SOES orders executed first and fast. The SOES system operates on a first-come, first-served basis, and it gives market makers a chance to rest and reset their quotes after they have fulfilled the SOES obligation. So being second or third in line often means missing the opportunity. Levine's Monster Key pushed Datek's orders to the head of the queue by automatically bidding the current price or up to 20 percent above it. This was a valuable advantage in a rising market.

All of these things helped in small ways, but the biggest thing Levine did was to invent the Island. He modestly deflects credit for the idea to his friend Citron, saying, "One day, Jeff noticed that with hundreds of Watcher traders doing tens of thousands of trades, sometimes one Watcher trader was trying to sell a stock on Nasdaq's SelectNet system while another Watcher trader was simultaneously trying to buy the same stock on SelectNet."

SelectNet is a Nasdaq system available only to market makers. Anyone could send orders to the market makers via SelectNet, but only market makers could hit the bids or lift the offers that came across the SelectNet screens. They were under no obligation to do so. If two Watcher traders had entered orders, one to buy and one to sell, at the same price, there was no incentive for the market makers to execute the orders. Market makers make their money on the spread, the difference between the bid and the offer price.

"Because only Market Makers could execute SelectNet orders, sometimes both traders were unfairly left without executions," Levine says. "There was a system available for matching limit orders, called Instinet. It was slow and expensive, but it was all there was, so we applied for access."

The application was denied. Instinet, sensitive to the prejudices of its market maker and institutional clients, wanted nothing to do with SOES Bandits. In fact, Instinet had pulled its terminals out of Harvey Houtkin's shop after market makers objected to his presence on the system. Datek never got on the system in the first place.

"They sent two attractive women out to meet with Jeff and me," Levine continues. "After a lot of back and forth about why we were being denied access, they finally told us that Instinet 'did not want your kind of business.' Period. We told them that we really needed a matching system for our then tens of thousands of trades per day, and if they didn't let us use theirs we'd be forced to write our own. They chuckled and left."

So Levine got to work building a system that would keep track of every SelectNet bid and offer entered by traders using Watcher and would match buy and sell trades. It was hard work with plain tools. "While the concept of matching these SelectNet orders off is very simple, the system design and implementation details are complex," Levine says. "Nasdaq's systems are notoriously hard to interface to, and it took a lot of work to get the matching algorithms just right. We did the whole thing on off-the-shelf PCs because that's what we had and that's what we knew."

If Island saw a buy order destined for SelectNet, it would look to see if there was a pending sell order in that stock already on SelectNet. If it found a match, Island would cancel the SelectNet sell order, and when it received confirmation that the order had been canceled, would execute a trade between buyer and seller on its **67** own system. If it didn't find a match, Island would send the incoming order to SelectNet, but it would "remember" having done so, in case a match came in before a market maker executed the order.

"People got more executions, those executions were faster, and expensive SelectNet fees were avoided. It was very good. So we decided to offer this 'we'll enter your SelectNet orders for you and you'll get more executions faster' service to anyone who wanted it," Levine recalled. "I wrote a very simple API [*application programming interface,* the protocol by which programs communicate with each other] to the system and started giving it to people." Word got around.

David Whitcomb, professor of finance at Rutgers University's Graduate School of Business, got a call one day from a journalist friend who invited him along on an interview with Josh Levine. "We went to a grubby office in a grubby building in a grubby part of Wall Street. There were coffee stains on the desks, wires everywhere, kids in T-shirts and jeans sitting at computers, and if we were the kind of people who are impressed with appearances, we'd have left," Whitcomb says. Instead, he asked to sign up as a customer, the first non-Watcher client of Island.

Whitcomb and a partner had built a small trading firm around an expert system designed to recognize market patterns that preceded movements in stock prices and enter limit orders the way an ace trader would. "The key is having another side so you can execute, get in and get out quickly," he says. Whitcomb had access to the Instinet system (he had done some consulting work for Bill Lupien, and he wasn't the classic SOES Bandit trader), but although Instinet was liquid, it was slow and expensive. Island, by contrast, was cheap and fast. Whitcomb and his partner had to do some reprogramming to connect to Island, but it was worth the trouble.

A lot of other people felt that way too. "As the number of orders in the system grew, so did the value of using the system, making it progressively easier to get more people on the system," Levine says. Liquidity begets liquidity. Traders who want a deal done fast go where there are lots of other traders. So the more traders Island attracted, the more orders there were moving through, and the more orders there were moving through, the more appealing Island was to traders. It was a virtuous circle of growth.

The changes in Nasdaq's order-handling rules imposed by the SEC after the discovery of collusion by market makers combined with the day-trading gold rush to spin that circle faster and faster. The little ECN started by two kids miffed because Instinet had refused to serve them had, just six years later, left Instinet in the dust. "Propelled by the surge of online trading volume, the Island ECN (which is owned and operated by Datek Online) leapt ahead of the venerable Instinet to seize the #1 position and become the single largest ECN in the world," wrote Credit Suisse First Boston analyst Bill Burnham. In the last three months of 1998, Island's volume went from being 52 percent smaller than Instinet's to being 75 percent higher. The secret to success: Island had become one of the top market makers for the stocks most favored by day traders—Amazon.com, Yahoo, and Dell Computer, among others. Meanwhile, Datek Online became the fastest-growing online brokerage, and the fifth largest.

There was trouble in paradise, but one had to dig deep to find it, and few seemed to care. An initial public offering of stock in the still privately held Datek Online was eagerly awaited in the spring of 1998. Then, *The New York Times* printed a devastating article outlining investigations by the SEC and the Manhattan district attorney's office into stock manipulation, money laundering, and unspecified violations of Nasdaq rules that cast a pall over the IPO. Datek Online denied that it had done anything illegal, and by early 1999, there had been no closure. The Manhattan district attorney's office refused to either confirm or deny that an investigation was underway.

Meanwhile, though, Island's phenomenal example had inspired others. The bluest of blue chip securities houses, Goldman Sachs, joined hands with online brokerage E*Trade to purchase half of a small ECN, based in Chicago, called Archipelago. Although it was only one-twelfth the size of Island, observers noted **69** that if both Goldman and E*Trade began to funnel trades through Archipelago, it wouldn't be small for long.

Archipelago, unlike Island, had linkages to all the other players in the market and was a true global market player, a spoke in a wheel whose hub centered on a nondescript office complex in Chicago, the base of operations for a low-profile software firm.

One February afternoon in 1999, Stuart Townsend welcomed a visitor to the Wacker Drive complex that housed Townsend Analytic Systems and its sister companies. In the plain but spacious front office, across the lobby from a stack of newly delivered workstations, in front of a sixties-retro couch with teardrop-shaped formica elbow rests, on a monitor no thicker than half a ream of bond paper, a graph of an index blipped upward again. Stuart Townsend clicked a mouse to shift the display, opened a window on the U.S. stock market, and perused the prices at the Pacific, Cincinnati, Philadelphia, and New York exchanges. Another click brought up the futures exchanges in Chicago; another click, there were the London metal markets; click again, here was the Nasdaq Level II screen; click, for options in Geneva; click, stocks in Milan; click, futures in Paris. Virtually everything traded on any exchange anywhere in the globe-girdling financial markets was accessible at the click of a mouse.

Some markets were still beyond the reach of the system, of course. Mostly they were markets beyond the reach of any system. Markets that don't have an organized exchange to give them a central point of price reference. Government bonds, for example. They don't trade on an organized exchange, and prices aren't available to the public. Ooops—make that *weren't*.

In a conference room a few steps from the couch, a team from Zion Bank watched another screen. A regional bank based in Salt Lake City, Utah, Zion had wandered far from home on an acquisition spree and bought the Discount Corporation of New York, thereby becoming a primary dealer in U.S. government securities.

"So here they are, a little regional Utah bank, trying to figure out how to compete against the big guys in New York," said Charlie McQuinn, a consultant to the bank, explaining the project to the visitor. "They decided that since they are a regional bank serving Ma and Pa America, they could make primary dealer rates on treasury and fixed income available to the little guy. Of course, they would have to do it electronically; otherwise it would be too expensive to go down to the little guy."

Working with Townsend, Zion developed a system to provide the little guy with the ability to trade, at the click of a mouse, bonds, repos, commercial paper, and other government debt instruments issued by the U.S. Treasury and its agencies—Fannie Mae, Freddie Mac, and others. For the first time ever, the little guys would have access to real-time prices for a range of government paper whose real prices used to be known only to a small group of big insiders, primary dealers and their best customers, who packaged the bonds for resale, through brokers, to the little guy. Like the old Nasdaq market makers, these primary dealers made most of their money exploiting an information advantage and a spread. "Little," by the way, was a relative concept. Customers on this system would include municipal and county treasury managers, trust departments of small banks, institutions, and perhaps well-to-do individuals who might trade up to five million dollars at a crack. But in a market that included central banks of major countries, they were indeed little by comparison. "The minimum at the other primary dealers is twenty-five or fifty million dollars per trade, so we're picking up the odd lots," McQuinn said.

Stuart Townsend strode ahead of the visitor, leading the way toward the back office with the easy confidence of a man who saw the future and his place in it. It would be a future of totally transparent markets, with equal electronic access for everyone, markets so efficient that the spread between a bid and an offer would have been reduced to almost nothing, because everyone would know simultaneously what the true, fair price was and no one would be able to exploit a monopoly on information, because everyone would know everything that mattered about anything.

In the back office, arrays of Gateway computers were racked on glass-doored shelves like books in a library. "We use Gateways because as the machines age, they move out to become people's **71** workstations," Townsend observed in an aside. Computers cycled in and out at the rate of about ten a week, every cycle bringing in the newest and most powerful available and pushing out what had been the newest and most powerful just a few weeks before. The computers, the routers, the servers tracked and sorted and transmitted 30,000 price changes per minute, for 33,000 different stocks and futures, 150,000 options, a universe that, with foreign instruments thrown in, covered half a million financial instruments. Townsend was about to add a fifth T-3 cable, which would give this room two more such cables than the entire University of Chicago, his alma mater. Two routers directed electronic traffic over a private network, a frame relay linking various institutions and trading rooms. Other routers connected to the Internet through several different Internet access providers, providing not only backup, but backup to the backup in case of a failure at one or two of the providers. Two batteries the size of refrigerators backed up the power system.

Monitors mapped the system for attendants, so that in case of trouble, a quick glance at the screen would show what needed to be fixed. Other monitors showed bids and offers flowing through Archipelago. "Dell dropped this morning. We were watching, and at times we had ten bids and simultaneously two or three offers, for size," he said. "Probably offers coming in from the floor of the Chicago Board Options Exchange, where the options traders were buying and selling Dell options and executing stock orders with us to hedge them. At times, Archipelago was on both sides of the market, it was moving so fast."

Three years before, those orders would have gone much more slowly into a decidedly different kind of market. The technology shock had hit with such force that it was turning the global economy into one gigantic trading pit.

Then Stuart Townsend began to talk about his plans for Europe.

Part Three

THE GLOBAL TRADING PIT

Chapter 5

Capitalist Roaders

Day Trading Without Borders

Chi va piano, va sano e va lontano.
Who goes slowly, goes soundly and far.
—Italian Proverb

A dark green Lexus GS300 barreled along the highway from Milan toward the mountains at a hundred miles an hour one February afternoon in 1999. Inside, Mr. Hugo Assi juggled a cell phone in one hand and the steering wheel in the other. "In recent years, we saw the sunset of a dream, a dream that had lasted for fifty or sixty years," he reflected distantly, in measured, slightly accented English. No one knew better than he the infrastructure of Italian finance, and no one was more committed to revolution. "Italian capitalism is very weak," he mused. "It is made up of a very selective, very small number of families that control Fiat, Olivetti, and the entire capitalistic system, including the stock exchange."

Assi had capped a career in the high-tech industry with a special assignment at the Bank of Italy: to link the country's banks in an electronic payment network and build electronic trading systems for bonds, options, futures, and other securities. He had seen it all; he knew what had to be done; there was no longer any question in his mind. Economic stagnation was a clear and present danger to the Italian masses. The people had believed in the illusion of social security, relied on the promises of a welfare state. But now it was frighteningly clear that the promises would not be kept. The people would have to provide for themselves. But how? Italians had never developed the habit or the culture of popular capitalism. "Investments were for rich people. The illusion of social security meant that people had no push to invest," Assi growled bitterly.

The only hope for the masses was the opportunity to share in economic growth. But growth on the scale required could not be led by the few big, tired Italian companies on the stock exchange, and even if it could, the people were in no position to share in it. Before they could share in growth, someone had to break the fingers that gripped the Italian economy in a stranglehold and smash the power of the ruling families. An oligarchy of bureaucratic behemoths was shutting off challengers from access to capital, cutting off the air supply to entrepreneurial ventures. "This is what is limiting the Italian economy," Assi observed with a degree of understatement that reminded one of his central bank experience. "A few families not permitting small companies to become big enough to be quoted on the stock exchange means an economy without enough oxygen to grow really big."

No one took the old cant of Marx, Lenin, or Mao seriously anymore, of course, least of all Assi. He understood the system far too well to swallow such naive claptrap. It was indeed true that, at the turn of the millennium, the masses would begin to wrest away ownership of the means of production from the ruling classes. But they would not do it through armed struggle. Power would not come from the barrel of a gun, but from the click of a mouse. The vanguard of the revolution would not be a well-disciplined Party, but fiercely competitive discount brokers and fast, ubiquitous online trading systems.

This would, of course, require a massive cultural revolution, a
spontaneous capitalist uprising. Here and there, it was already be-

ginning. Curiousity vied with fear, as Italians began to subscribe to financial publications, watch market news on television, even form investment clubs to trespass on the territory of the very rich, the stock exchange.

No question at all, there was something very un-Italian, even un-European, about it. For companies to raise money on stock exchanges, for investors to buy and sell shares of stock—this was all a very Anglo-Saxon way of doing things. Assi had the statistics in his head. "As a matter of fact, the amount of financial information consumed per year in Europe—a total of $3.5 billion—is purchased 41 percent in the United Kingdom, 13 percent in Germany, 13 percent in France, 4 percent in Italy, and 17 percent in Switzerland. Do you appreciate the difference in approach?"

Continental European financial culture was a debt culture. Companies in search of growth capital went to the banks, which made lending decisions peripherally influenced by financial information but powerfully motivated by family, corporate, political, or other connections. This culture was generally risk-averse, always preferring the tried (even if not necessarily the true) over the new. It was a culture of personal relationships, privileged information, inscrutable, Byzantine, secret.

By contrast, the Anglo-Saxon world, especially in its American avatar, was public, transparent, straightforward, and efficiently impersonal. There were banks, of course, but they operated increasingly as mere conduits to the capital markets. The British and the Americans built trust not through personal relationships and old family connections but by a system of checks and balances that treated all comers more or less equally. Public financial reports prepared in accordance with uniform accounting standards, and audited, made it possible for complete strangers to make educated bets on product, strategy, and management before investing in someone else's vision. Entrepreneurs with a good idea could approach these strangers by making a public offering, raise capital, and grow as Microsoft, Intel, Yahoo, Amazon.com, and any number of others had done.

"This is the only democratic solution to the problem of Italian **77**

capitalism," he said. In the first phase of his plan to make it a reality, Assi had formed a relationship with Townsend Analytic Systems and a venture with the oldest private securities brokerage
firm in Milan, a company called Cofimo, which provided a point of
entry to the stock exchange. The next phase of his plan called for
approaching upper-middle-class Italians through their banks, edu-
cating them to the opportunities in the market, and providing
them with software to take advantage of those opportunities.

Assi was not alone. He was a key figure in an elite group with
representatives in every financial center of Europe. There were
connections in Zurich and Geneva, Paris and Frankfurt, Amster-
dam and London. They worked autonomously, but were known to
each other and exchanged information as needed. Their common
goal: To transform the European economic system by bringing the
power of electronic trading systems to individuals.

In Berlin, Dr. Guido Sandler, chairman of Berliner Effekten-
bank, chuckled with peculiarly Germanic ambiguity at the inefficiency of the stock market. "Look at the economic power of the
European countries, and look at the development of our equity
markets! Until last year, we had only eight hundred German equities. That's roughly the number of new issues you see in the U.S.
every year! And three-quarters of all trades are done within just
ten stocks! So the market is not very efficient, and not very deep.
We have a very strong debt culture in Germany."

The inefficiency of the market was, to some, its most attractive
attribute. As small as the German stock market was, Sandler explained, it was divided among several regional exchanges, each of
which functioned as the main arena of liquidity for its own local
stocks. This created a tremendously profitable arbitrage opportunity for traders.

At the end of 1998, the Deutsche Börse in Frankfurt, Germany's biggest exchange, had decided to include all eight hundred
stocks on its electronic trading system, Xetra. A costly mistake,
Sandler said, because while the regional exchanges that listed
many of these stocks were small, they were very liquid in their own
stocks. Sellers knew that there would be buyers on the regional ex-

change, buyers knew there would be sellers, and the fact that buyers and sellers met regularly on the regional exchanges meant that the prices quoted there best reflected the current supply and demand conditions for the stocks. There was no compelling reason for buyers and sellers to trade on Xetra instead of on the regional exchanges, so the prices quoted on Xetra were out of line with the prices quoted on the regional exchanges. Therefore, traders could buy a stock on Xetra and sell it on the regional exchange, or buy it on the regional exchange and sell it on Xetra, for an arbitrage profit. "It was a rip-off for everybody who had access to intraday trading systems, because the prices were better on the regional exchanges than in Frankfurt. We in our company made quite some profits on that," Sandler guffawed. "And it was a pleasure to rip off Xetra!"

Sandler had a plan to put trading technology in the hands of individuals, but he did not speak in terms of democracy or revolution. In fact, he seemed to lack entirely Assi's Mediterranean passion for the romance of social transformation. Rather, Sandler approached the task with plodding, inexorable, Teutonic determination.

His bank was exclusively devoted to equity financing, and besides trading stocks for its own account, Berliner Effektenbank was involved in a wide range of exotic financing activities. "We are the first in Germany to do concept IPOs, very early stage IPOs where we present a business idea to the market and individuals can buy in to the value added in the process of developing the company. Once the company starts to report profit, these investors are not interested anymore. This is a type of risk capital which we have at present here in Germany that is not even available in the U.S.," he said, not without pride. Sandler's bank also made a market in Germany for seventeen hundred high-risk stocks. "Small cap U.S. stocks, Russian stocks, even Chinese stocks," he said, "the type of risky investment you don't sell to traditional investors."

Of course, the investors whom he courted were anything but traditional. As the generation that had built Germany's closely held, often family-owned companies passed from the scene, problems of choosing successors and dividing inheritances in many cases led the estates to sell the companies. "So the kids take over, and for the first time they have substantial wealth in hand. Historically, in this century we have seen deflation, collapse of currencies, wars—so older folks tended to invest in real property, not in stocks. But the generation now in charge and holding liquidity hasn't had the bad experiences of their parents. These are the ones who are making the waves now," Sandler explained. "A lot of liquidity is pushing into the market, and the market is not big, so prices go up, and that attracts more interest. This is the cycle we're going through right now in Germany. We now see a group of young people coming in who in some individual stocks are better informed than we are. They have done their homework, they are comfortable with new technologies, they are willing to take more risk, and they want to have the tools to take advantage of this situation."

Sandler found these people most interesting indeed. Rich, sophisticated, well-educated people with time on their hands, interested in trading not because they needed to make a living but more as a hobby, a game of skill, an intellectually challenging diversion from their regular professions. "They are not risking the whole property they have, but perhaps 10 to 15 percent, a million or two to start out with, so they can really do something," he said. A few of his customers were American, and he expected the number of Americans to grow as his bank made more sophisticated, online trading technologies available.

Sandler had decided to focus his attention on the upper-middle-class investor. There were sound reasons for this. While market regulations and trading practices differ from country to country, generally speaking, margin is not available to European individual investors. In the United States, traders and investors can double the power of their money by taking advantage of margin credit. Margin is really a loan, secured by the stock itself. It allows a person with only fifty thousand dollars to buy a hundred thousand dollars worth of stock. If the price of the stock falls, either the

trader may add money to the account to ensure that the broker will not be at risk, or else the broker may sell the stock to recover the margin loan.

Margin gives traders more bang for the buck, and because margin is not generally available in Europe, traders in European markets have to start out with more cash than their counterparts in the United States. But for traders with the cash to play, the European stock markets offer some interesting opportunities of a type not seen in the United States for years. For example, spreads between bid and offer prices tend to be much wider than in the United States. A trader can buy a stock, cut the spread by offering it for slightly less than the current best offer, and make a quick profit. Spread cutting had been an important part of the game played by American SOES Bandits in the late eighties and early nineties. But the SEC mandated market reforms, and the pressure of competition had narrowed Nasdaq spreads almost to the vanishing point by the end of the nineties. With spreads often as thin and sometimes even thinner than a sixteenth of a point, there was little to be gained in the U.S. markets by spread cutting anymore. But in Europe's less efficient markets, the game could still be played profitably.

Partly because of the relatively high prices of European stocks, and partly because of the (by U.S. standards) exorbitantly high commissions, the European trading game did not look quite the same as its U.S. counterpart. But it was clearly evolving in the same direction. Industry analysts expected that about ten million Europeans would be using online information and brokerage services by the second year of the new millennium. Among them would be day traders, a group that Sandler himself found rather distasteful. "There is a day-trading room in Berlin already," he sniffed. "Who are they? They start with twenty or a hundred thousand marks only, and it is just like gambling. They might as well go to a casino."

Others were considerably less disdainful of the day-trading phenomenon.

Daniel Huber had been a professional trader for a major Swiss bank before he decided in 1994 to go partners in a financial information company to profit from the vulgarization of Europe's stock markets. First Quote, a venture based on Townsend software, would be his ticket to the races. The privatization of big, state-owned utility companies like Deutsche Telecomm had brought many Europeans into the stock market for the first time, and they clearly liked what they found there. "We are at the beginning of the bubble you see in the United States," Huber said. Evidently impressed with the ability of entrepreneurs with good ideas to raise capital and launch companies in the United States, Europeans had set up their own small cap exchanges, flattering by emulation the Nasdaq. "Local European investors are jumping on the opportunity to buy the small caps," Huber remarked, citing the example of one company that had an opportunity to do an IPO either in Europe or the United States. In the United States, it could have raised only $150 million in a U.S. offering, but it managed to get $280 million by doing the offering in Europe.

Small-time European traders had also found a way to trade the big-name stocks on a leveraged basis, through the warrant market. Warrants are a species of option. Typically, a big institutional investor makes a deal with a bank to issue the warrants on shares owned by the institution. The institutional investor's motivation is to earn additional return on the stock portfolio by pocketing its share of the warrant proceeds. Warrants give European traders of modest means a chance to get a lot more bang for their marks, liras, or francs. Warrant prices are low, so a trader can buy a big position. When stock prices move, warrant prices move; so warrants give small traders the hope of making money trading stocks they can't afford to buy directly. Wide spreads, volatile prices, and high leverage mix a potent cocktail.

"There's big money to be made, but it's a dangerous game," Huber says. Once the warrants are issued, the bank and the institution hedge their risk using mathematical models that require them to buy and sell the underlying stock in response to price changes. These models are similar to the "portfolio insurance" that achieved notoriety for its contribution to the October 1987 stock market crash in the United States. Some traders blame wide swings in European stock prices on dynamic hedging by institutions trying to protect themselves against the risk of warrants they have issued.

Volatile markets are a thing of beauty to Extreme Investors in the United States. They buy stocks on the way up and sell them short on the way down. Unfortunately for traders in the European markets, barriers to playing the downside by shorting stocks made it all but impossible to do likewise.

In the United States, it is relatively easy for traders to sell borrowed stock in anticipation of a fall in the price, then buy it back after the price has fallen. Buying at a low price and then selling at a higher is economically identical to selling at a high price and then buying at a lower. Both have in common the golden rule of trading: Buy low, sell high.

So, one of the fundamental principles of the Extreme Investor's game in the United States is to look for stocks that show weakness when the market rises and sell them short when the market turns down. On European exchanges, this strategy won't work. "Very few banks allow their private clients to go short," Huber says. "For institutions, it's not a problem, but for private individuals, it's not common to do. So 90 percent of the traders in Europe just know how to buy. If a stock doesn't follow the market up, trading just dwindles away. Everybody is long and holds the stock even if the price falls by 10 percent. No one plays the downside."

The ability to profit in down markets, combined with much lower commissions, deeper and more liquid markets, and the availability of margin, all made the U.S. markets more congenial to many European Extreme Investors than their own backyards, and thanks to the Internet, the U.S. markets were even closer and more accessible than their own backyards. Huber and his partners hoped to link all of the European and U.S. markets on a single, electronic trading platform that would give individual investors in Europe access to trading power historically available only to professional money managers.

Others had their eyes on the same prize. **83**

A clear sign of the times: In 1998, a German entrepreneur opened a day-trading room in Berlin, the city that perhaps only baby boomers now remember in connection with a famous wall. He named his firm Momentum AG, after a Houston, Texas, firm, Momentum Securities, that had been profiled in *Der Spiegel*, Germany's leading news magazine, several months before. Soon afterward, the German press marveled at the phenomenon of a middle-aged former hairdresser scoring thousands of marks a week, playing options and futures markets just like the professionals at the big German banks. In fact, she was using professional trading software that linked her to Interactive Brokers, a member of the New York–based Timber Hill group, 60 percent of whose customers were institutional traders.

Interactive Brokers had begun in 1998 to offer fully electronic trading, over the Internet, to customers in the United States and Europe. Timber Hill had made its name in the New York and Chicago markets trading options and futures during the eighties. In 1990, the company had been one of the first American outfits to trade on the Deutsche Terminbörse (DTB)—later renamed Deutsche Börse—and quickly captured 10 percent of the volume there. Timber Hill soon expanded to the other major European and Asian exchanges.

The firm was an early adopter of advanced technology. As early as 1983, Timber Hill equipped its floor traders with handheld computers to continually reprice options. At the time, other traders used printed pricing sheets that were updated only twice a day. By 1998, through the Interactive Brokers unit, it was offering customers direct online links to fully electronic exchanges and to traditional trading floors, where its traders received customer orders on their handheld devices, executed them, and sent the customer an electronic confirmation.

Although Interactive Brokers did not specifically target day traders as a customer base, Managing Director Robert Prior said that the firm's software was in fact being so used by several new, European day-trading firms. Speed and ease of use were big selling points. "All you need is a PC on your desktop and a connection to our network," Prior said, noting that while Europeans were trading the Nasdaq, Americans were playing the European markets, and some traders were using the system to bet the spread between American indices like the S&P and European indices like the DAX, the index of leading German stocks. The only thing standing in the way of more Asian participation was the time difference; U.S. and European markets trade in the dead of the Asian night.

But in summer of 1999, announcement of a joint venture between Japanese venture capital firm Softbank and the National Association of Securities Dealers (NASD) signaled that the time difference would not be an obstacle to Asians much longer. Called Nasdaq-Japan, the new venture aimed to make trading opportunities in at least one hundred of the largest Nasdaq stocks available to Japanese individuals during their own market hours. Press reports suggested that Americans might also use Nasdaq-Japan to trade outside of U.S. market hours, even though the Nasdaq was likely to extend trading hours domestically. The existence of two exchanges trading many of the same stocks would probably offer arbitrage opportunities to traders equipped with the technology to exploit them.

Chapter 6

Inside the Archipelago

The Technology of Revolution

T he technological and market revolution that spread the Extreme Investing game to all continents is in large part the story of a little, Chicago-based, husband-and-wife software shop: Townsend Analytic Systems. Other companies and entrepreneurs have shaped one element or another of the new, global electronic market, but Townsend has at one point or another had a hand in every part of it.

Yet serendipity and coincidence are about the only constants in the story of the Townsend group. MarrGwen Chapman Townsend certainly did not set out to change the world, though she came of age in the 1960s, a time when many other people did. Slight, modest, with reddish brown hair, girlish even today, MarrGwen has a quiet, self-effacing manner that seems ill-suited to the job of changing the world. She graduated from a quietly patriotic Austin high school in 1969 and went on to Southern Methodist University, with half an idea of doing something to help the poor in Latin America. She mentioned that shadow of a goal to an advisor, who told her

that she would be useless in Latin America without a profession and suggested economics because MarrGwen was very good at math.

She didn't know what economics was, but she took a course, and she liked it. And when a University of Chicago economics professor visited the campus to teach a class one semester, she decided to take the class. When she got around to registering for it, though, the man at the registration desk told her that the class was full. She told him she really wanted to take the class, and she asked if there was a waiting list. There was, so she put her name on it.

He looked at the name and then at her. "MarrGwen. That's an unusual name," he said.

She explained that she was named after an old friend of her mother's in Austin.

"Oh," he said, a little oddly.

To her surprise, she got into the class. Very much to her surprise, later, she learned that she had leapfrogged that waiting list because the professor from the University of Chicago had many years before been in love with a girl from Austin named Marr-Gwen, the same MarrGwen after whom she had been named.

She did quite well in the class, so well that she decided she would like to take a graduate degree in economics. She knew almost nothing about the University of Chicago, except that it was supposed to be a good school. But she applied and was accepted, so she went to Chicago.

It was a long way from sunny Austin.

A big, cold, lonely place.

Everywhere she looked, there were serious, nerdy guys.

So, MarrGwen did what any Texas girl from a sleepy little town like Austin would do. She went to the secretary at the economics department to ask for the names and phone numbers of some of the other girls in her class.

The secretary glared at her and said, "Girls? We don't have girls at the University of Chicago."

"Oh," said MarrGwen, timidly.

"We have women," the secretary snapped.

"Oh," said MarrGwen, "well . . ."

The secretary began to move her index finger down a long registration roster. She paused, some way down, cleared her throat, and then continued, without looking at MarrGwen. Her finger moved all the way down the list, turned a page, and went all the way to the bottom. Then she folded the list and put it away, cleared her throat again, and said brusquely, "Well, there are no other women. You are the only one in your class." The secretary immediately got busy with something else and was careful to avoid any eye contact with MarrGwen.

It promised to be a long winter.

But MarrGwen was studious, and everyone else at the University of Chicago seemed to be intensely serious about study too. They had to be, because they had something to prove. The ideas of the Chicago School economists were radical, and they were opposed by powerful champions of plain-wrong conventional wisdom who controlled the commanding heights of economic power. Now, though, it seemed that Chicago could be on the verge of victory.

At the beginning of the seventies, the Bretton Woods System, an economic order that had ruled the world since World War II, suddenly collapsed. In the late 1970s, rampant inflation and simultaneous economic stagnation presented a challenge that conventional wisdom could not even name, but for which Milton Friedman, of the University of Chicago, offered a cure. A few years later, he would claim his Nobel Prize, and after him, a whole parade of Chicago School economists would pass through Oslo to pick up their laurels.

The revolution in economic thought drew power from a simultaneous revolution in technology. MarrGwen worked with complex economic models, running them first on mainframes, then on minicomputers. She began to spend time with an almost equally quiet and serious young man, similarly devoted to studies and technology, named Stuart Townsend. They programmed together, married, and continued to program together. They began to do some consulting, writing software for currency futures trading, and that led to a major project for the Chicago Board of Trade.

The Board of Trade asked them to develop a computerized version of its Market Profile, an analytical tool that recorded the prices of all trades and the times at which they had occurred in a way that let pit traders see at a glance the shape of the market. MarrGwen and Stuart Townsend hooked up a computer to an FM radio signal that broadcast tick by tick price information and wrote the software to turn this information into a real-time Market Profile. As a result, traders no longer had to be on the floor to get up-to-the-second information, and many decided to trade from home.

"The problem we ran into immediately," says MarrGwen, "is that these people were using PCs, and if they wanted to do something else with the computer, they would shut down our program, open another program, do what they wanted, and then when they were finished, click on our program again. Then they would call us and say, 'What's wrong with my data? It's missing from 10:30 until 11:00.' We'd say, 'What were you doing from 10:30 until 11:00?' They'd say, 'I was writing a letter to my mother,' and we'd say, 'That's the problem. It has to run all the time.' "

When Windows came out, they rewrote the program to take advantage of the multitasking capability. In the process, they broke it up. "We had some customers who didn't care about the technical analysis and charting, but wanted to do number crunching and volatilities, so they wanted the piece that dealt with data but not the other two," says MarrGwen. "We ended up with separate clusters, which meant we were well positioned to go into networks." They wrote a protocol that allowed their programs to work in a network environment. They adapted them to work with data feeds from different vendors, collecting, processing, storing, charting, or otherwise manipulating data.

Along the way, a group of German banks approached them for help linking up with Germany's new electronic futures exchange, the Deutsche Terminbörse (DTB). The exchange used DEC computers, but several member banks used IBMs and did not want to switch. They asked the Townsends to design risk-management software for options and futures trading that could receive data from the DTB but run on their IBM computers.

The DTB project led indirectly to another similar project in Austria. Once again, a group of banks with IBM computers needed **89** help linking to a new exchange that used DEC machines. But this project was more comprehensive. Here, they had to design a complete point-and-click trading interface to allow banks to use IBM machines to trade on the Österreichische Termin-und Optionenbörse (OTOB).

They wrote the software in Chicago, and in order to test it, they built their own electronic exchange, writing an order-matching program that would simulate the flow of orders through the OTOB. After they had tested the software, they put their electronic exchange on the shelf. There seemed to be no further use for it. The Townsends had, of course, no way of knowing at the time that a scandal would soon blow apart the Nasdaq or that the electronic exchange program on their shelf would be reborn as one of the most important ECNs in the market or that in the spring of 1999, years after the Austrian project had concluded, Goldman Sachs and E*Trade would ante up about fifty million dollars for the opportunity to become minority owners in that ECN.

In the early 1990s, data vendors who used Townsend products invited them to go on sales calls to visit a new type of customer: SOES Bandits. "We were doing software for Level II quotes, high performance; that's a lot of data and you want it fast," MarrGwen recalls. She and Stuart noticed a bottleneck in many of the SOES rooms. Although traders were able to watch the market on their own screens, they didn't have the capability to enter their own orders. They shouted their orders across the trading room to an order-entry person who sat at a Nasdaq machine. "We said, there's another way to do this. So we got the interface from Nasdaq and created an electronic order-entry program, probably the first of its kind," she says. "The funny thing was, at the time people didn't like it, because it wasn't noisy anymore. Everybody was trading with the mouse instead of yelling, and the other traders didn't know when something was going on. They'd been used to that level of energy. So they wanted bells and buzzers so the software would make noise while they were trading. It was a sales issue. People who operate the trading rooms obviously wanted people to trade more, because that's how they make their money."

But automatic capability was so far superior to the old way of doing things that most trading rooms eventually came around. During these first years, Townsend had the market for trading software pretty much to itself. The only other developer working on products for the SOES Bandit game was Josh Levine, of Datek, and Datek didn't set out to commercialize the Watcher software, just traded with it.

The Townsends did not confine their efforts to the SOES Bandit market. They wrote software to provide price quotes to traders in the oil industry, and they wrote software to provide stock market quotations for television news broadcasters like CNN. They worked with data vendors like S&P Comstock and PC Quote, among others, providing the so-called front end, the display that subscribers to these services see when they log on.

The financial information business is divided, like Caesar's Gaul, into three parts:

1. Originators, who gather or create information. The New York Stock Exchange, the Nasdaq, the New York Mercantile Exchange, and Chicago Board of Trade, are a few examples of the originators of financial price information. Financial news originators include Bloomberg, Reuters, Dow Jones, and similar organizations.

2. Data providers, who deliver information. Standard & Poor's, Comstock, PC Quote, and Virtual Telecomm/First Quote are among the data providers. Some data providers, such as Bloomberg and Reuters, also originate financial news. Other providers merely collect and deliver financial information originated by others.

3. End users, who include the investors, traders, analysts, and curious consumers of information.

As long as trading was mainly a job for professionals at big banks and brokerage houses, the financial-information business tended to be dominated by big, proprietary systems like Reuters and Bloomberg. In order to get access to the information, subscribers needed specialized terminals and systems. It was costly but profitable for providers to develop such systems and deliver information to specialized trading desks at powerhouse financial institutions.

But as market reforms and competition among discount brokers made it possible for more people to trade more cheaply, technological advances, especially on the Internet, made it economical to deliver information to ordinary computer screens, on ordinary desks, in ordinary home offices.

The Townsends were among the first to see the potential of Internet trading. By 1995, they had added to their software a communications layer using the TCP/IP (Transition Control Protocol/ Internet Protocol) enabling it to run over wide area networks.

One evening, over dinner, Stuart Townsend happened to mention the remarkable growth of day trading to a friend, Gerald Putnam. An institutional broker, Putnam had drifted in and out of several firms before starting his own brokerage, Terra Nova, to specialize in derivatives. It was a sort of anonymous matchmaking service that brought buyers and sellers together and allowed them to trade without disclosing their identities to each other. Terra Nova had worked out an arrangement with the Townsends to distribute Townsend software to Terra Nova clients. "We weren't burning up the world," Putnam says, with decided understatement.

Putnam's timing was off by about a decade. The derivative business had boomed during the eighties, but by the early nineties, it was coming on hard times. In 1994 and 1995, a series of headline-making scandals, including the Orange County bankruptcy, a massive loss at Procter & Gamble, the implosion of value at supposedly safe mutual funds, and the collapse of Barings Bank, helped bring these hard-to-understand financial instruments under a deep shadow of suspicion. Financial regulators fretted publicly about immeasurable risks to the international banking system, securities regulators demanded tougher accounting standards, and business backed away from the derivative market.

Stuart Townsend told Putnam that SOES firms were ordering

equipment and software in big numbers. "You ought to take a look at it," he advised.

So Putnam got in touch with Harvey Houtkin. "The Godfather of Day Trading! He was the only one who had an organized class. I went to it and spent a week there with the intention of starting a day-trading business. I came back armed with some knowledge, filed applications to get Nasdaq electronic services brought in, and opened a trading room."

Opening a trading room was a logical way to enter the business, and it was the way that Harvey Houtkin and his competitors had gone, but it was not the best way, as Putnam discovered.

Trading rooms were expensive to set up and run. Opening a trading room meant leasing office space, buying computer hardware, buying or licensing software, and paying attorneys to deal with various regulatory and compliance issues.

Then came the scramble to generate revenues: marketing to attract prospective traders, training to develop the prospects, coaching them while they came up the learning curve, sometimes even arranging for lunches to be brought in so that traders would not have to leave their desks to eat. Though some day-trading firms charge a seat fee to cover part of the fixed cost, commissions are the mainstay of the business, and traders only generate commissions when they are doing trades. But the life cycle of a trading prospect tends to be exciting and short.

Good traders who make money keep trading and generating commissions, but these are rare. Far more common are poor traders, who lose until someone stops them, or until they have nothing more to lose, and then quit generating commissions.

Stuart Townsend explains, "Until day trading started, the place where these people went to speculate, to gamble, was in the futures pits. People called up their broker, made a trade, found out if they won or lost money. Ten percent made money; 90 percent lost money. The business was churning customers—bringing in new customers to replace those that went broke—and the companies lived on always getting new customers in, and that went on for a long, long time."

But a futures broker doing business over the telephone can consider almost anyone in the world to be a prospect. By contrast, the pool of prospects available to the operator of a trading room is limited by physical distance. As long as traders have to come to one spot to trade, all of the prospects will have to come from the population that lives within a convenient driving distance. Even in a big city, this population is not infinite. Combine a limited population with the fact that 90 percent of those who start will drop out, and some very simple arithmetic is all it takes to infer that there must be a better way.

While Putnam was discovering these facts of life, the Townsends were wrestling with similar physical constraints. They had entered the day-trading business by licensing their software to run on-site at SOES Bandit firms. Most licensees were not technical types, so they demanded support, a lot of support. Support meant putting people on planes to fly back and forth between Chicago and wherever. It would make much more sense to run the software at one central site and let the customers link in through a network. The Townsends couldn't do this alone because they didn't have SOES lines. Only brokers and market makers who had passed through the regulatory and compliance filters could have SOES lines.

Terra Nova had a SOES line, though. And by cooperating with Townsend, Gerald Putnam could extend his pool of potential prospects beyond the circumference of Chicagoland to, literally, the entire world.

So Terra Nova and Townsend Analytic Systems got together to set up a service center, perhaps best understood as a private-label day-trading brokerage business. "We were able to offer it to people with the skills to go out and find customers, but without the technology skills," Putnam says. "They could build a trading room in another state, connect to us over a network, and we would do all of the heavy-duty regulatory compliance and technology work here."

Aspiring SOES Bandit firms who hooked their customers into the service center could get all of the technology, telecommunications, and market access they needed, without a major capital commitment. Their customers could trade using Townsend Analytic System's Real Tick quotation and order-entry software, sending their SOES orders to the Nasdaq market makers on Terra Nova's lines.

The service center was perfectly suited to Internet trading. Why lease a space and buy computers when you can let customers come to you over the Internet, using their own computers? Christopher Doubek, who had managed the growth of the service center at Townsend Analytic Systems, moved (literally) across the hallway of the office building on Wacker Drive to become president of Terra Nova in February 1999. Going down a list of Internet day-trading firms listed on a popular financial website, he identified most of the firms on the list as customers of the service center. "My philosophy is not to get rid of competitors, but to make money off of as many different profit centers as I can," he said. "What you really want is to be making a tenth of a tenth of a tenth of a penny off of everything that happens in the world."

That philosophy also guided the development of the next collaborative venture between Putnam and the Townsends: Archipelago, an ECN distinctive for its openness.

Attentive observers might have noted that a battle between openness and its opposite had been going on in the electronic markets for some time. The inventor of Instinet, the first ECN, had intended to limit membership to institutions. But Bill Lupien, who took over as chief executive of Instinet in the early 1980s, opened its membership to brokers, market makers, and specialists, in addition to institutions. Later, membership criteria tightened. Lupien had left the company before Harvey Houtkin invented SOES Banditry, but Houtkin and traders like him found their business unwelcome on Instinet.

In fact, if Instinet had allowed day-trading brokerage firms to participate in trading on its system, it might have continued to enjoy a monopoly as the only ECN in the market. Josh Levine of Datek would probably never have invented Island. Levine says that he took his order-matching problem to Instinet first, but Instinet's **95** representatives told him forthrightly that Datek's business was not welcome. So he wrote his own program to match buy and sell orders against each other. When Island subscribers sent in their orders, the program sought a match in Island's book. Traders whose orders found a match on Island got cheaper, faster executions than they could get on the Nasdaq's SelectNet system.

When Levine wrote Island, he knew there were many traders who were using his Watcher software to send buy and sell orders to SelectNet. Their offsetting bids and offers were passing each other on their way to and from the Nasdaq SelectNet system. When the orders got to SelectNet, market makers might or might not choose to execute them. If a market maker did execute the order, the trader had to pay a service charge.

Island offered to match orders for approximately half of the SelectNet service charge. If an order sent to Island could not be matched with another order on its book, Island sent the order on to SelectNet and ate the balance of the service charge. "It was a brilliant idea, probably one of the best ideas ever thought of in the brokerage industry," Putnam says. "It helped revolutionize the industry, that simple concept."

In late 1996, the SEC announced new rules intended to put an end to the scandalous practices that its investigators had discovered in the Nasdaq market. Among other abuses, market makers often chose to ignore orders that they did not want to execute or send into the market. The SEC rules required market makers to do one of three things: (1) execute the order, (2) expose it to the market, or (3) send it to another market maker or to an ECN.

The rules had been announced in August 1996, with an implementation date of January 23, 1997. But MarrGwen Townsend says that it took a couple of months before the people on Wacker Drive recognized the significance of this change. "We read the rules and found they had defined an ECN as an alternative to a market maker, and there was nothing that said any broker dealer couldn't have one. We recognized the opportunity in November. We talked to the SEC. They couldn't figure out any reason why we couldn't do it, so we said 'If we show you we have the technology, would you give us the no action letter,' and they said 'OK.'" (A "no action" letter is an official statement that the regulators have no objection to what is being proposed.)

It would have been all but impossible to invent an order-matching system from scratch between November and January. But the Townsends had already invented one. They still had, on the shelf, the order-matching program that they had written to test the trading interface they had developed for the Austrian options exchange years before. They rewrote that program and turned it into an ECN. "It wasn't the same program," says MarrGwen, "but the knowledge of how to do it is the hard part. Once you've got that, you can rewrite it without great difficulty."

Answering the "how" question was easier than answering the "why" question. Josh Levine had invented Island because he could see that traders needed an order-matching system. Datek already had a lot of customers whose orders would provide liquidity to Island. Speed was everything in the day-trading business, and Island's liquidity helped traders get orders executed quickly.

Instinet also had a clear reason to exist. It provided a liquid marketplace where market makers, brokers, and institutions could trade among themselves.

Bloomberg, the financial information company that competed with Reuters, had set up its own ECN shortly after Reuters acquired Instinet. Called Bloomberg TradeBook, it also served the high-end institutional brokerage, market making, and specialist clientele.

With Island providing liquidity to SOES Bandits, and Instinet and Bloomberg TradeBook providing liquidity to the big institutions and market makers, why would anyone want to use a new ECN that did the same thing?

The answer was, they wouldn't. In fact, the market did not need an ECN like the ECNs that already existed.

But there was a gap in the market, an unmet need that none of the existing ECNs could fill. Each of the existing ECNs was a self-contained unit, independent, unconnected to the others. In fact, the name "Island" could have been applied to each of the existing trading platforms. Orders sent to Island were either executed on Island or (after the order-handling reforms) exposed to the national market, where they might or might not find a match. Orders in Instinet and Bloomberg TradeBook were either matched internally or sent to the national market, where they might or might not find a match.

Island did not connect to Instinet. Instinet did not connect to Bloomberg TradeBook. Bloomberg TradeBook did not connect to Island. Although the market was, as a whole, very liquid, the liquidity was fractured and fragmented among these self-contained, electronic trading systems.

What happened if an order came to Island and there was no matching order on Island, but there was a matching order on Instinet or on Bloomberg TradeBook?

Since the systems were independent of each other, and there were no links between them, nothing happened. The orders went unexecuted.

To be sure, the orders might eventually meet in the national market, but on the other hand they might not meet at all. The orders on Instinet or Bloomberg TradeBook might be matched with another order that came to the national market hundredths of seconds ahead of the order that went through Island.

Very simply stated, it seemed to the Townsends and to Putnam that the market needed a mechanism to link all of the various, independent pools of liquidity into one gigantic order-matching system.

That was their answer to the "why" question.

It was brilliant.

Instead of designing an ECN to do what the other ECNs had done, they decided to design an ECN that would tie all of the other ECNs together.

Instead of trying to attract customers who would trade with each other on a self-contained ECN, they would build a system through which any customer could access the customers of all of the other ECNs.

"We did something different from what everyone else did,"

MarrGwen explains. "Everyone had said you need to have a lot of liquidity in order to operate an exchange. What we said was, We have the whole national book at our disposal. We could have just had one customer, and we would still have been able to operate an ECN because all we needed to do was have access. Of course, we had to pay wherever the order went, whether it was Instinet, or Island, or Bloomberg, but we had access to all of the liquidity and all of the market makers."

They decided to call their new ECN "Archipelago" because instead of being a discrete island, it was a whole, linked chain of islands.

The idea was so good that Bloomberg TradeBook adopted it about a year later; its marketing materials promised institutional clients "full electronic and anonymous access to the rest of a Nasdaq system that encompasses some 500 broker/dealers and half a dozen ECNs, together trading 750 million shares a day on average." But Bloomberg TradeBook offered that access only to the big boys. Archipelago offered it to anybody who wanted it.

Archipelago was the only ECN in the market that seemed willing to make its services available to everyone, without discrimination. Instinet and Bloomberg TradeBook had no interest in the little guy. Island, by contrast, had decided to present itself as the Robin Hood of the financial markets, a pose that made it difficult to enjoy very friendly relations with the Sheriff of Nottingham and his rich friends in the market-making business. ("Anyone who profits from current inefficiencies in the marketplace should be rewriting their résumé," Island's new president, Matt Andresen, told *Fortune* magazine in March 1999.)

Archipelago's very different character was illustrated by, and a major factor in, the decision of E*Trade and Goldman Sachs each to buy a 25 percent stake in Archipelago in January 1999. Said E*Trade spokesman Lisa Nash, "We certainly saw this as a great opportunity to make a financial investment in a company we believe will be growing, leading the pack, pushing the envelope of what technology can do to help consumers—particularly because it is open access. If you don't find a match within their book, they **99** send the order to other market makers." Nash said that E*Trade saw several possibilities to make use of Archipelago in its own operations, possibly sending customer orders through the ECN, possibly using it as a platform for after-hours trading. The global reach of Townsend Analytic Systems apparently didn't hurt either. "From our perspective, if you look at the Internet, there is no border; it's a global capability from the get go," Nash elaborated. "It is growing rapidly in Europe and Latin America, so there's much more opportunity outside of the U.S., both for access to domestic markets, for cross-border access, and for access to the U.S. market. Our goal is to enable customers from around the world to trade in markets around the world."

A few months later, in June 1999, JP Morgan announced that it, too, was taking a stake in Archipelago. JP Morgan and the Mutual fund company American Century together bought 20 percent of the ECN.

Archipelago was expected to seek SEC approval to transform itself into a full-fledged exchange, a move that would put it on (at least) an equal regulatory footing with the New York Stock Exchange and the Nasdaq.

Chapter 7

On the QT

How the Biggest Traders
Cover Their Tracks

rik Tonley, vice president and senior equity trader of the Northern Trust Company, buys and sells stock on behalf of portfolio managers for one of the premier money management firms in the country. The portfolios are big, and so are the orders Tonley deals in: hundreds of thousands, even millions, of shares. So his orders are certainly capable of moving the market. Therefore, he's the kind of trader other traders love to watch. Perhaps the most challenging part of Tonley's job is making sure there's nothing for them to see.

He occupies an office midway up the Northern Trust headquarters building, a structure so solidly grounded in this city that its foundation cornerstone was the benchmark by which the rest of Chicago was measured. Trim, of medium height, with graying temples and a carefully clipped moustache, Tonley looks like a man who knows far too many secrets to ever really relax. His brown eyes steady, his voice deliberately calm, his words few, he leads a guest back to a conference room with a stride as invariable as a yardstick. A few minutes into his meeting, someone interrupts to **101** claim the conference room for another meeting. Tonley shows no impatience, no annoyance, nothing at all. He doesn't frown, and he doesn't smile, just nods, rises, and walks with the same, carpet-measuring stride to a vacant office, settles in with his guest, and resumes talking precisely at the point where he had been interrupted. This uncanny demonstration of self-control in a trifle says more about Tonley than his whole résumé.

Emotions are treacherous; they betray strategies. So, Tonley never lets his guard down and always wears his poker face. A little excitement in his voice, a flicker of interest in his eyes, noticed at the wrong time, by the wrong person, could cost millions of dollars. People who make such costly mistakes don't last long in jobs like his.

Tonley's job is to execute decisions made by fund managers who are trying against stiff odds to beat the market. Studies have demonstrated and repeatedly reaffirmed that the market index consistently beats fund managers. Institutional investors have known for decades that active managers who endeavor to beat the index by picking superior stocks seldom succeed in the short term and almost never in the long term. While it might not be quite correct to say that stock-picking fund managers on the whole do more harm than good, a lot of investors seem to think so. In recent years, prodded by articles in the popular investment press and by information accompanying their 401(k) plans, they've been pouring more and more money into funds whose passive managers promise merely to buy stocks that track the index, instead of taking a near-hopeless shot at beating it.

It's not that active managers don't have good ideas. They do. And if they could implement them speedily and secretly, they might very well beat the index. But the market is very efficient. This means that all relevant information about a stock quickly finds its way into the stock price. When information gets out that fund managers are interested in a stock, the price soars. Tonley's job is to make sure that the fund managers at Northern Trust get the stock they want before it soars too far to be a good investment.

As at other big money management institutions, investment

decisions at Northern Trust follow a chain of scrutiny that begins when an analyst looks at a company and decides to recommend the stock. The recommendation goes to an investment committee, where it vies against numerous other recommendations from other analysts for a spot on the fund's shopping list. The manager or management team looks at the prospects for the company and decides at what price the stock has value. Enter Tonley.

"The portfolio manager may say, 'I like XYZ; it closed today at 150, I would like it at 155 or less.' My job is to accumulate several million shares at or under that price. I have to be judicious in my selection of a broker to find institutions interested in selling. But as soon as I open my mouth to a broker, that information becomes, for practical purposes, uncontrollable," Tonley says. Once they know that there is a buyer for several million shares in the market, sellers call their brokers to cancel sell orders in anticipation of a higher price. So supply shrinks. Meanwhile, people who have had no interest in the stock at all, or who may have been trying to make up their minds about it, are prodded onto the buy side by the knowledge that there is another big buyer in the market. Shrinking supply and rising demand—a deadly combination for a trader whose job is to buy low.

Tonley guards every scrap of information like a pit bull on a meat truck, but in order to buy, he has to express an interest to someone. He may begin with a call to the New York Stock Exchange, to ask a direct access floor broker to have a look around and see what is happening in XYZ. After checking out the situation, the floor broker calls back with a report to say which firms have been buying heavily and which have been selling. "If I have a good relationship with one of the sellers, I may call and I may be able to put together a block transaction," says Tonley, "but I've had to give up information to the direct access broker." The direct access broker now knows that Tonley has some sort of interest in the stock. That may not be enough information, on its own, to tell the broker what Tonley has in mind, but combined with other bits of information, it may be.

Why would this be a problem? Suppose the next call the floor broker gets is from someone interested in selling. After telling the caller basically what he told Tonley, the broker passes on the very relevant information that there could be a big buyer testing the market. So the seller decides to hold back and see what happens to the price.

Instead of calling a direct access broker on the floor of the exchange, Tonley may decide to use another channel. "I may call my trusted local broker, my friend. He may be my child's godfather. I know he'd never compromise my information." But in order to put the trade together, that broker has to call his firm's block-trading desk, which specializes in trades that start at ten thousand shares and go up to several million. The broker would not mention the name of the client. Very likely, Northern Trust will be referred to only as a code number in the conversation between the broker and the traders on the block desk. But just asking the question may provide enough information to move the stock price. "He calls his block desk, says Institution 129 wants to know what is going on in XYZ, and they might make a position offer. Now they know there's an institution in the Midwest interested in the stock, and since the sell-side institution wants to become a significant player in as many securities as possible, because that's how they make their money . . ."

He doesn't complete the sentence. He doesn't have to. Front running—trading ahead of a client—is illegal, and Tonley is careful not to use the word. But block-trading firms do trade for their own accounts. One of the services they offer their clients is anonymity. They stand between the customer and the market, buying when the customer wants to sell, selling when the customer wants to buy. Like a specialist on an exchange floor, they try to position themselves so that they will have inventory when customers want to buy. So the block-trading desk, knowing that there may be a big order coming in the stock, may start phoning potential sellers, buying ten thousand shares here, thirty thousand there, trying to minimize the market impact, but clearly putting pressure on the price.

There are all sorts of penalties for betraying customer confidences. But it's not unknown on Wall Street for a few young brokers or traders who were, maybe, classmates at business school to get together for a beer and talk about what they're doing now. One tells a story about a big deal, and to top him another brags about the order that just came in today, from a big institution in the Midwest. Thus, a tip is born. Someone at the table is bound to buy some of the stock for her own account or recommend it to one of his favorite clients.

If it's a Nasdaq stock, of course, it's quite likely that Tonley will have engaged a big market-making firm, the "ax" in the stock, to work the order for him, and day traders will certainly notice this closely watched firm staying on the bid with an order for, say, one thousand shares, getting hit, getting hit, getting hit, but staying to get hit again. If the ax put an ad in the morning's *Wall Street Journal,* it could not send a clearer signal to the day traders that there's a big buy order in the market and if they get in quick they will be able to make money. The SOES Bandits can play havoc with Tonley's order. "They may send multiple small orders to the market makers on the offer, who for fear of being picked off for a thousand shares, raise their prices a half a point," he says.

From an Olympian economic perspective, of course, it's a good thing that information leaks lead to almost immediate price rises in the stock Tonley is trying to buy. A market is efficient when prices reflect all available information about a stock. Something would be wrong with the market mechanism if Tonley were able to get into the market and buy two million shares of XYZ without anyone noticing.

But it's Tonley's job to beat the market mechanism, somehow. He may try to do his buying fast, so he's in and out of the market before anyone notices. Perhaps at some other institution, a portfolio manager bought XYZ when it was a small, speculative tech stock selling for $40. Tonley's portfolio manager is willing to get into the stock at $150; the guy who bought at $40 would be happy to get out at that price. The two might try to meet in a crossing session. Three organizations (Posit, the Arizona Stock Exchange, and Reuters Crossing Network) offer to match big buy and sell orders for institutional traders. They match orders several times a day, at **105** a price at the midpoint between the bid and the offer, or at the day's closing price.

On the plus side, these organizations allow traders to save the spread and trade without driving the price of the stock up. On the downside, the odds against finding a match for an order are slim. Most traders, while they're in the crossing cycle, take their orders away from the New York Stock Exchange floor. "While you're waiting for the cross, a print may go up in New York, and you miss out because you're not there, because you're sitting in the crossing network. Or there may be a seller in a different crossing network, so you don't cross. It's like a harbor and it's nighttime and these tall ships are floating in the harbor, some with buyers and some with sellers, and there's no efficient way for the buyers and sellers to hook up with each other. They have to take a chance and aim for one ship and hope, and every once in a while they get lucky, but it's not guaranteed," Tonley says.

It's called market fragmentation, splintered liquidity, Balkanization, and sometimes less printable names, but by any name, it's a huge problem. ECNs may have made the problem worse. Customers of an ECN have their orders matched against other customers on that same ECN. The model used by Archipelago and Bloomberg TradeBook, which search for matches not just internally, but also on other ECNs, is not universal. As the market mainland breaks into more and more islands, some argue, it becomes less and less likely that buyers and sellers will find each other quickly, conveniently, and economically. (The force of this argument is somewhat weakened by the fact that ECNs like Instinet and Island grew and prospered because they brought more efficiency and liquidity to the market than it had before. Abusive practices by Nasdaq market makers had made that market a laughingstock among professionals.)

Tonley uses Instinet, of course, and when his guest asks about others he mentions that he may find time to test Bloomberg TradeBook. Anonymity is one of the advantages of using these networks. Institutions don't have to identify themselves. But they do have to post their orders where the orders can be seen. Naturally, no institutional trader in need of two million shares of a stock would be so fatuous as to post an order for that quantity on any ECN. Some ECNs allow traders to put big orders into the system, but hide them. A bid for a hundred thousand shares would be in the system, but only show as a bid for a thousand shares. When the first thousand is executed, a bid for the next thousand shows automatically; and when that is executed, the next shows, and so on, until the entire hundred thousand has been executed. Though the feature has value, it doesn't solve Tonley's "ships in the night" problem.

Professionals like Tonley, trading for big institutional accounts, are responsible for the lion's share of volume on the Big Board. And according to one database, single orders to buy or sell more than half of a stock's average daily volume are common. In one study, Professors Eric K. Clemons, of the University of Pennsylvania's Wharton School, and Bruce W. Weber, of New York University's Stern School of Business, reported that information leakage can reduce investment returns on such trades by almost 3 percent, "a considerable proportion of expected annual returns on U.S. equities of about 10 percent."

Consequently, many big institutional traders have become convinced that the market as it exists no longer serves them. Because they cannot tell the market their real buying or selling interest without moving the price, they withhold big orders. Thus, the market is less liquid than it could be. That liquidity is further splintered as the market Balkanizes into competing submarkets: the various exchanges, the various ECNs, the various block-trading firms, the various crossing networks, etc. In the early 1970s, the SEC and Congress had pushed for development of a single, nationwide, integrated market system. In the late 1990s, the SEC suggested that much of that work had been undone by events. The two-tiered Nasdaq market showed how badly the market had disintegrated: Instinet subscribers obtained much better prices trading Nasdaq stocks with each other than the public obtained in the national market.

As the SEC weighed new regulatory proposals to remedy the problem, it gave its endorsement to an experimental technology **107** that seemed to be a step in the right direction. Over the objections of the New York Stock Exchange, the SEC ruled that Optimark ought to be admitted to the Intermarket Trading System.

Designed by a submarine warfare expert, Terry Rickard, in partnership with the redoubtable Bill Lupien of Instinet fame, Optimark promises to solve the most vexing problems of big institutional traders by offering them a way to put big orders into play without the risk of costly information leakage. Incidentally, if enough big traders adopt it, Optimark threatens to make the already challenging SOES Bandit game even tougher to play.

After selling his stock in Instinet, Bill Lupien had withdrawn far from the markets, to a four-thousand-acre ranch near Durango, Colorado, that was once owned by Western novelist Louis L'Amour. He spent several years developing a PC-based order-routing system called TomCat, designed to pool all of the fragmented puddles of liquidity into one giant pond. The technology worked, but the product flopped. It didn't solve the real problem in the market—big buyers and big sellers were afraid to put their orders in anywhere because doing so would certainly move the price against them. Since the orders were being withheld from the market, they couldn't be found even when all of the existing puddles had been pooled.

"After giving it some thought, I realized that there is a communication and search problem in the securities market, and those are problems that you deal with in antisubmarine warfare all the time," said Terry Rickard. "Given all this babble of communicating voices across the markets, how do you search out and find who should do what for whom at what price and size?" Before teaming up with Lupien, Rickard, a Ph.D. in engineering physics, had been senior vice president and technical director of the San Diego–based defense contractor ORINCON. By applying mathematical techniques honed in the cold war, he came up with an algorithm to bring big buyers and sellers together instantly in a way that allows no information leakage, because no human being ever sees the information that traders input. Northern Trust's Tonley is

such a huge fan that he almost comes close to expressing emotion when he speaks of Optimark. "It's the first ECN that gives you not only anonymity, but also complete invisibility. No one else can see your indication of interest, not even Optimark themselves," he enthuses.

Traders use the system by putting in a "profile" of their interest in a stock, indicating the range of prices at which the trader is willing to buy or sell a range of quantities of the stock. For example, a trader whose portfolio manager wants two million shares of XYZ could instruct the Optimark system that he would be willing to pay a slight premium over the current market price in order to get the whole order executed immediately, but would only be willing to pay a lower price for a partial execution. Optimark allows the trader to input orders not only for one price and one quantity each (as on an exchange), but for a number of prices and quantities, along a spectrum of satisfaction levels. Traders can use a numerical scale ranging from 0 to 1 (zero to one) to indicate their degree of satisfaction with each price and quantity on the profile, and they can express "if-then" preferences that make one order contingent on what happens to another.

Once these orders have been put in, the Optimark system searches near and far for stock at the price: internally, among profiles submitted by other institutional traders, and externally, in the global market. That is, it uses electronic linkages to search the entire, far-flung market—domestic exchanges, ECNs, brokerage houses, foreign exchanges, and any other sources of liquidity for the stock—to locate buy and sell orders that might fit the profile. Using all of the available data and some heavy-duty mathematics, Optimark then computes an optimal price and executes the transaction.

"We intend to be very big users of Optimark," Tonley says. "I would use Optimark instead of several of the ECNs I'm now using. But I think a lot of the sell-side traders are hoping that Optimark fails because it will threaten their livelihood. It will start to level the playing field and take away some of the unfair advantages that brokers and ECNs now enjoy and increase competition, and I think that's better in the long run for investors."

Optimark went live in the spring of 1999.

People who had studied the prospects for the system said that the biggest hurdle would be to attract enough participants fast enough to deliver liquidity on the scale that institutional traders required.

If it succeeded, it would get big orders executed quickly and efficiently, at a price that optimized everyone's satisfaction. By eliminating the need for institutional traders to slowly work their big orders through an antiquated set of market structures, it would also reduce if not totally eliminate the opportunities for day traders to hitch a ride on those orders.

Could it work? Skeptics said that it was far too rational to succeed. Even though the markets were in the process of radical change, two things could be relied upon to endure—greed and fear—and there seemed to be no place for them in Optimark.

Yet that could hardly be true because among the first brokers to sign up for access to Optimark's liquidity was Harvey Houtkin, the original SOES Bandit himself.

Part Four

BANDIT
BOOT
CAMP

Chapter 8

A Total Immersion Course in Day Trading

On October 26, 1998, about eight registered students and twice as many visitors crowd the classroom as another training cycle begins at the Montvale, New Jersey, headquarters of Harvey Houtkin's All-Tech Investment Group, Inc. The registered students have paid five thousand dollars to learn day trading from the original SOES Bandit himself. The visitors are thinking about doing the same.

No one here calls the game Extreme Investing; it would be considered a pejorative phrase, not so much because of the word "extreme" as because of the word "investing." Houtkin defines an investment as "a trade that went bad." His name for this game is "direct access electronic trading." The first rule of the game is to forget everything you ever knew about investing.

Five thousand dollars is a premium price, even though All-Tech promises to rebate the tuition by giving alumni discounts on their trading commissions if they stay with All-Tech after completing their training. By comparison, Broadway Trading in New York City charges only about fifteen hundred dollars for its training program. **113**

Broadway's founders have written a best-selling book about this business, and their training program includes a manual, keyboard practice, and lectures spread over four days. For thirty-five hundred dollars more, All-Tech puts aspiring traders through a month of full immersion in the markets, under the guidance of full-time faculty, before allowing them, if they qualify, to trade with real money on the floor. Winning five thousand dollars in the market might take two weeks; losing it, a single morning. The trainees here probably get what they pay for: a slightly better chance of coming out ahead in the game.

Every day that the markets are open, from 9:30 in the morning until 4:00 in the afternoon, All-Tech's trainees sit at authentic trading stations, each equipped with a computer identical in all respects to the machines on the real trading floor located just a few steps down the hall. They receive the same market information and use the same software as the real traders. For the duration of the training session, they participate in a simulation so accurate that even the seasoned traders who teach the course sometimes get carried away by the action.

The simulation is realistic because with one exception it is real. The only difference between training and trading is in the routing of orders. The account numbers and passwords used by traders send orders directly into the stock markets. Those assigned for training purposes route orders to a room in All-Tech's back offices where technicians intercept them, and then try to mimic the market's likely response under the circumstances. An attractively priced order in a fast-moving market will be snapped up immediately; an order going into a slow market may take a long time to fill; some orders will simply languish. The technicians adjust their responses accordingly, but where the market would simply ignore an unrealistic order, the back office at All-Tech sends the trainee who placed it a brief rejection note explaining why it is wrong.

On the first day of this training cycle, the room is packed, and in the back row, people are sitting in the aisle. The first day of each session is open to visitors who might be thinking of attending the whole session but want to get a feel for what it is about first. The visitors include a former chief financial officer of a bank who lost his job in a merger, got a good early retirement package, but is already tired of having nothing to do; a manufacturers' representative in the sporting-goods business looking to change his career; and a housewife with unfulfilled needs for achievement, among others. All of the visitors will be gone by the second day, and the eight or nine registered students will discover that the room is not uncomfortable at all when there's space to spread out and stretch.

As a general rule, these classes are predominantly male, but in this cycle, half of the registered students will be women. Olga is a white-haired, seventy-three-year-old former secretary for a public intermediate school in New England. She is taking the course with her daughter, Joyce, who recently lost her job as a receptionist in a law firm. Olga and Joyce saw a magazine article about direct access electronic trading when they stopped into a brokerage office while on vacation early in the year. They have already spent two weeks in phases one and two of the training program and, for reasons that become obvious, have decided to repeat those first two phases before moving on. Olga has never worked with computers before, and she is a little bewildered by Windows. Joyce takes notes as if she were taking dictation, and though she has all the words down pat, she somehow seems to have missed the general thrust of the message.

Fortunately, All-Tech's training program is something like a club with a one-time membership charge. Once students have paid for training, they can stay as long as they want or come back as often as they want, with no additional fees. Olga and Joyce are set for a very long stay. They've just moved from their hotel into a small bed-and-breakfast inn, determined to stick with the program until they've mastered the game.

Lenore is an environmental engineering consultant, originally from northern New Jersey, but now based in Minnesota. She's been active in the stock market ever since she was in college, about two decades before. She's tired of consulting, tired of travel, looking for a career change, and all but convinced that day trading **115** will deliver the variety, excitement, and money she is looking for. For the duration of this course, she's staying at a house she owns in northern New Jersey, but she talks about spending the rest of the winter trading from All-Tech's Boca Raton, Florida, office. Then she might have a special data line installed in her Minnesota home so she can trade from there during the summers.

Vilai is a Thai immigrant whose business card identifies her as a commercial real estate broker in central New Jersey. Like Lenore, she's been playing the market for a long time, mostly as a "position trader," shifting in and out of likely stocks every three days or so. She's been successful at that game and now she wants to take her trading to the next, potentially far more lucrative step.

Among the men, Herb is an environmental engineering consultant from Boston, bored with his work, looking to do something different, something new, something that can make him rich. He's already an avid stock player so this is an obvious course for him. He will be doing the course in quick bites between consulting assignments—two weeks in, a month or so off, two weeks back, and so forth until he's covered all the basics.

Randy, on the other hand, is a middle-aged former mining engineer from West Virginia, who has been between jobs for several years, taking care of a four-year-old child while his wife runs a florist business. The life of a house-husband is eating away at his self-esteem, but there aren't many jobs in West Virginia. He found out about All-Tech on the Internet. Then he read several books about market analysis and visited several day-trading firms before deciding to take this training program, hoping it will provide a new life, complete with money and self-respect.

Mark shuffles into the room gripping a walker, dragging one foot. He doesn't look much older than thirty-five or forty, and until he contracted a neurological disease, he had his own metal-finishing business in New Jersey. Guillain-Barré syndrome put an end to that phase of his life. The disease attacks the spinal column. He spent several months in bed, paralyzed, before recovering, slowly, some nerve function. "This is something I can do on my butt," he says during a break, "if it works."

Paul just graduated from college, where he played varsity base-ball for four years and studied business. He says that he works for a construction company and the company is looking at day trading as a good way to manage its investable cash. The company, he says, is paying his tuition and will provide capital for him to trade. Only much later in the course does he let drop that his father owns the company.

Sonny, about the same age as Paul, works in a family-owned garment-manufacturing business in Brooklyn. He has a friend who took this course and has been trading and making money. It looks easier than haggling with retailers about rags, and though it has risks, Sonny says everything in life has risks, and after all, nothing could be riskier than the garment business. His conversation be-trays a greater-than-average familiarity with games of chance and a tendency to conflate trading with gambling. For example, he consistently uses the word "marker" when he means "margin" and simplifies the instructor's explanations of complicated trading strategies by restating them in terms of craps, blackjack, and poker.

The instructor, Don, introduces himself in a voice that quiets all side conversations immediately. He's just under six feet tall, with a fringe of white hair around a deeply tanned dome. He looks like a monk of the markets. As many monks do, he came to his vocation from another, very different way of life. Don owned a string of beauty salons in New Jersey. He had never bought a share of stock until 1990, when his stepson talked him into trying the SOES Bandit game, and as it turned out, Don had a knack for it. He left the beauty business and traded at All-Tech for seven years. He was about to retire again and move to Florida when the company asked him to take charge of the training program.

He explains that the training program has eight full-time instructors who divide their time between the Montvale headquarters and the twenty-four branch offices nationwide. For the benefit of visitors, he notes that the branches offer one-week boot camp training modules for people who can't take a full four weeks to come to headquarters. These mini–boot camps present much of 117 the same material, but faster, with less time for the cycle of practice-repetition-correction-practice that makes the long course so intensive.

For the benefit of those who are staying, he talks a little about what lies ahead. He tells them that in the first phase of training they will learn how to "read the market," how to interpret the patterns of price movement that they see on the screen, how to buy and how to sell, but most importantly, how to control risk.

This kind of trading is different from any other trading they have ever done, he explains. Previously, they may have bought and sold stock through a broker, delivering their order either by phone or by e-mail. The broker then submitted their order to a market maker. But direct access electronic trading eliminates the brokerage function. It allows traders to put their buy and sell orders into the market themselves, immediately. Although traders can use the technology available here to order stocks on any major market, most of their trading will probably be done on the Nasdaq.

As a condition of their status as Nasdaq "market makers," institutions like Goldman Sachs, Merrill Lynch, and Morgan Stanley Dean Witter must commit to buy stocks from people wishing to sell, and sell to people wishing to buy. They have to be ready to do both at a publicly stated price.

The market makers decide for themselves at which prices they are willing to buy and sell any given stock. Their appetite for a stock and therefore their buy (bid) and sell (offer or ask) prices usually depend on the volume of buy and sell orders they are receiving from their own customers. Customer order flow gives them a sense of where demand is headed for the stock, and that information allows them to position themselves profitably.

The Nasdaq's systems aggregate all of the market makers' published bid and offer prices, pick out the best buying price and the best selling price available, and post it. At any given moment, this best price is the market price of the stock. Of course, some people think the stock is worth more, and some think it is worth less, but ordinary investors don't have any gauge of the strength of those opinions. Extreme Investors do.

Day traders like those at All-Tech can use the Nasdaq's Small Order Execution System (SOES) to buy and sell stocks at these "best" prices, directly engaging those market makers. The market makers have no choice about buying or selling in response to a SOES order. Execution is automatic. Without SOES, this kind of trading would be impossible because big market makers aren't in business to buy stocks when they are about to fall in value or sell them when they are about to rise. SOES forces them to do exactly that, and gives the trader a chance to get out of a bad position fast, hitting a market maker's bid or lifting the offer at the very moment the market makers are having second thoughts about this stock. But SOES is not the only way to buy and sell.

Traders can also place orders into the market through electronic communication networks (ECNs). ECNs are not market makers, and therefore they are not obligated to post buy and sell offers for stocks. They are merely channels that traders can use to bid for stock or to offer stock for sale. They are private for-profit operations, and trading through them means paying a toll, but there are times when trading through them can be quite profitable. Some traders, for example, place small orders through ECNs in order to make the market look stronger or weaker than it really is. A trader with a lot of stock to unload may put a very attractive bid into the market through an ECN in order to make it look as if demand for the stock is growing. If the market is teetering on the thin edge of equilibrium, such an order may shake things up enough to allow the cunning day trader to shed a position or cover a short, profitably, before the rest of the buyers and sellers in the market recognize the ruse.

But people in this class will learn to recognize the ruse, and perhaps to set their own snares instead of stumbling into snares that others have set.

A third alternative is to use a special trading system that some of the instructors refer to as the market maker's private club— SelectNet. Only market makers can take advantage of the buy and sell orders that flash across the SelectNet screens. Like SOES, SelectNet allows traders to send bids and offers to market makers, **119** but unlike SOES it does not promise automatic execution. The market makers have every right to do as they please with orders that come in to them over SelectNet.

So, the savviest traders use SelectNet as a barometer of the market climate. Market makers have a lot of information that small traders lack. Market makers have a stream of orders from their own customers, and often another stream of orders from customers of other brokerage firms that have sold their customer orders to the market makers. So, the market makers don't have to rely on taking the pulse of the market from a distance. The market flows through them; they are its gatekeepers.

The market maker firms also have traders hunting for profit in the stream of market order flow, and those traders have a big information advantage over the SOES Bandits. But they can't help leaving tracks. When market makers choose to hit a bid (sell) or lift the offer (buy) on SelectNet, they give away important information.

Jesse Livermore and his peers used to send small orders to the stock exchange in order to test the market's appetite for a stock. With the right software, casual stock players, part-time day traders, career changers, and full-time direct access electronic traders can use SelectNet to take the same kind of readings that Jesse Livermore did, before they commit to a strategy.

"There's a lot of information on these screens," Don says, noticing the perplexity in the gape-mouthed, wide-eyed faces of the students and visitors looking at him through the flickering twilight of a training room lit, now, only by the computer monitors and the overhead screen. "You can get bogged down. Don't worry. We'll teach you to read the market, how to tell when it's moving and when it's dead, when to trade, when not to trade, how to recognize the movement of stocks. There's a lot to learn, but you can learn it."

"This is different from any other type of trading," he repeats. "The mind-set you need is very short-term. You have to divorce yourself from an investing mentality. You can't let things go against you." A long-term investor may hold a stock even while it is falling, confident that in time it will come back. A day trader doesn't have that luxury.

This is a game like tennis, he says. You expect to lose some points. The idea is to make sure that winning points outnumber losing points. "It will cost you twenty-five dollars to get out of a losing trade. Ridiculously cheap!" he barks, referring to the commission that All-Tech charges on every trade. "There's no good reason to hold on to a losing trade. We're adamant about it because we know that of ten traders who don't succeed, nine fail because they hold on to a losing position. Not only hold on to it, but add to it. Not only hold on to it and add to it, but keep it overnight. That's how you turn a one-eighth point loss into a twenty-thousand-dollar loss. You've got to keep big losses out of the picture. If you don't, you could be right 90 percent of the time and still lose more than you make."

To underscore the point—it's one he will come back to again and again during the next two weeks that constitute Phases I and II of the program—Don lists on the whiteboard four possible outcomes for any trade: (1) small gain, (2) small loss, (3) big gain, or (4) big loss. "If you eliminate number four, you will only have small gains, big gains, and small losses. You can make a good living that way." Someone asks how much money they can expect to make. He says there are no guarantees—some day traders make a million dollars a year, some lose a hundred thousand in a month and wash out. "If you are successful, there's no reason why a guy with fifty thousand dollars in his account can't make five hundred dollars a day," Don says.

But the money won't come easy and it won't come fast. There's going to be a learning curve, at least three months long. This learning curve is like a rite of passage—you have to descend into it and come up alive before you can succeed. You have to be able to come back in order to keep trading, and eventually win.

A balance of fifty thousand dollars gives the day-trader an adequate cushion to absorb losses during the learning phase, provided the trader is astute about cutting losses. Fifty thousand in the account means "buying power" of a hundred thousand, because All-Tech gives its traders two-to-one margin. That is, All-Tech's traders can, in effect, borrow a dollar for each dollar they put into their accounts, thus doubling their buying power. Two-to-one mar- **121** gin is the maximum allowed by federal banking and securities regulations. Don mentions that regulators are considering a proposal to increase margin to four-to-one, but until that happens, two-to-one is the maximum. He points out that two-to-one margin already means a trader can lose twice as much as he or she has invested. It's a sobering thought. "Some people sit in front of the screen and stare at a losing position praying it will come back. Day after day, week after week. And they only hold the losers! If you buy expecting a stock to go up, and it goes down, and you hold it for a week, and it comes all the way back up, you'll not only be extremely lucky—you'll probably just break even. Because when these stocks come back to where they bought them, they can't wait to get out. They end up selling where they bought and miss the move up that they bought the stock for in the first place, and they've been tortured for nothing!"

He takes a deep breath. The ability to lose more than you invest is only one reason why holding on to losing positions makes no sense in this kind of trading.

The other reason is that direct access electronic traders see more clearly than other investors where the market is going. They can tell when losses are about to grow, and because they have the magic bullet, SOES, they can get out of those bad positions fast enough to avoid serious damage.

Most people who buy and sell stocks have very limited information about the currents of supply and demand within the market. The stock prices that appear in newspapers or on most online information sources are the so-called "National Best Bid and Offer" or "Inside Market" prices. The best bid is the highest price that an investor can receive when selling the stock; the best offer is the lowest price at which an investor can buy the stock. The Nasdaq systems pull together all of the bids and offers for each stock and put them in order, in two columns, with the highest bid on the top of the left-hand column and the lowest offer on the right. The price at the top of each column, the National Best Bid and Offer, or Inside Market, is the only price that most people see. In Nasdaq parlance, this is called Level I information.

Yet underneath each "best" price is a long list of other prices—lower bids and higher offers, arranged in descending order on the bid side and ascending order on the offer. The price levels appear in different colors, the best price always appearing in yellow at the top, with progressively less desirable prices appearing below in green, light blue, red, and at the bottom, dark, purplish blue bands.

Traders with access to Level II information can tell at a glance not only what the market is doing, but what it is about to do. The width of the colored bands is an important clue to the strength or weakness of the stock. Perhaps there is only one market maker bidding to buy XYZ stock at the best bid price—only one name in the thin, bright, flashing yellow band. Or perhaps there are five market makers bidding at that price. If there are five names flashing in the yellow band at the top of the bid price column, the price is unlikely to fall—at least, not for a few seconds. But a day trader needs only a few seconds to plan a strategy, make a trade, and take the money off the table.

If there is only one market maker in the yellow band, and if that market maker is a small one, the best day traders prepare themselves for a fall in the price. They get ready to short the stock. They look around, like hunters, and if they see that there are several major market makers lined up on the offer, or sell, side, they load their guns.

With a little practice, it's not difficult to tell in which direction prices are about to move. "We can see price changes coming," Don says. "The market moves up and down, and we don't care which way prices move, just as long as they keep moving. We need volatility." As he tells the story, day trading is entirely a momentum game. The trader's job is to recognize a move shortly before, or perhaps just after, it begins, and hop on for the ride. Given that this is the trader's job, it is clear that a trader who holds on to a losing position is not doing the job.

"Compare trading to getting on an airplane. Just before takeoff, the pilot announces that the plane is going to London and suggests that if London is not in your plans, you get off. Well, if you'd gotten **123** on expecting to go to Los Angeles, wouldn't you get off? But people get into a trade expecting a stock to go up or down, and stick with it when it moves in the opposite direction. *Why?*" There is real perplexity in his voice.

He knows why, of course. As he says to someone during the break, teaching people to trade is like teaching them to walk on top of a narrow brick wall. The technology and information in the training room are identical to that on the trading floor. So the wall is the same width here as it is there. But in training there is no real risk, because trainees are not trading with real money. They're learning to walk on a wall one-foot high. When trainees graduate and start to trade with real money, the wall is suddenly a hundred feet high. It is still the same width, and they have already proven that they can walk on that wall, but a hundred feet above the ground, everything changes. Greed and fear unbalance them.

But balance, discipline, and control are more important than ever because the game is getting harder than it used to be. Don tells the trainees that they will be operating in hostile territory because the market makers don't like independent day traders. The market makers call them SOES Bandits, and while all SOES Bandits are disliked, the ones most closely associated with Harvey Houtkin believe that they are disliked more than most, because Harvey Houtkin invented this whole game. It gives them a strong sense of belonging, a sort of "us-against-them" gangsta feeling. So Don explains that after the SEC punished the Nasdaq market makers for abusing their power and position, and forced them to open the closed system to the little guys, the big guys only grudgingly complied. They've been trying ever since to roll back those changes, not all at once, but slowly and incrementally, by small, sudden changes in obscure rules, the kind that don't make headlines.

So, changes in Nasdaq rules have reduced the number of shares that market makers are required to provide in a SOES order, imposed a five-minute rule that makes day traders wait five minutes (forever) between SOES orders in any given stock, and most recently made it much more difficult to short stocks.

Shorting, or selling borrowed stock in anticipation of a price fall and then buying it back for a cheaper price after the price has fallen, is half of the Extreme Investing game.

Buying low and selling high makes money; so does selling high and buying low. It doesn't matter in what order the buy and sell orders happen, as long as the buy is lower than the sell.

The opportunity to sell short makes these traders as happy to see a falling market as a rising one.

Of course, the best time to short a stock is when it is clearly falling. If a stock has begun to fall, it is likely to fall even farther, so shorting a falling stock is like shooting ducks on the water. Not very sporting, but a reliable way to fill the larder.

Although traders love the opportunity to short, the people who manage companies don't like to see their stock shorted. People who manage companies tend to get rewarded when their stock price rises and suffer when their stock price falls. The thought that someone might actually be profiting from the very thing that makes them suffer is abhorrent. Stock exchanges pay close attention to the desires of people who manage companies because those people have the power to decide which exchange will trade their stock. Even though shorting stocks makes eminently good sense in pure economic terms, exchanges therefore have an "uptick rule" that makes it more difficult for traders to short stock.

The uptick rule forbids traders to short stocks at the very time when shorting is most likely to make money for the trader—when the stock is falling. It requires traders to wait for an "uptick," a rise in the price, before they can sell short.

Like other exchanges, the Nasdaq has an uptick rule. But, until the summer of 1998, traders had been exploiting a loophole in the Nasdaq rules. The loophole let them set up a special sort of position called a "hedge," and with that position in place, the traders could short stocks when the stocks were falling. Someone in power eventually noticed the loophole and closed it with a sudden rule change.

The day traders at All-Tech and elsewhere interpreted the change as a sneak attack by powerful Nasdaq market makers bent **125** on the destruction of the SOES Bandits. Don yields himself to misty reminiscence, recounting with fond nostalgia every beloved detail of the dear departed loophole, then glowers and grumbles when he gets to the dastardly manner in which the powerful market makers snuffed out its beautiful, frail life. Something in his voice makes it clear that if it's a fight they want, they've got one now.

"We have advantages over market makers," he growls, warming to the theme. "We don't have to be on both sides of every stock. They do. We can pick our shots, and when we get hit, we can get out. They have to stay—they can change their prices, they can adjust, but they have to stay. So remember, the market makers are most vulnerable when they're busy. They are in fierce competition with one another, and when they're busy handling orders, they aren't paying attention to us. That's when we want to be trading like a sniper. Get in, take the money, disappear into the jungle. That's why they hate us. While they're busy, we pick their pockets!"

And by the way, he adds, don't worry too much about that new rule that seems to prevent traders from shorting a falling stock. Even as he speaks, the financial engineers are at work mining a new tunnel through the regulations. "They're trying to come up with something and are very close to coming up with something that will let us get around it," he says. In the meantime, there are still ways to identify shortable stocks and make money when they fall.

Someone asks whether he means, perhaps, that it might make sense to check the news before the market opens and put in short orders on stocks that have announced bad news the night before, after the market closed. And if this makes sense, mightn't it also make sense, on the upside, to put in orders to buy stocks of companies that have announced good news overnight? Presumably, the bad news will drive the stock price down when the market opens again or the good news will push it up, so putting in an order before the open should mean you have a head start on the action, right?

Don shakes his tanned tonsure emphatically. "When you hear news before the market opens, the best advice is simply be warned that the stock will be active. Wait and trade in the direction it goes.

It's uncanny how often good news drives a stock down and bad news pushes it up. You'll see market makers buying a stock they've just downgraded, and you'll also see them selling stocks they've just upgraded. It stinks!"

How the market will react to news is unpredictable. Sometimes, on no news at all, stocks will "gap down" in the morning. That is, the market makers decide to mark down the prices at which they buy and sell that stock for no apparent reason. Often the reason comes out later in the trading day and is greeted with cynical cheer by traders whose deeply rooted convictions about the integrity of the market makers have by the order of these events been rooted a little more deeply still.

And so the first day ends.

The trainees slowly gather their notes and papers, not saying much to one another. They look confused, shocked, dazed by the strange things they have heard, hesitating a little, unsure what to make of it all: market manipulation, conspiratorial intrigues, and the ominous hints of the forces within themselves they may never have imagined or may have simply preferred not to face. They pull together their materials and leave the room one at a time.

By the next morning, having had a chance to spend an evening mulling over all they heard and then sleep off unwarranted anxiety, everyone seems comfortable with the prospect of the future, confident that he or she will be able to avoid making those stupid mistakes Don warned against yesterday. Some are already planning for a soon-to-be-expected rise in personal disposable income.

"Every morning, you will get a printout of the previous day's activity in your account," Don says, addressing some administrative point.

"Should we save these papers for our income tax purposes?" white-haired Olga asks in a tremulous voice.

"Yes, absolutely," Don says, then hesitates. "Once a year, you get an accounting of all activity during the course of the year, both buy and sell."

"We're going to end up paying a lot of income tax," Olga volunteers.

127

Don advises her to talk to her accountant about these matters.

"I want to buy a houseboat," Olga says, "on the Boston waterfront. I think that would be so nice."

Don talks a while longer about margin and happens to mention that traders can post a portfolio of securities as margin.

"So I didn't have to sell my stock!" Olga's daughter Joyce cries, aghast.

"You sold your stock?" Don asks, puzzled by her outcry.

"Tsk, tsk, tsk," Olga shakes her white head, with the air of one whose good advice could have prevented that if only it had been followed.

The daughter turns—they are sitting at opposite ends of the room—and gives her mother a look of such glum remorse that Olga says no more.

Don looks at Joyce like a sympathetic uncle. "Well, you can buy them back," he says. "Everything has gone down; you probably did a good thing."

"I sold them in September," Joyce says. The market in September was at its lowest point for the entire year, having just collapsed in August.

"Well," Don says. A question about margin saves him from having to say more.

It takes most of the morning to work through the dull but necessary details about margin requirements and various rules that have a direct effect on how much, how frequently, and when a trader may buy or sell. After the coffee break, though, Don starts into the meat of the course and begins to peel away the veils that everyone came to see fall, the ones that conceal the secret to success in the market.

"Remember, I want to take money away from the market makers when they're busy, not when they're waiting for me," he begins. So the first order of business is to set up what he calls a "speedometer," a special ticker that monitors all market activity in approximately forty stocks. The ticker shows buys in green and sales in red.

Since every stock transaction involves both a buyer and a seller, it's necessary to explain that a "buy" means an order coming into the market to buy and a "sale" means an order coming in to sell. When buyers initiate the action, the transaction shows up in green; when sellers initiate, in red.

The "speedometer" registers the identity of the market maker involved in the transaction and the price at which the stock changed hands, but if the ticker is moving slowly enough to read that information, the market is too slow to trade. "I don't want to read it," Don says. "I just want to see that speed. I want to find out when the market is active." He says that he wants to see the speedometer at a rate of at least "3" before he'll consider getting into the market. The 3 is an arbitrary number that describes the speed of a ticker just fast enough to make it uncomfortably difficult to read the information scrolling through it. In an ideal market, the the ticker would be at a 4 or a 5, an illegible blur of colors.

A fast ticker is more likely to display long scrolling series of either green or red prints that mean a price trend in the making. A flat, choppy market, one where short moves up are followed by short moves down, will register on the ticker like a Christmas decoration, blinking green . . . red . . . green . . . red. When a wave of buy orders hits the stock, the ticker prints a long series of green and the trader knows to prepare for rising prices. A long series of red prints in a fast market signals the trader to look for ways to play the short side.

"Excuse me, what chart are we creating now?" Olga asks.

"The speedometer," Don answers.

"Oh. The speedometer. Oh . . ." Olga says, looking from the big screen at the front of the room where the speedometer is displayed, to her own personal screen, and back.

"I'm sorry, I put in CSCO and hit Enter and the whole chart went away," her voice quavers.

Don goes over the steps she needs to take to bring up the speedometer again. It takes a couple of passes through the instructions before she finally says, "Oh, all right. Yes. I've got it. Thank you. Thank you very much."

The speedometer is just the first step, though. It's also a good idea to keep an eye on the behavior of the market by watching an **129** index of the leading stocks. Different traders like different indexes. Some watch the Standard & Poor's 500 futures index. Don prefers to watch the Nasdaq 100, or NDX index, because he feels that it gives a better picture of the forces at work on the Nasdaq market, which is the focus of SOES Bandit trading.

"What about the Dow?" someone in the back of the room asks.

"The Dow is just thirty industrial stocks. It has nothing to do with us," he says dismissively.

He sets up the window for a chart of the NDX, an intraday graph that registers every move in this index with only a one-minute delay. While waiting for the graph to come up, he mentions that the data for the tickers, graphs, and charts he will be creating comes from one of several intermediaries that purchase raw data from the Nasdaq and transmit it to customers. Nowadays, anyone can subscribe to these intermediaries and receive these real-time quotes. In the training room, the data is provided by S&P Comstock, which All-Tech uses as a backup data service in case PC Quote, the service that provides data for the floor traders here, should go down.

By the time he has finished this explanation, the graph of the NDX shows a long, flattish choppy run followed by a quick upturn. It's all happening now.

"If you don't know where a stock, or the market, was, then knowing where it is now is insignificant," he says. "You need to know where it has been to know where it is going." If the ticker is moving fast, printing a lot of green, and if the graph of the NDX is starting to go up, it means the tide is rising, and a rising tide sooner or later lifts all boats.

He sets up a "market maker" window, and types a stock symbol into a little box at the top. It takes almost a second for the window to give the inside market and the double column of bids and offers, in colored strata, beneath. At the beginning, he recommends that the trainees try to watch no more than one stock at a time. They can set up any number of market maker windows on these screens; but if they try to watch more than one, the odds are they'll get confused in the heat of market action and send out a buy or sell order

for the wrong stock.

Everything is in place now. The ticker is moving; the market is heading up. "I expect my stock to follow the overall market," Don begins.

Olga interrupts. "What's the name of that ticker that goes across the screen? Does it have a special name?"

"The ticker," Don says.

"Oh. Just 'the ticker'?" she repeats, still not quite sure.

"Just—'the ticker,' " Don says again, gently but firmly.

"Oh. All right."

He continues.

"Say that stock price hasn't moved, but the market is up. Then you see a lot of buys at an eighth. Sometimes they come in forty, fifty at a time—whoosh! You pounce on that! When you see the market up and you see one or two prints in the stock at an eighth, get in as early as possible." (Note: The traders and instructors here don't ever talk about stock prices in whole numbers, just by the fractional increment between whole numbers. So a stock selling at 35⅛ is said to be selling at an eighth, and if it moves up an eighth, it's selling at "a quarter" not "thirty-five and a quarter.")

Stocks don't usually move straight up indefinitely, though. They usually show a kind of sawtooth pattern, moving up three steps, falling back one, moving up two, falling back one, moving up four, falling back two, that sort of thing. "That's the movement we need to get in sync with. What we think doesn't mean anything. The market is going to do whatever the hell it's going to do. It requires that you be able to recognize the movement, the rhythm," says Don.

As he talks, the graph of the NDX shows a leg down. In a few minutes, the market has come down almost to the level of the previous day's high point. Don draws a line from that high point, across. He tells the class to watch the NDX graph approach the line. "Rarely does the market move smoothly through a level like that," he says. Traders put in orders at key levels, some to buy in expectation of a bounce back up, some to sell and take profits or stop losses.

The NDX continues down, bounces, bounces again, and then cuts through the line. The market closes as prices are still trending **131** down. The next morning, the first trades will occur at far lower prices—a so-called gap down.

*   *   *

Along one side of the room, an observation window admits a little light from the adjacent hallway. Otherwise, all of the light in the room comes from the screens. A big projector, attached to the ceiling, beams the display from Don's computer onto a white screen at the front of the room, and pale reflected light rebounds in a broad haze. The individual screens on the trading desks absorb the trainees' intent faces in a lambent, dim, bluish-white glow: the neutral sum of the red and green numbers blinking and scrolling through the tickers, plus the spectrum shimmer of levels expanding and contracting in the market maker windows, plus the varicolored flash of charts shifting from foreground to back, and the lights of the other software tools coming up and going down, as the opportunistic neophytes try to find a stock on the move. The light creates a mood so strong that to walk out of the door of the training room and into the ordinary fluorescent office light of the hallway gives one a little shock of disappointment; so every day, fewer trainees go to take breaks. They leave this room only when necessary and hurry back again to their screens.

The light inside the room is fluid, motile, aqueous, and dim. The sound is a similarly disorienting sum: the barely audible, constant, subdued hums of the computers, plus the tense quiet of extreme concentration, punctuated by infrequent gasps, muttered curses, and meaningless little sporadic outcries, plus the lecture, in which the pauses get longer and longer, because the lecturer is also fascinated and drawn in by the market action and often stands quietly watching, rapt, then delivers suddenly, as though talking in his sleep, a burst of observations and analysis and jargon.

So because of all of this, the room seems to disconnect, when the door closes, from what is just outside. It is not like closing a door to an ordinary room. This disconnect is something like the

feeling of cutting away that comes just when an airplane lifts off from the runway, breaking gravity with a jolt—that light, momentary, weightless feeling. Or something like the feeling of going down through the water on a scuba dive, hearing strangely amplified and distorted sounds that come from the water, and the loud rhythmic whoosh of air through the regulator that almost seems to be the sound of someone else breathing, the odd disconnect of hearing what no one else quite hears because in fact it is the sound of one's own breathing, and seeing what no one else sees quite the same way because it is the world as seen through the glass of only one person's diving mask. Similarly, the sights and sounds, even the atmosphere, inside this dark, screen-lighted room, are alien to those of the hallway beyond the window.

From time to time, small groups of observers come to stand by the hallway window and look in. On their own side of the window, the trainees, like fish in an aquarium, pay no attention to the muffled comments and finger pointing of the observers beyond the glass. The powerful attraction of their screens drowns out everything else. Even the lecture shifts from the foreground, fading to the relative importance level of the TV color commentary on a big game.

All of this is part of the adjustment to screen-based life. Even the sense of time changes; the day's rhythm shifts from whatever it was to market time. The day used to begin with morning, but now it begins only with "the open." Early birds who arrive in the training room in the morning before the open and turn on their computers see that nothing is happening. The screen is yesterday's screen, all the last array of red and green prices on the speedometer ticker frozen in place at the position they held precisely at 4:00 P.M. yesterday, the market maker windows a dull monochrome because at yesterday's close all of the bids and offers were immediately moot. In market time, nothing has changed since yesterday's close. Market time stopped at 4:00 P.M., and it has not begun yet, so even though it may look like morning outside the room, inside there is no light or living color.

The day begins in market time at 9:30 A.M., when the ticker jerks into action and the colors come up in the Nasdaq Level II, or market maker, window. It's the open! The ticker moves again, new **133** trades begin to draw a new day's price line on the chart, and there is money to be made again.

On the third day of the training session, the new trades start to sketch a line on the chart that begins some distance below the point at which yesterday's line stopped printing. The market had been falling yesterday when it closed, and this morning the first buy and sell transactions happen at prices well below yesterday's close. In trading parlance, this is a "gap down." Market makers have decided to mark down their prices, perhaps because on the basis of orders received overnight they see more selling than buying pressure, or perhaps because they see a chance to buy cheap and ride their positions up for a quick profit.

Don is of the opinion that the market makers deliberately set the opening prices low in order to profit from a rapid move up. "I expect the first significant move this morning to close the gap," he says, just at the open. "Most professional traders want to 'fade the gap.' They know that most of the time it will close. It may take a few minutes, but don't get suckered into the first move down. Wait for the up move and get in." "Fade" means to trade in the opposite direction. When the market opens gap down, traders fade the gap by buying; when it opens gap up, at a higher level than the previous day's close, they fade by going short, expecting the market to sink back and close the gap. The gap usually closes within the first fifteen minutes of trading. Today, that's what happens. After opening gap down, the market sinks slightly, chops around for a few minutes, then moves decisively back up to close the gap, reaches yesterday's closing price, and then edges a little higher. Within fifteen minutes after opening gap down, the market has made what proves to be its only big move of the morning. Traders who missed the opportunity to 'fade the gap' in these fifteen minutes may as well have missed the whole morning.

"What if the market had gone down instead of up?" someone asks.

That would have been a strong signal to go short, in expectation of a major move down, is the answer. It would have meant that the gap was not just another market maker ruse, but rather that real selling pressure had built up overnight, and that yesterday's closing price had been just a way station on the road south, and that the market would keep falling until some new, lower price level gave it a floor to hit. But there are no such major moves in store this morning. After the market closes the gap, the ticker slows way down, and the NDX chart shows short chops, up and down, back up again, back down, moving horizontally in a narrow range.

"You can see a lot of indecision in the market now," Don interprets. "The market is just going sideways, with no direction." The stock CSCO is up in the market maker window. One of the trainees notices a small order record pop up in the CSCO ticker at a price well away from the market. "Somebody got ripped off," Don laughs. Somewhere, someone phoned or e-mailed a broker an order for a stock, and influenced perhaps by early morning news that the market had gapped down, sold at a price a half-point below the present market. But because he or she didn't have real-time quotes, the seller probably didn't know any better, and if the broker is a smooth enough talker, perhaps never will.

This market is now too slow to trade, but traders don't make money sitting still, and even in a poor market there may occasionally be a good opportunity. Vilai asks whether it might make sense to look at a market news feed, see what stocks are being talked up, and check them out.

"Nah," says Don, with the intonation that suggests he's tried that before. "You look at the news and see, say, ten headlines, pick one stock, watch it, jump to another, watch it, to see which one is going to make money. Instead, we have a ticker that will search the entire market and report which stocks are making sharp moves."

Thus he introduces a software tool called the Analysis Client. It does exactly what he says it will do. He keys in some preferences: stocks priced between twenty and eighty dollars per share, with a bid-offer spread no greater than ⅛ point, and at least ten market makers, four of whom have changed their prices within the last five seconds. Then he clicks the mouse, and a small window pops up among the other charts and windows and tickers. The Analysis Client begins to print the names of stocks whose prices are on the **135** move, even though the market is not, in red if four market makers have reduced prices within the past five seconds, in green if they have raised prices. "This identifies stocks that are active *now* and eliminates the need for news," he concludes.

The Analysis Client flashes an intermittent green series of SUNW—the ticker symbol for Sun Microsystems. The stock is on a run. Don keys the symbol into the market maker window, and the display changes from CSCO to SUNW. At the top of the window in a gray sort of capstone frieze is the Inside Market—the current best bid and asked, the day's high and low, arrows to indicate upticks and downticks, etc. Underneath, in quick-shifting bands, or levels, are all of the prices away from the inside market. On the right column, the offer prices are moving up. It looks as though a pump is pushing the prices up from the bottom of the offer column. They literally move up in the window, all the way to the top, and disappear for a second. Then they appear on the left column, as though they rose out of the top of the right-hand column and spilled over into the left. They flow into the top of the bid column and push the older bid prices toward the bottom.

The market pressure and direction are clear; just a glance at the direction of the flow from offer to bid column tells the whole story. In order to buy the stock, bidders have to pay up, meeting the sellers' ask price. As they meet the ask prices, what had been the "offer" or "ask" becomes the new "bid." Of course, seeing bidders willing to come up, the sellers raise their ask even farther, and the bid and offer keep rising until eventually the bidders decide it's not worth paying up any more. The bidders fall away, at which point the whole process reverses itself. As prices fall, it seems as though they well up from the bottom of the bid column, lower and lower bid prices moving inexorably to the top and over, to land in the offer column and push the high offers to the bottom there.

At the moment, though, SUNW is still moving up and moving so fast that a trader who puts in an offer to buy at the specific bid price on the screen now would probably not be filled. The stock is hard to buy. That's why the price is moving up. "If you expect to be filled on the bid, the stock has to be ticking down!" Don says. "If you want to sell at the offer, the stock has to be ticking up." There are only two ways to buy a stock moving as fast as this one: either use SOES and take the stock from the next market maker in line at the inside market price prevailing at the very moment when the electronic SOES order hits, or else bid a price somewhat higher than the present market. The second way is riskier, since the market has to move up in order for the trader to merely break even on the trade and then move up even more if the trader is to make money.

Vilai asks, "When you see a stock move like this, does it make sense to check the news then?"

"You could, but it doesn't make any difference. There could be news, but the stock is moving," Don says. Why waste time finding out why? The important thing is to get on board.

The trainees settle in to trade, some buying SUNW to catch the momentum, others picking their own targets from the Analysis Client. After a while, Olga says, sweetly, "Don?"

He walks back to her station.

"I'm watching this," she says uncertainly, her finger trembling a little as she points at a window on her screen. "Is this what I watch to see when it's time to buy a stock?"

"What?" Don asks, condescending, but disbelieving.

"I want to know when it's time to buy a stock," Olga explains with a patient tolerance, as if that ought to be a clear and reasonable thing to ask for.

"Well," Don says, stammering just a little, "yeah, you watch this . . . you watch this to see when it's time, depending on how the market is moving . . . and just now, while I've been talking, it's moved! It's too late."

"Oh," says Olga, with a little disappointment. "It's already moved?"

The flurry of action stalls a little before noon. Most of the trainees leave for lunch. A few stay behind even though nothing is happening on the screens, just in case. One asks Joyce how she is doing. "I got some hits, and I missed some," she answers, a little evasively. Then she continues warmly, "It's like craps. I like that, too." Once on the subject, she talks about casinos in a tone many women reserve for memories of old boyfriends. She went to Vegas five times, she says, even though she doesn't really like Vegas. She's familiar with the two Indian casinos in the Northeast, knows them well, by name and identifying characteristics, but doesn't really like them; the wry twist of her lip and the way she shrugs them off suggests that these two didn't behave themselves quite the way gentlemen ought. "I like gambling in the Caribbean," she continues, romantically. "It's more intimate, more . . . intimate."

The person talking to her has the poor judgement to spoil this tender moment by asking about a comment she made yesterday, about having sold some stocks before coming to this course. She stiffens, answers curtly, "I don't want to talk about that; I'm very upset about that," and turns away to find more pleasant company at another desk.

Everyone is back to their trading stations on time, checking what has happened in the lunch hour, talking about good trades they made that morning. The market begins to get active and move up.

"Ha! Got that one!" says Herb.

"You got it?"

"Bought at a sixteenth, sold at a half."

"Congratulations."

"Way to go, Herb!"

Herb tilts back in his chair. "I made a half on that this morning too. That's the second time."

One or two other voices pipe up to brag a little about a gain of a quarter or a half. No one talks about losses, though the probability that there have been some may be inferred from the people sitting silently, heads tilted in toward their screens, as though to escape notice.

Don picks this moment to put everyone through keyboard and mouse drills. On command, the trainees must bring up the appropriate window, send an order using SOES, an ECN, or SelectNet. The buy orders go well. Then Don instructs the class to bring up a sell window and short a stock.

"Shit!" someone exclaims.

"Why not hold!"

"The market's still going up!"

"Look at the ticker!"

They aren't joking. Even though they aren't making or losing any real money at this, even though it's just a drill, for mechanical practice, a paper trade, the trainees grumble and resist the instruction to sell, because the market is still going up.

But it's important to know how to do these things, Don says. And the market is just moving enough to "grind," or snatch sixteenths, eighths, maybe a quarter out of the horizontal sawtooth chart. There are no runs.

The trainees come to their senses, a little reluctantly. They look around and remember that this is just a training room, not a trading floor.

The back talk stops.

Buying and selling correctly is surprisingly difficult. Bringing up the order window and sending the order to the market isn't a problem, but in this course, the trainees learn that every decision to buy must include a decision to sell, and every decision to sell must include a decision to buy.

Don sends a buy order and immediately brings up a sell screen. He points to the left-hand, or bid, column on the market maker window. On this transaction, he has defined a stop loss point ⅛ below his buying price. If the market moves down, he intends to place a SOES sell order in time to get out of the stock with a loss no greater than ⅛ point. There are several market makers in the bid window at each level, so the price that would give him a ⅛ loss is more than halfway down the bid column. But if the stock turns against him, the intermediate levels can quickly disappear. In order to ensure that there will be time for his order to be filled before that happens, he draws an imaginary line a little more than halfway up the bid column. If the ⅛ price level hits that line, he will send his sell order and take the loss.

"Before you get into a stock, you have to know when, at what point, you will get out, how much of a loss you are willing to take," he stresses. "While I'm in this position, I'm also looking to the market to see what it's doing. It's moving up. Now, I need you all to **139** join me in praying for more three-eighths to print in the stock ticker. Prayer helps. Just keep it down when you're on the floor; don't let everyone around you hear. . . . Ah! It's working! Look at the three-eighth prints! At this point, since it's not going against me, I'll just sit and wait, but be ready to bail if it moves against me." The market is flat, chopping sideways, directionless. Suddenly it shoots up. The stock follows. "I'm establishing a new exit point as this goes up," Don says. He takes a substantial paper profit before the close.

Because it's important to be able to get out of bad positions before they move too far in the wrong direction, new traders are advised to avoid the most volatile Nasdaq stocks. Traders need volatility, and Dell, Yahoo, and Amazon deliver it. But these and a few others move too far, too fast for most apprentices to trade comfortably. "You have to be willing to risk three-quarters of a point, at least, on these," Don explains, and on a typical thousand-share lot, that's $750. "If you want to trade stocks that volatile, limit yourself to one or two hundred shares. That way you can participate without taking so much risk."

Newbies are also advised to limit themselves to trading no more than three stocks. In order to tell where a stock is going, the trader has to know where it's been. "You don't want to try to watch too many because then you recognize movement too late," Don says. "There was a six-month period when I traded the same three stocks every day. Some days, when the market was not active, I made five trades; other days I did fifty. I recommend you do the same."

*   *   *

In principle, it all seems simple enough. Determine the direction of the market. Find a stock that is moving. Buy if it's going up, and sell if it's going down. Cut your losses; let your profits run. Simple rules, clear, easy to remember.

Promptly contradicted by other rules equally simple, clear, and easy to remember.

Because every rule of trading is qualified by its opposite.

Find a stock that's moving up, and buy—but buy when it comes down. Don't predict—but do anticipate. Let your profits run—but take the money off the table as soon as you see it (and don't be greedy). The only rule that is absolutely inviolable is the rule of cutting losses—always define a loss limit before getting into a trade, and always get out when losses reach the limit. Yet remember that in the volatile markets that are best for trading, the stock may jag down through the limit loss level and then up again. So the trader who follows the loss-cutting rule with mechanical consistency will be shaken out of some very good trades.

The aspiring traders need to know that trading isn't just a matter of following the rules. They learn it the hard way. In the back of the room, a quiet, middle-aged man in a black turtleneck shirt and a herringbone-weave jacket spent the first several days of the program trying to follow the simple rules exactly. He began by identifying stocks that were moving. He waited and watched a moment to make sure the move was real. When it was clear that the move was strong, and real, he bought. The stocks turned down. Mindful of the rule to cut losses, he sold as soon as they had fallen a sixteenth, or an eighth. Vexingly enough, just after he had taken his loss, the stocks started up again. Once burned, twice shy, he waited a little longer for confirmation of the new move, to make sure it was truly real this time, and when he was confident, he bought—just before another bounce down. Over and over, day after day, every trade a loser. His experience was not exceptional. Clearly, following the straightforward rules was not the secret to success.

It seemed that the secret to success was to do two contradictory things at the same time. But that is illogical. So, like a Zen koan, the contradictory rules freeze the part of the mind that works by logic. Arguably, most of what happens in the markets is neither clear nor logical. Trading requires a broader perspective. At All-Tech, in the fall of 1998, just when it was needed, the broader perspective arrived in the flesh.

Mike joined the faculty of All-Tech about four days into phase one of the training program. He was an imposing figure, square **141** head set directly between wide fleshy shoulders, his umber hair swept back in a bristle above a thick face, a tense jaw, and a neck whose presence was merely suggested by the tie knotted against his collar like a red ribbon on a prize bull. Mike was almost as wide as he was tall; he spoke in a voice hoarse from shouting and unmistakably Staten Island in its accent.

He'd worked his way up from the bottom to the middle of the hierarchy on the New York Stock Exchange, where at the pinnacle of his career he had managed all floor operations as head clerk for a major brokerage company. He left that job to join a small Florida hedge fund as a trader. Things went so well there that the fund's principal manager, applying the rule to take the money when you see it, fled the country with everyone's investments. After a stint in sales with another brokerage, Mike joined the All-Tech faculty.

No one could doubt his authenticity. True, Mike had never had a seat at the power table on Wall Street. But for people still trying to elbow their way into the dining room, what he had seen from below-the-salt sounded marvelous and new.

"You can trade any stock on momentum," he said, hitching up his pants. "You want to buy strong stocks in a weak market and sell weak stocks in a strong market. Don't just trade the momentum of the tape, but let the stock tell you where to be. A stock that goes down when the tape is up, it's just like that stock is waving a flag. If you have an up tape, and you see the market losing its momentum to upward, that weak stock will sell down a lot more quicker than a stock that was strong on the up tape."

"The ideal place to be a buyer is on a low, or a pullback. You will make more money if the stock goes with you, and lose less if it goes against you. But how do you know whether a stock is digesting a move before going higher, or else in trouble? I check the industry. If the industry charts are up, that tells me the industry is doing well. I don't know why, but I know it's up for some reason. There are leaders and laggards in each industry, so some stocks don't move as fast as others, but if the other stocks in the industry are up, my stock should go up too. If the rest of the group is going higher, but my stock is not, maybe there is something wrong with it."

"Charts are history lessons. It's a good idea to know where a stock has support and resistance," he says, pointing at something on the screen.

"Excuse me, I can't see the screen."

"Hey, I'm a one-man eclipse, I tell you." He smiles, sort of, and moves aside a bit. "Momentum tells you when to get in. If I see the market trending up, I know I want to be a buyer sometime. If I have profit in a stock and the market starts down, shouldn't I sell somewhere? I want to be a buyer on the pullback, and I want to go short around a high as the market loses momentum. When I was a trader at a hedge fund, we basically traded the elasticity of the tape, from the highest high to the lowest low. Am I going too fast?"

A little.

But so is the market. Even when it is slow, there are too many things going on in it for anyone to think anything through clearly.

That is one of the main lessons of the program—never quite stated that baldly, but no less true.

The trainee traders have to be aware of everything, and focus on any one thing means turning attention, however briefly, from something equally important that will certainly become even more important as soon as it is ignored.

For example, a basic understanding of technical analysis is important. Technical analysis postulates that prices move in certain repetitive patterns, and therefore the trader who correctly identifies the pattern in which prices are moving now can anticipate their next move. Don and Mike frequently speak in technical trading jargon, noting that stocks seem to have found a support or to be breaking through a resistance level. The software at the trading stations allows the traders to pull down charts of two-hundred-day, twenty-day, five-day moving averages, and intraday trend lines, and superimpose one trend line on the chart of another, and identify the point where the short-term moving average crosses the long-term lines, which point marks a reversal of the long-term trend. The software will also calculate and chart the overbought and oversold indicators for the market index or for individual stocks. When the market is "overbought," technical traders anticipate a **143** fall; vice versa when it is "oversold." There are more technical factors and charts and calculations, but they are introduced with a warning that day traders cannot really rely on them for more than ancillary information, certainly not for decision-making guidance. Even though the software performs them in seconds, the calculations are too time-consuming for day trading. More to the point, because these technical analytical tools map out only what has happened in the past, they never include what is happening right now, the only thing the day trader should care about. Technical factors cannot be ignored because there are in the market many technical traders who do make their decisions on this basis and at certain points, in certain circumstances, these traders will determine the prices. But the trainees should only think like technical traders at those points and in those circumstances. At other points, in other circumstances, they must think entirely differently.

Think is the wrong word. In order to day trade, they must move beyond thinking altogether, to intuitive action. Understanding why a particular move made sense is an exercise for later. There's no time to think about reasons when the move must be made.

This is something that only begins to make sense, intuitive sense, with long practice. So, day after day, the lights in the training room go down, the screens come up, the trainees practice catching the moves, while Mike and Don, from the front or the back of the room, utter aphoristic, oracular apothegms to the rhythm of the jiggering prices, in an incantatory, quasi liturgy of initiation.

Thus:

Trading—what you put in is what you get out . . . If the stock lags the market down, people are reluctant to sell, so when the market turns, that stock will be the first to go up . . . News will make a stock more active . . . Some stocks are active every day . . . The trend is your friend . . . When the stock jogs, you need to buy at the bottom . . . When the market is doing nothing, don't try to create something . . . The three-day rule: if the stock goes up three days, it will turn down on day four, and vice versa, if it has been down for three days, it will turn up on day four . . . When the market turns, don't give a long position time to go against you . . .

When the market approaches yesterday's high, expect turbulence . . . Follow the path of least resistance . . . Always know what stocks you want to buy and sell, and at what price; carry the list in your head . . . Emotions are deadly . . . All rules can be broken except the rule to stop losing . . . Discipline means doing what you need to do when you don't want to do it . . . The only truth in the market is what's happening before your eyes, so trade the truth . . . The ticker is your music; don't stand up and dance when there's no music playing . . . Higher highs and higher lows spell upward momentum; new lows and lower highs spell a sell-off . . . Emotions are deadly . . . When you get into a stock, know your tolerance for pain . . . If you want to stare at pictures, go to a museum . . . Listen to Kenny Rogers; you got to know when to fold 'em . . . Some days the tape follows the bond market; some days it follows the futures . . . Some stocks trade with the tape; others trade on their own timetable . . . Constantly reevaluate your position . . . Be flexible . . . Pick the right entry point . . .

Olga raises a hand and, in some consternation, asks, "But when should I buy?"

Mike answers with a shrug, "About ten seconds before the stock goes up a point."

Her head seems to tremble a little, and she apparently thinks she is alone in her confusion, but everyone is like her, alone in confusion by now.

Toward the end of this segment of the program, a psychologist replaces Don and Mike at the front of the classroom to warn the trainees about another source of confusion besides the contradictions of the market. After so many days of solitude, sitting in the darkness with only their screens for company, each person merely peripheral to the other, the trainees seem to welcome a day with the screens off, the lights on, and an ongoing conversation about something besides price moves. They talk about stress, a commodity of which everyone has plenty, not all of it from the vexations of trying to predict the market. Some are shifting jobs; some recovering from illness; some have just moved or are just about to; some have difficult mates and some have no mates; and most in- **145** terestingly, almost all have misgivings about the morality of trading for a living. It doesn't seem productive, they say; it seems somehow wrong to make a living doing something that really produces nothing. This is a difficult problem, and the psychologist warns that if they do not resolve it one way or another, their trading will suffer. Some try to rationalize a solution, only to have their rationalizations attacked by others with the vehemence that comes from the experience of having tried to live with an insupportable rationalization. There is no solution forthcoming from the psychologist either. She merely points out where the problem lies and suggests that each trainee try to deal with it in some constructive way.

She warns about several additional sources of stress, such as boredom, fear, troublesome relationships, financial pressures. She warns that smokers are apt to smoke more, drinkers to drink more, overeaters to overeat more once they move into the real world on the trading floor. She equips the class with several stress-management tips, prescribes regular exercise and occasional deep breathing sessions, and hands out her cards, in case anyone should need more extensive counseling down the road.

Oddly, the very brief experience of talking to each other seems to make a real difference in the atmosphere of the program. The next day, the lights are off again; everyone is again absorbed by the screens and by the trades, the apothegmatic chant of principles and rules punctuating the silence. But it is a more relaxed silence, and people seem a little more willing to confess to losing trades, a little more willing to shout out winning ideas.

Mike walks back to Sonny's station and exults, "Beautiful! That's a beautiful trade!" He announces to the class that Sonny had looked at the stock, looked at the stock, and saw it breaking a half. "It faltered for a second; he wasn't sure. But he saw bids coming in; he bought, stayed with it; it rose." Then, turning back to Sonny, "You keep your eye on that index. If you think the market is going to fade, make a sale."

That afternoon, Olga returns from lunch to find a trade that she had booked before leaving (breaking the rule never to leave trades untended) has made a thousand dollars.

Progress is being made. The trainees have grasped the basics at last. Now they are ready for the last segment of the training program, the one in which they forget what they have learned and do things completely differently.

For the final two weeks, they move into another room. During phases one and two, which they have just completed, they worked in a room with only one window, the one facing the hallway. In the new room, there is no window on the hallway, and the windows to the outside are covered by dark blinds. In the upper corner of the room, CNBC plays constantly. The darkness is deeper, the silence quieter. And, as if there have not been enough contradictions to deal with yet, the instructor is a Jew for Jesus.

This is not immediately apparent. It takes a good ten minutes to become clear.

Trim, slightly built, with a neat gray beard, a sharp, dark suit, white shirt, and classic power tie, he enters the room briskly and introduces himself as "Manny, that's short for Emmanuel, a nice Jewish name, because I'm a nice Jewish boy." He pauses to ask that people put lids on their coffee cups. "Nothing is worse than to walk in somewhere and it's dirty, so please."

He asks if anyone has a ticker up on their trading stations. Everyone raises a hand. He walks around and looks, shaking his head. "The ticker is not the speedometer," he says. He will have nothing to do with that speedometer nonsense. Nonplussed, the trainees delete their speedometers.

He begins to speak, calmly, matter-of-fact, now and then with a crescendo of emotion, though, as he recalls the old days, when he was head trader in the New York office of a major midwestern brokerage. He has been in the markets, trading actively, for over thirty years, and he was with Harvey Houtkin almost from the beginning. He was there when the SEC officials came in to sit alongside Harvey's SOES Bandits and observe the collusive skulduggery by which the market makers attempted to shut them out of the market. He talks about his experience in just enough detail to establish his authority.

Then he says, in an evangelical crescendo, "This may not be your business. This is not a science, and it's not a slot machine. **147**

Tell yourself that if you lose a certain amount, you're quitting. Draw the line. This may not be for everyone. You're putting tremendous pressure on yourself, tremendous anxiety. You don't need it. You will face two monsters. The first is fear, and when you get past fear, then greed is waiting there for you. We can exorcise the spirit of fear, but not the spirit of greed. And by the way, if you are successful, give a tenth of it to the Lord! It will come back a hundredfold, believe me."

A stranger silence than the one they have known settles over the class.

"Okay," says Manny. He turns around in a crisp, businesslike manner and, as though turning around took him from one mode of thought into another, goes to his computer and, step by step, deconstructs what the trainees have learned to date.

He replaces the speedometer with a single ticker, displayed banner-style across the top of the screen, that contains only those stocks in which the trader has an active interest. None of them are top-tier Nasdaq stocks, none of them among the hundred stocks in the NDX index. Those top hundred stocks are too volatile and too hard to get in and out of because too many day traders are involved in them. Manny, although he is a day trader, doesn't care much for day traders in general. He still has a professional market maker's attitude toward the upstarts. So he sets up the ticker so that it will display only price changes by market makers and eliminates all ECNs from the display. "You only want to see market makers," he says dismissively. "The market makers are the only ones who determine where the stock is moving. If Goldman is raising prices in the ticker, the stock is going up."

He gets rid of the charts too. He gets rid of everything except the market maker window, which gives best price and the day's high and low in Level I and the names of the market makers and their diverse bid and offer prices in the Level II section. "Before the beginning, this existed," he says, "the market maker windows and the ticker."

A trading minimalist, Manny dismisses momentum trading and technical charting with a shrug. "You can look at a stock and see the speedometer rip, but will it determine whether or not you buy the stock? No! I can't follow the pack. I have to be a step ahead. You want momentum to follow you. You don't want to follow it."

The key to his strategy is a pattern he has noticed in his decades of trading: stocks that are beaten down today tend to come back tomorrow. This observation inspired a simple but effective trading method.

Each day, before the open, refer to the *Investors Business Daily* newspaper to identify the previous day's losers. Identify those that have lost about three points. Check the volume of shares traded to be sure it is at least two hundred thousand. Check the seven-day chart of the stock to make sure that the decline was not part of an ongoing trend, and check the news to make sure that there is not a very sound reason for the stock to go farther down. Then, watch the futures.

There is something about that number three. "Three pays you back a lot more than one or two or four or five. Nobody knows why; that just comes out of experience," he says. "Somehow any stock that's down that number, for some reason or other, when the market goes up, those stocks always come back."

At the open, there are three possibilities. If the market, after falling the previous day, turned up somewhat near the close, it may gap up, and several of these stocks could therefore open gap up. The gap up is usually followed by a fall, then another attempt to rise. "If they gap up, wait," Manny counsels. "If it goes up, it always comes down, jiggles, then makes an attempt to go up again, depending on where the futures are. If the futures are up, it will play up; if the futures weaken, there will be a jiggle, and when the futures strengthen again, buy the stock, ride it up. That's what you do in a gap up."

The second possibility is a gap down, especially likely to occur if the market had been falling sharply at the previous day's close. "As soon as the futures start turning up, there will be a jiggle, then up again—but take warning when the stock gaps down. I'd be very leery about how far up it's going to go. I'd be careful. If it was down the day before, then gapped down at the open and went down a lit- **149** tle farther, then jiggled and tried to come up, I'd ride it until it stops, then SOES out, even if I sacrifice an eighth of a point to get out."

Gaps are tricky business. The best situation is one in which the stock, after falling three points the day before for no apparent good reason, opens in a sort of limbo, in a dull but improving market. "What you want is the dormant stock. Maybe they go down a teeny or two in sympathy with the market at the open, but as soon as the market improves, that stock is up. Look at the ticker. When it shows green, green, green, that's your time. Bring up the stock, size up the market, check the futures, see where it's at, and if it's moving, get on board. You aren't going to have too many people on these stocks, first, because they're secondary stocks and, second, because the other people are still looking around. But you're already focused on the stock, so you have a better chance of getting in than the guy looking for momentum. By the time he gets in, you want him in, to take it up further. If the market turns down again, these stocks are going to give up some ground, and that's another opportunity! If your futures are down, that's another opportunity, because when the futures start up again, it will move. It's only down because the futures are applying pressure to it. But I will not get into the stock more than twice—three times, you just give it all back."

This game of playing stocks that were down the day before has a strict time limit. It works only in the morning and usually only between the open and 10:30. Sometimes the opportunity window stays open as late as 11:30, but generally that's only if the market has been sluggish and things have gotten off to a late start. Most days, this action is over by 10:30. At this point, the trader's attention turns from the up side to the downside.

"This is the second step of the day. Between 10:30 and 11:00, you're looking for negative stocks in the Analysis Client. Run them through the mill, check out the same criteria, down three sticks [points], volume of at least two hundred thousand, but the more the better, and at least ten market makers. When there's only a
150 few houses trading a stock, I guarantee you they're sleeping to-

gether; there's collusion. You don't want to play with that game. So go through the five steps: down three, volume two hundred thousand, and check the news, and the seven-day chart, and the futures. Find the worst ones, the worse the better; the game has changed."

The game now is to play the short side. The key to winning is to recognize that the market makers will try to bring these losing stocks up in the afternoon in order to unload their own positions. The worse the news, the likelier it is that the stocks will stage a sucker rally and then fall back again. A serious downgrade, litigation, the resignation of the CEO—all are stimulants to the appetite of the short-side helluos. But shorting these stocks is a waiting game.

"This begins to play out its game around 2:00 or 2:30," Manny says, "Wait. The stock may be activated at 1:00, or at 2:00. Some may not even go until 2:30. But all of a sudden it begins to make the move; the ticker shows green, green, green. Remember to look at the highs and the lows. When the stock is midway between the high and the low, that's the ideal situation because from there to the low there's room for me to make money. Watch the futures. As soon as the futures start going down, you're going to see a levelling off here. Look for the first downtick. That's the stock I'm going to short." (The uptick rule requires that the trader wait for an uptick after the first downtick before shorting, but at this early stage of the action, the uptick will come along soon enough.)

Prudence dictates that the first short sale should be relatively modest, say, five hundred shares, just in case the entry point is not timed right. If the stock goes up a quarter to three-eighths more, it is time to short the next five hundred. The success of the strategy depends on the fundamental weakness of the stock and on the fact that it has merely been dragged up from its low of the day by the overall rise of the market. Stocks damaged by really bad news won't keep moving up when the market turns—in fact, they'll be the first to fall. "You'll find them. They're out there, a point and a half up from the low, and all of a sudden the futures are going **151** south—short that stock. There's money here!" Manny exclaims with relish. "Don't let it pass you by."

The instructors who addressed SOES Bandit wannabes during the four weeks of the All-Tech training program disagreed about many things, but agreed on one. Each of them found an occasion to cite one trader as a guide and inspiration: Jesse Lauriston Livermore.

It is the Livermore of the bucket shops whose spirit and memory matter here—not the later Livermore of the stock-manipulation scandals or the ultimate Livermore of the Sherry Netherland Hotel men's room. It is the brash, young Livermore who matters, the consummate student of prices and their changes, the fellow whose uncanny intuition gave him a strange feeling about the price movement of the Union Pacific Railroad stock and led him to short it, inexplicably, just before news of the San Francisco earthquake broke.

The notion that when prices reach certain trigger points, they will either fall back or, if they break through, soar far is vintage Livermore. So is the talk of internal enemies—greed and fear—that are more daunting antagonists than any unpredictability or contradiction within the market itself. But only Manny talked with passion of these latter things.

"I'm not solely responsible to All-Tech," he said, early and often. "I'm not solely responsible to All-Tech. I'm responsible to the Almighty God I serve. I'm convicted in my heart! We have to be honest with people. This is a high-risk business! It's not as easy as it used to be! It's important that you explain to your spouse what's involved. If you work this kind of job deceitfully, it will hound you. How will you explain a loss of fifteen thousand dollars? Please, work together with your spouse. And would I recommend anyone leaving their job to do this? No! It's not in compliance with what goes on here, but I am my brother's keeper and I have to sleep at night."

The game of SOES Banditry had made its easy money long ago. Now, things were harder. In fact, many of the big, early profits of

the SOES Bandits had been simple consequences of the inefficiency of a collusive cartel. As economic theory suggests, the exploitation of those inefficiencies by the SOES Bandits quickly made the market more efficient—and therefore harder to make money in. The Nasdaq was like a cherry orchard, the SOES Bandits like a flock of birds. The easy fruit had now been picked.

And the fight over the hard fruit was taking some of the day-trading industry's brightest stars out of the trading room and into the courtroom.

Part Five

THE BAD
AND
THE UGLY

Chapter 9

The Dirt

Day Trading Secrets Spilled in Court

A snarl of litigation coiled through Texas courts and arbitration rooms has revealed facts of the day-trading life that aren't taught in any training course in the country. Day trading came to Texas courtesy of Jeff Burke and Chris Block, the founders of Block Trading, whose story is recapitulated in the first chapter of this book. Texas has always attracted the kind of people who make risky bets, from cowboys through oil wildcatters to high-tech entrepreneurs. Enough of those bets had paid off that Texas had an ample pool of well-heeled high rollers psychologically conditioned to believe they could beat the odds. Burke and Block prospered, and so did their imitators, one of whom founded the industry association of day-trading firms, the Electronic Traders Association, headquartered in the main office of Houston-based Momentum Securities.

The legal war of attrition in Texas has made it possible to learn details about how day-trading firms do business, and about the character of the people who have emerged as the industry's leaders, that would never have come to light if they had not gone for **157** each other's throats. It's not a pretty or an edifying picture. The lawyers and the plaintiffs and defendants are tangled thicker than diamondbacks at the Sweetwater Rattlesnake Round-up and forked tongues sometimes seem to be one thing they all have in common. Allegations, charges, and countercharges in the files of suits and countersuits include violations of securities laws, usury, theft of documents, corporate espionage, breaches of contract, defamations, and even racketeering.

It makes sense to begin the process of untangling these poisonous strands with the case of Kevin Burke against Dr. Gene Burke because it is the simplest, most straightforward, and possibly the most bizarre of them all. The public court records of this extraordinary lawsuit contain a map to a sort of buried treasure discovered by Mr. Kevin Burke and his wife Kristi. The treasure was buried in the twists and turns of Texas usury law. Mr. Burke is described in court papers as "an unsuccessful day trader," but "unsuccessful" seems hardly the right word to describe a man who has, after all, found a way to make millions of dollars from day trading, whether his trades win or lose.

Kevin Burke won approximately $3.5 million from Dr. Gene Burke, no relation, who had made the mistake of lending him money to meet margin calls. Even as the judge was ordering Dr. Burke to turn over various investments to pay the judgment, Kevin Burke had another lawsuit in the works seeking nearly eleven million dollars from other lenders who had allegedly made the same mistake as the good doctor.

Dr. Gene Burke's son, young Jeff Burke, was the flamboyant, Ferrari-driving cofounder of Block Trading, a wild operation even by the loose standards of the Extreme Investing scene. Although the firm went bankrupt in the fall of 1998, it was still at the peak of glory when Kevin and Kristi Burke were day trading in the Dallas office. Its growth had been so impressive that Jeff Burke and cofounder Chris Block served stints as magazine cover boys for *Inc.* magazine and even made the pages of *Details*.

Dr. Gene Burke was nowhere near as high-profile as his famous son, but he had a discreet sideline to his medical practice as a specialist in addiction medicine. Every day, Dr. Burke received a fax from Block Trading with a list of customers who had margin calls due the following day.

A margin call is a demand that the trader put more money into his or her account. Securities and banking regulations allow people to buy twice as much stock as they actually have money to pay for. Sometimes, in the frenzy of trading, Extreme Investors go past the limit and buy even more than that. More often, they make trades that lose money, on paper, and therefore reduce the equity in their accounts. Whether the traders break margin rules by trading beyond their limit or by making trades that lose money so that they no longer have enough equity to support the volume of stocks they have bought, they receive a margin call. When traders receive a margin call, they must either deposit more money in order to bring their account equity up to the legal minimum, or liquidate some of the securities in their portfolio. Traders tend to be reluctant to liquidate securities in order to meet a margin call, especially if this means turning a "paper" loss into a cash loss, as it often does.

Block had offices all over the country. According to Massachusetts state securities regulators, sixty-seven of sixty-eight trading accounts at Block's Boston office lost money. That may not be quite representative of Block's overall operation, but it is probably close. Texas regulators say that well over 90 percent of all traders in all day-trading firms inspected in that state lose money.

So there were a lot of margin calls. When he received his daily fax from Block, Dr. Gene Burke reviewed it to see which margin calls from Block's national network of trading rooms he was willing to help traders meet with a short-term, usually overnight, margin loan. When he had made his decision, he faxed a letter of authorization to Block Trading's clearinghouse, instructing the clearinghouse to transfer money from his own account to the accounts of the traders he was willing to help. Dr. Gene Burke loaned as little as ten thousand dollars and as much as six hundred thousand dollars to traders in the various offices of Block Trading nationwide. He had never met most of the traders, but the loans were very low risk, both because they were short-term and because he carefully **159** selected which margin calls he would cover. Dr. Gene Burke made twenty-three loans to cover margin calls for Kevin and Kristi Burke from June to November 1997. He charged $100 per day for every $100,000 loaned, a rate that was supposed to work out to 18 percent, annualized. However, some quirks in the way Dr. Burke calculated interest due made the real interest rate much higher.

Dr. Burke considered a loan made on Monday afternoon and repaid on Tuesday to be a two-day loan, not a one-day loan. So he charged not one, but two days of interest—not $100, but $200 per $100,000 loaned, for an annualized rate of 36 percent.

"By doing business this way, Defendant obtained an eight-day yield on loans made during the four days from Monday to Friday," noted Kevin Burke's attorney, in his motion for summary judgment. "In common language this is known as loan sharking."

The court agreed. Texas law takes a very dim view of usury. Perhaps because it's a Bible-belt state, or perhaps for some other reason, Texas has some of the most draconian usury laws in the United States. In Dr. Gene Burke's case, the penalty was three times the usurious excess interest, plus the entire principal of the loans. That is why Judge Montgomery ordered him by summary judgment on October 23, 1998, to pay Kevin and Kristi Burke the sum of $3,596,740—plus 10 percent interest.

Kevin Burke's victory in this case ought to ring the come-and-get-it bell for anyone who has ever day traded in Texas, win or lose. There is another dimension to this story, though, because before he began to trade at Block, Kevin Burke had traded at Cornerstone.

Owned by Russell Grigsby, David Burch, and David Jamail, with Grigsby sole officer and director, Cornerstone had been incorporated in 1993, with its main office in Austin. Kevin Burke began to trade at the Dallas office of Cornerstone in July 1995.

He traded so heavily that he claims to have been Cornerstone's biggest customer in Dallas, and his trading fit the classic Extreme Investing pattern, quick in and out moves and hundreds of thousands of dollars of volume. According to his affidavit, he didn't make much money from his own trades—only ten thousand dollars from July 1995 until July 1996. But he did generate a lot of commissions and margin calls.

It's worth noting, by the way, that Burke blames his lack of success at trading on everything but a lack of skill. He alleges that Cornerstone was illegally using unlicensed brokers to enter transactions for him and says that errors by these order-entry brokers cost him "thousands of dollars." He also claims that losses were caused by power outages in the Cornerstone offices during trading hours and by "failed air conditioning in the summer." Even though Burke wasn't making much money from his trades, Cornerstone was, and so were some of the other traders around him.

Cornerstone made money even from his losing trades because it charged commissions of $20 to $25 per trade, according to an affidavit by the Dallas branch manager. That's $20 to $25 to buy, and another $20 to $25 to sell, for a total round-trip commission charge of $40 to $50 on each trade.

Since Burke traded heavily, often on margin, and without notable success, it is to be expected that he might generate a lot of margin calls, and in fact he did. Unlike Block Trading, Cornerstone did not fax daily margin call reports to a well-respected specialist in addiction medicine, so that he could help the trader out with a usurious loan. Cornerstone kept the business of margin lending more or less in the family. Relatively more successful traders helped relatively less successful traders with margin loans—"funds," according to Burke's attorney, "equity" according to the attorney for the defendants in this suit, who claim that the loans weren't money and therefore don't come under Texas usury statutes.

The charge for the loan of funds or equity, depending on which attorney is right, was a trifling two-tenths of one percent of the principal, no matter how long the loan was outstanding. Written out in decimal form—0.2 percent, or .002, of the principal—this looks insignificant. But since most of the loans were only one-day loans, Burke was paying an effective interest rate of approximately 73 percent per year.

In fairness, it must be noted that the interest rate was reduced **161** in October 1996, a few months before Burke left Cornerstone, to one-twentieth of a percent per day, or an annualized 18.25 percent. However, even this amount is arguably in excess of what Texas usury laws allow under the circumstances—at least, that's what Burke's attorneys are arguing.

Texas laws provide different levels of penalty for different levels of usury, and the attorneys on this case are also arguing over numerous other technical legal issues. But the bottom line is that Burke's attorneys are seeking more than eleven million dollars in penalties for usurious interest, including all of the principal that other traders at Cornerstone loaned to Burke during most of his tenure as a customer of the firm.

Kevin Burke's attorney on this case is one Charles M. Hamilton, of the firm of French & Hamilton in Dallas. Mr. Hamilton did not return phone calls seeking comment on the case, or on an intriguing connection between this case and another. Among the attorneys of record on Hamilton's motion for summary judgment appears the name of John A. Lee, of the firm of Andrews & Kurth.

John Lee is the lead attorney for Momentum Securities in another lawsuit against Cornerstone. He's also the brother of James H. Lee, founder and president of the Electronic Traders Association. It is rumored in Houston that James Lee has been funding Kevin Burke's costly lawsuit against Grigsby and the other Cornerstone traders, as part of his own war of attrition against Cornerstone. He strenuously denies this. "Don't kid yourself into thinking we have anything to do with it," he says. "I found out about it because I was contacted by the lawyers to be an expert witness."

James H. Lee got to know the day-trading business by backing a trader who worked with Block in the early 1990s. (The connection between Lee and the founders of Block went back to Houston's Memorial High School.) In 1995, he founded his own firm, Momentum Securities. Lee's new venture was an almost immediate success, with revenues of over $10 million in 1996 and 1997, according to his attorney.

This was Extreme Investing indeed. "Momentum customers normally purchase and sell securities in 1,000 share lots, buying or selling $50,000–$100,000 worth of securities in each transaction, and enter millions or tens of millions of dollars' worth of transactions each day," reads Momentum's second amended petition to the District Court of Harris County, Texas, in Case No. 98-05914. On each trade, Momentum earned a commission of approximately $15. That's $15 to buy and $15 to sell, for a round-trip commission of $30. "Many of the more experienced Momentum customers transact as many as 100–300 transactions a day, and a single customer may thus produce up to $4500 ($15 × 300) in gross revenue to Momentum each business day," the petition states.

It would be hard to imagine a better business. Momentum expanded rapidly, opening branch offices in Austin and Tyler, Texas. When Block fell on hard times, Momentum acquired some of that company's most profitable offices in California and elsewhere. According to its petition to the court, if it had made its financial reports public, Momentum would have ranked among the ten fastest-growing companies in red-hot Houston.

James Lee located his headquarters in the posh Galleria district of Houston, a neighborhood where Rolls-Royces are a common sight. The floor is cushioned with costly Persian rugs, the walls hung with collectible old securities certificates. Bearded Jefferson Davis and uniformed Robert E. Lee stare shot-eyed from rebel-gray bonds of the Confederate States of America, and next to them hang colorful, flag-bedizened bonds of pre-revolutionary China, decorated with elegant calligraphy, and inflexible promises to pay. These decorations give one pause.

Back in the trading room, a long, crescent-shaped trading desk arcs along the wall of glass, its backdrop a smoggy panorama of Houston. Traders sit on both sides of the crescent. There are about fifty traders, young, wearing the wardrobe that is standard to the profession: shorts, T shirts, baseball caps, sneakers, no socks. There is an un-trading-room-like quiet about the place. Perhaps the wall-to-wall carpet hushes the noise, or perhaps it is the huge, high-backed, CEO-style chairs, burgundy leather with brass studs and brass casters, visually impressive but so ill-suited to actually sitting and trading that some traders have propped stuffed brief- **163** cases in their seats behind them to spare themselves the agony of back pain.

A bell chimes from a trading station, a synthesized female voice says "Partial," like the voice in an elevator.

A human voice groans from somewhere on the crescent. "Fuck! There's some sick fucking shit going on!"

Someone answers, "This is ridiculous!"

The bell rings; the synthesized voice says "Partial." Another bell rings.

"I just lost it! Three thousand fucking shares!" a human shouts.

"Partial," the synthesized voice apathetically declares.

A young, blond man, college age or a little older, in a T shirt and shorts, holds his head in his hand and groans, "Don't look at me! Don't look at me!"

The chime tolls. "Partial."

Maybe it's just a bad day.

According to court records, at least some customers used to make quite a bit of money trading here—between two hundred thousand and six hundred thousand dollars apiece. Momentum had a special relationship with them. It required them to sign contracts in which they agreed to trade exclusively through Momentum and not to own any interest in any other day-trading firm. Assured by these contracts that its business was sound, say Momentum's lawyers, the company invested heavily in advanced technology and made plans for an initial public offering of its stock to take place in 1998.

Yet, ten of its most active customers, who accounted for almost 40 percent of the company's revenue volume, allegedly held a series of "clandestine" meetings with Cornerstone in late 1997 and early 1998, with the objective of forming a competing trading cooperative, and signed a secret agreement to do exactly that.

"What happened next was a well-planned and organized attack on Momentum's business," Momentum's lawyers say. "Information was selectively leaked through the trading community that something 'big' was about to happen to Momentum. Rumors were purposely spread and exaggerated. Several of Momentum's customers who had signed the secret agreement to move to Cornerstone and raid Momentum, including DeAyala, a former professional football player, became increasingly belligerent and aggressive in Momentum's offices, creating an open atmosphere of discontent and openly inciting customers to pick up and leave Momentum." Then, one day in mid-February 1998, the group of traders named in Momentum's suit against Cornerstone walked out and encouraged others to go with them.

Momentum accused these traders, and Cornerstone's Russell Grigsby, of defaming it by spreading the word that Momentum ran a dirty business, routinely engaging in practices that broke laws and violated trading and market regulations.

The attorney for Cornerstone and the traders being sued responded to Momentum's lawsuit by denying that Mr. Grigsby ever said any such thing. But then he went on to state that even if Grigsby had said those things, they wouldn't be defamation because they were true! Momentum's illegal activity, he said, includes "violation of NASD and SEC regulations, unlawful trading in tax losses, wire fraud, intimidation, and duress, as well as activity prohibited by the Racketeer Influenced and Corrupt Organizations Act." According to Cornerstone's attorneys, it was this pattern of illegal activity, not a secret agreement to form a competing trading operation, that led the group of traders to walk suddenly and dramatically out of Momentum's trading room in February 1998.

Their attorney claimed that Momentum illegally charged some of the traders low commissions in return for a piece of their action to be deposited in the individual retirement accounts of Momentum's principals. He also said that Momentum illegally reassigned, canceled, or rebilled trades in order to get around SEC and NASD rules. "With the push of a button, the trader can reassign his trade to a different trader's account, thereby deceiving the NASD and the SEC as to the true source of the trade," the attorney for the defendants wrote.

The case took a particularly strange twist in April 1998, when James Lee of Momentum apparently managed to develop a "mole" who worked at Cornerstone's Houston office. According to docu- **165** ments filed in court records of yet another suit, this one Cornerstone against Susan Harrison, the alleged mole, she began to pass along to her brother information she overheard about Cornerstone's business plans and trial strategies. Her brother ran Momentum's Tyler, Texas, office, and passed the information up the ladder. Later, he passed along copies of memos his sister had typed, outlining trial strategies Cornerstone planned to use to defend itself against Momentum. Eventually, he introduced Jim Lee to his sister. She brought a packet of documents including confidential information about Cornerstone's business practices, customers, financial position, and legal strategy and gave it to Lee in a meeting at Houston's Restaurant in May 1998. A follow-up meeting was held later in May at P. F. Chang's, a restaurant and bar, and she delivered more information. In a deposition, Lee admitted that he had "parallel" talks with Susan Harrison about employment opportunities at Momentum. In June 1998, as Cornerstone management began to get suspicious, Susan Harrison left to join Momentum in Houston.

The legal implications of the facts and allegations wound up in the skein of suits, countersuits, and arbitration hearings involving Momentum may be more severe than any of the parties imagined when they launched their war of attrition.

In a vigorous denial of Cornerstone's allegations that Momentum ran a dirty shop, Momentum's attorneys wrote the following, in a submission to the court:

> Needless to say, the allegations regarding improprieties and breaking the law were absolutely false. Since its inception, Momentum and its principals have strived to maintain the utmost of integrity in the operation of Momentum's business, and full compliance with applicable laws and regulations. In its efforts to comply fully with the rules, Momentum has spent hundreds of thousands of dollars in compliance fees and expenses, and has conducted numerous internal audits at its own expense. Momentum's books and records, trading records, and procedures have been examined by the NASD, the United States General Accounting Office, and the State of Texas (the latter two within the

last four [4] months) and the firm has been found to have a perfect compliance record despite malicious prosecution by Cornerstone after the walkout that led to at least one of these examinations.

When a visitor reads that passage to Texas securities commissioner Denise Voigt Crawford, a flush of red begins in her neck and ascends into her face. Her jaw tightens; her eyes narrow. Policy prevents her from making any direct comment on any individual firm or investigation, so she thinks for a moment before she says anything. Then she says, simply, "This agency has never given a clean bill of health to any day-trading firm."

Chapter 10

Cops & Robbers

*The Hard Facts
of Bandit Life*

Denise Voigt Crawford is a tall, sharp-featured woman who grew up on a ranch at the edge of the Texas hill country near the town of Bastrop, in a region where, for generations, "the men ranched and the women kept house or taught school." She looks a little like a schoolmarm herself, with blue eyes, wire-rimmed glasses, and straight blond hair parted down the middle and cut straight off at shoulder length. There is no mistaking her intelligence or her political savvy. She listens attentively as others ramble and measures out her own severely considered words with a garnish of sweet, old-fashioned Southern charm, bred-in, since in this part of the country, intelligence without charm used to be considered a vice in a woman—and may be still, in some circles.

Denise Voigt Crawford ("I really do hope you'll call me Denny!") has served as Texas state securities commissioner since 1993, under the distinctly different gubernatorial administrations of Ann Richards and George W. Bush, Jr. After ten years with the State Securities Board, first as staff attorney, then as general counsel, Crawford stepped into the top job just as the great Prudential derivatives scandal was breaking. She broke ranks with other state regulators who had worked out a settlement with Prudential and proved her toughness by threatening to pull the firm's license to do business in Texas. The deal she eventually negotiated did force Prudential to close its Dallas office to new accounts for several weeks but allowed it to continue to operate provided it reimburse wronged Texans and pay a $1.5 million fine to the board for selling risky derivatives without proper disclosure.

Prudential got off easy. Unusually for state securities regulators, Crawford can make a criminal case out of market malfeasance, and she boasts that Texas has more such indictments than any other state. "We need to put people in jail to provide deterrents," she says.

Although she has several investigations of day-trading firms underway, with criminal referrals expected shortly in two cases, Crawford is careful to make the point that she does not have any sort of animus against day trading. "It's true that some people make money day trading, and a few make very large amounts of money," she concedes. But most don't. Most lose some money, and some lose a lot of money. "One family lost everything. They're now living in a trailer and literally could not afford shoes for the children," Crawford says. "In the securities markets, there are always winners and losers, but to find so many losers is disturbing. Our estimate is that more than 90 percent of the people who try day trading lose money. That's a rough estimate, based on records of firms we've visited."

The Texas Securities Board conducts regular inspections of companies under its jurisdiction. All day-trading firms that the inspectors have visited have had problems. Some of the problems were just technicalities, "but most firms have major problems," Crawford says.

The most serious problems, to date, are misleading advertising that overplays the upside and underplays the risk of day trading and failure to screen customers for financial sophistication or risk tolerance. "Day-trading firms, by and large, take as customers anyone with money to spend," she says. Training, usually conducted **169** by the day-trading brokerage or by an affiliate, is simplistic and generally inadequate. Firms teach the mechanics of using their software and give people some basic principles, such as "Don't carry positions overnight" and "Cut losses," but don't get down to the basic facts of financial life that many unsophisticated wanna-bes need to know. "Customers are not educated about fundamental market risk, such as if you lose an eighth of a point often enough, you'll have nothing left," Crawford claims.

When confronted by regulators, day-trading brokerage firms often aver that they have no fiduciary responsibility to their customers because they are not soliciting trades. That is, no one at the day-trading shop suggests that traders buy or sell any particular stock. But regulators are beginning to press the argument that the day-trading shops do solicit a "trading pattern," the quick-action SOES Bandit game, and therefore do have a responsibility to screen customers and perhaps even require traders to be registered.

It's fairly common practice at day-trading firms around the country for traders to raise money by borrowing from family, friends, or third-party backers. Usually, the trader splits the profits with his or her backers. Regulators take a dim view of such arrangements, since the trader who invests on behalf of a third party usually has the illegal status of an unregistered investment adviser or dealer. The "Heads I win, tails you lose" compensation arrangement is all upside and no downside for the trader. The trader wins if trades pay off, but someone else bears the losses if they don't. Therefore the trader has every incentive to make risky bets that will pay off big if they pay off at all, and no compelling reason to be prudent.

Other problems and potential problems with day-trading firms include operating without a license, failure to maintain proper records, and—on the horizon—money laundering. "We have not yet brought a case based on money laundering, but that does not mean money laundering is not going on," Crawford says, weighing each word with her habitual caution. "We will see it down the road."

In May 1998, the Texas Securities Board shut down a company founded to manage money for a group of Colombians with a great deal of money and an intense interest in secrecy. The circumstances are suggestive, but regulators moved against the company on grounds that it was doing business without proper registration and did not probe deeply into the background of the Colombian investors. They did not allege money laundering or present any evidence that any of the Colombian millionaires who invested funds with this company had done anything illegal.

Juan Carlos Nieto, identified in the administrative court records on this case as "a Colombian citizen who has a significant educational and employment background in the areas of finance and international business" had founded Infinitum Capital Management, a Virgin Islands corporation, and Infinitum Management Company, a Florida corporation, to make investments on behalf of clients identified in administrative court records as his "family members and long-time family friends." Nieto testified that his father, an economist and jurist, was a member of the board of the Colombia Stock Exchange and a judge on the International Court of Justice (World Court) at The Hague, in the Netherlands, where he deals with alleged war crimes in Yugoslavia. Nieto also testified that his clients included a well-respected economist and attorney who had served as a governor in Colombia and been "a secretary in the government at least two or three times." He said that another client owned the largest tuna-fishing fleet in the world and was a major shareholder in one of the biggest mortgage banks in Colombia. There were several other clients too, all Colombian and all with well over a million dollars of net worth.

Nieto set up his companies to maintain several walls of separation between his clients, himself, and the people who actually traded with the money the clients had invested. This was in order to keep the identity of his investors secret. He explained to the court that confidentiality was extremely important to his clients because being wealthy is dangerous in Colombia—wealth tends to attract kidnappers. His secretive ways were not at all intended to evade regulations, he said, but merely to protect his clients. **171**

He decided to put his investors' money to work in the SOES Bandit game because he saw it as a high-return, relatively low-risk opportunity. Before he set up his own operation, he visited several day-trading firms to learn how the business worked. Then he began to hire traders, none of whom had any previous experience in the securities industry. The traders worked as independent contractors. They paid Nieto $3,000 for about three days of training in the principles of SOES Banditry, followed by a few days of paper trading. Then they were turned loose in the market to trade accounts averaging about $150,000 apiece. Traders received a share of net quarterly profits, that is, the increase in the value of the portfolio, minus losses and minus any costs or fees incurred by Infinitum to cover margin calls. Their percentage share went up as the profits went up, and the traders also received a $1,500 monthly payment in return for signing a noncompete agreement that bound them to Infinitum and prohibited them from competing in SOES trading with Infinitum for three years after they left for any reason.

The traders did not know the people whose accounts they were trading. Although they were authorized by a signed power of attorney to trade on behalf of these investors, they never had any personal, telephone, or written contact with the investors. Only Nieto knew whose account each trader was trading.

Some of the traders were extremely good. One made $100,000 on a $150,000 account between June 1996 to May 1997, for a return of 67 percent. Another returned 65 percent for his client during the last five months of 1995 and a whopping 200 percent in 1996. Their performance was the more impressive, considering that none of them had had any previous trading experience. Some traders reportedly lost money too—but none of Infinitum's Colombian investors complained, at least not to regulators.

The Texas Securities Board didn't move against Infinitum to protect these clients, for whom some trading losses may well have been an acceptable cost of doing business. Instead, Infinitum was shut down for the brokerage industry equivalent of hunting without a license: operating an unregistered securities dealership. An

attorney for the board says that allowing companies like Infinitum to do business without registering would be unfair to companies that do register.

Whether or not Merrill Lynch, Goldman Sachs, Morgan Stanley Dean Witter, and their peers need the protection of state securities regulators to shield them from unfair competition may be debatable, but the issue of registration is a big one for day traders, and it's likely to get bigger. State regulators have moved against firms on these grounds in Texas, Massachusetts, and Wisconsin. Colorado regulators attached stiff conditions when they agreed to grant a license to Generic Trading Associates in order to ensure that Generic's traders used only their own money. State regulators have established an informal joint working group to coordinate their approach to day trading, and they've made the issue of registration a top priority—understandably, since it's one of the few handles that allow states to get a regulatory grip on the business.

Most of the leading day trading firms require a minimum trading stake of between $50,000 and $100,000 to open an account. Many, if not most, of the people attracted to day trading don't have that kind of money. The problem is so common that it's the first point addressed on a checklist of salesmanship tips given to employees of Harvey Houtkin's All-Tech Investment Group. When prospects demur because they don't have enough capital, the salesperson is supposed to follow up by saying, "Have you considered getting either an investor or a partner?" All-Tech's tip sheet sternly instructs its salespeople not to offer to help finding such a backer, but some day-trading houses do perform a matchmaking service to bring together traders and capital, the two essential components to generating commission revenue.

Unfortunately, the sources of capital aren't always as well fixed as Infinitum's wealthy Colombians. Fred Sharp, a Maytag man, cashed in a $100,000 CD that represented his and his wife's entire life savings and used half the money to open an account for their twenty-five-year-old daughter to day trade at Block Trading. Brenda Richardson, a single mother in her fifties who worked as a pharmacist at Walgreens, wanted to provide funds for a college education for her only daughter, so she put her life savings in the **173** hands of a day trader. Both cases went to arbitration after Richardson and Sharp lost all or most of their money, much of it to commission charges. Richardson's attorney said that although she only had about $50,000 in her account, the trader entered $35 million worth of trades in roughly ten weeks, generating $35,000 in commissions for the brokerage firm and losses of about $48,000 for Richardson. (Trading on margin allows one to lose more than the amount invested.)

In another case before the arbitrators, a businessman who spent a lot of time traveling made the mistake of opening an account at a day-trading brokerage, apparently thinking it was something like an ordinary brokerage. The broker turned the money over to day traders, who reduced the businessman's net worth from approximately a million dollars to about thirty thousand. The broker didn't tell the businessman about this right away. He had gone out socially with the businessman and had met his girlfriend and apparently found her attractive. So he started to hit on her, "aggressively seeking to date her, making direct propositions of an intimate relationship," according to the businessman's claim before the NASD arbitrators. When she turned the broker down, he told her that she was wasting her time with the businessman because, after all, he was broke. She passed the information along, and that's how the businessman found out about his financial predicament.

Lawyers say that they are receiving more and more calls from people who claim to have been burned by day-trading firms. But even lawyers who specialize in representing injured investors have little sympathy for failed day traders. An attorney who specializes in securities industry arbitration in one large southwestern city said, "Day trading appeals to the greedy fuckers who are told they can make three times their money in weeks, and it appeals to the neophyte dumb asses who would believe anything. I got a call from one fucker, a real estate guy, who'd invested his life savings and wiped himself out after six weeks, and he wanted to sue them, and I said, 'Sue them for what? You're the fucking idiot who was doing the day trading!' "

In part, his attitude stems from the difficulty of winning cases in which people were wrecked by bad decisions they made all by themselves. In a courtroom, a busted trader might be able to convince a jury that the broker encouraged him to commit economic suicide and is therefore liable, but most disputes between investors and brokers go to arbitration, not to court. "The standard profile of a panel member is a seven-figure-net-worth, WASPy motherfucker who has sat on ten or twenty different panels and has an institutional bias—good luck trying to tell a panel that shit," the lawyer opined. He has taken a few cases on behalf of investors who relied on assurances by day-trading brokers and agreed to back traders. In these cases, he has evidence that the brokers misrepresented the qualifications and success records of the traders. His experience has given him a rare insight into the operations of day-trading brokers, a lot for whom he has scant respect but growing admiration. "They're making a killing on this shit," he concludes. "If you knew somebody who'd give me seed capital to open an online brokerage, let me know. I'd get into it tomorrow. I'm *serious* about that."

Conclusion

Reporting on the foregoing work began in the autumn of 1998 and ended in the early summer of 1999. The New York Stock Exchange and the Nasdaq, facing increasing competitive pressure from alternative trading venues, announced their intention to extend trading hours. The NASD, in a move to become a more prominent international force, announced a joint venture with Softbank to create Nasdaq-Japan. Initially, this new exchange would allow Japanese investors to trade the hundred biggest Nasdaq stocks. Eventually, it was expected to compete for listings in Japan.

The ECN Island, a subsidiary of Datek Online, announced its intention to apply for exchange status under new SEC rules, but Island was not the only ECN to see the merits of transforming itself into an exchange. In fact, a lot of very smart money was betting on Archipelago, the ECN whose story was told earlier in this book. In January of 1999, Archipelago had attracted support from Goldman Sachs and E*Trade, which bought half of the company. In June, JP Morgan and the mutual fund group American Century took another 20 percent. Other institutions were said to be lining up to invest, and Archipelago was expected to apply for exchange status later in the year.

Public interest in online investing, especially short-term trading, showed no signs of abating. Established brokerages like Merrill Lynch accepted the inevitable and announced plans to participate in the new electronic market, some with special pricing plans targeted to active traders.

But senior securities market regulators at the national level were expressing extraordinary concern about speculation by online traders, and state regulators promised more examinations and enforcement actions against day-trading brokerage firms. "We are always worried when people stop mining gold and start selling maps to the gold mine," said Phil Feigin, executive director of the North American Securities Administrators Association in Washington, D.C.

In December 1998, Massachusetts securities regulators had initiated proceedings against the original SOES bandit himself, Harvey Houtkin, and All-Tech Investment Group. Their investigation found that misconduct in All-Tech's Massachusetts office included the unauthorized transfer of funds from customer accounts using forged signatures, the creation of fictitious accounts, commingling of customer funds, and use of unregistered investment advisers, among other problems. In June 1999, All-Tech offered a settlement that was accepted by the state. The settlement barred All-Tech from doing business in Massachusetts or opening any new accounts for Massachusetts customers for two years, and required All-Tech to hire a compliance officer and make a $50,000 payment to the Massachusetts Investors Protection Trust Fund. In addition, All-Tech agreed to hire a consultant to "examine all aspects of All-Tech's securities business" and make regular reports to the securities regulators. Among the subjects the regulators were interested in learning about was whether any of All-Tech's customers made money day trading.

At least one academic study suggested that day traders did make money. Paul Schultz, after coauthoring the groundbreaking paper that exposed the collusion by Nasdaq market makers to keep spreads wide, had turned his attention to the profitability of **177**

SOES Bandit traders. In a paper published in 1998 by the prestigious *Journal of Financial Economics*, Schultz had concluded that "bandits do not have any more information than the market makers that they trade against and in many cases they have less information. But bandits still make money. . . . Unusually fast or skillful traders may find SOES trading to be more profitable than working for a Nasdaq market maker." Schultz attributed their success to the fact that, unlike employees of market-making firms, bandits were personally responsible for all of their losses and kept all of their profits, so they had a stronger incentive to follow stocks closely and concentrate on their screens. Although the bandits lost money almost as often as they made money, they managed to eke out a small average profit per trade, and by trading in high volumes, managed to make a living.

That said, it is a truism of investing that the more efficient a market is, the more difficult it is to trade profitably. By definition, an efficient market is one in which all relevant information is quickly reflected in the price. The early SOES bandits had prospered because of the very inefficiency of the Nasdaq market. As the market became more efficient, trading profits became smaller and harder to get. The price of success at trading is opportunity. The old opportunities no longer exist. But new opportunities are emerging as new technologies break down the barriers that isolated and insulated the markets around the world.

This book has been about making money the old-fashioned way—by exploiting the disintegration of an old order. Some of the money is made by traders, a great deal more by brokers. Much will continue to be made, and lost, before the old order of discrete national marketplaces fuses into a single, efficient system.

Part Six

THE EXTREME INVESTOR'S MANUAL OF ONLINE DAY TRADING

E xtreme Investors use sophisticated technology to buy and sell stocks in an attempt to profit from price movements that occur within a single market day. They trade in large lots, often a thousand shares at a time, in highly volatile stocks, on margin, and may place anywhere from fifty to three hundred such trades a day. Their risks are as extreme as their potential rewards, no more and no less.

Because the technology they use allows direct market access similar to that enjoyed by institutional traders and market makers, and because the time horizon on any trade is usually less than one market day, Extreme Investors are also called "electronic day traders," "direct access electronic traders," or simply "day traders." At its inception, this type of trading depended on the Nasdaq's Small Order Execution System (SOES), and day traders who successfully used the SOES system to profit at the expense of market makers were pejoratively tagged "SOES Bandits" by the Nasdaq's publicity machine. Even though Electronic Communications Networks (ECNs) have largely replaced SOES in the toolkit of Extreme

Investors, the name has stuck, but instead of being offended, many day traders take a perverse delight in their bandit image.

The purpose of this manual is to present concisely some useful tips for people who are interested in trying this type of trading and a summary of important trading principles that even experienced traders may find helpful to glance at from time to time. It is divided into five sections.

The first section presents some basic facts of the Extreme Investing life to help readers think about whether they have the financial and temperamental wherewithal to succeed before they learn the hard way that they do not.

The second section summarizes the essential "how to" information taught in the best day-trading training courses and supplements it with additional information drawn from a wide literature of stock and commodities trading.

The third section offers pointers on legal recourse for traders or investors who believe that they have been cheated by a day-trading brokerage.

The fourth section, The Extreme Investor Lexicon, is a glossary of the day-trading argot.

The final section is a short list of pertinent websites.

Look Before You Leap

In the best of all possible worlds, day-trading brokerage firms would offer a full and frank disclosure of risks to all prospective Extreme Investors, but experience indicates that this is not the best of all possible worlds. Early in 1999, after a spate of scandals, frauds, and regulatory actions, the Electronic Traders Association posted on its website a recommended risk disclosure form that read, in part:

> *The risk of loss in electronic day trading can be substantial. You should, therefore, carefully consider whether such trading is suitable for you in light of your circumstances and financial resources. In considering whether to trade, you should be aware of the following points:* (1) The national securities markets are extremely efficient and competitive. Successful Electronic Day Trading typically requires skill and discipline as well as experience and knowledge of the capital markets. There is no guarantee that you will be successful in implementing your investment strategy.

A substantial number of Electronic Day Traders will not be successful. Moreover, changes in market structure and competitive conditions also may affect your continued success. Only risk capital should be used for trading. Market structure and competitive changes in the markets may cause formerly successful traders to become less successful.

(2) Electronic Day Trading involves a high volume of trading activity and the number of transactions in an account may exceed 100 per day. Each trade generates a commission and the total daily commission on such a high volume of trading can be in excess of any earnings.

(3) Persons who are new to Electronic Day trading should strictly limit both the number of trades they do and the size of their trades to reduce the risk of large dollar losses during the learning process.

(4) Electronic Day Trading is designed to produce short-term profits. However, the activity also may result in losses that can exceed more than 100 percent of your initial capital. You are solely responsible for any losses in your account.

(5) Placing contingent orders, such as "stop-loss" or "stop-limit" orders, will not necessarily limit your losses to the intended amounts, since market conditions on the Nasdaq or any Alternative Trading System on which the order is placed may make it impossible to execute such orders. Similarly, using "market orders" can be very risky, since large gaps can occur in price movements of active stocks. You are urged in most instances to use "limit orders."

(6) Under certain market conditions, you may find it difficult or impossible to liquidate a position quickly at a reasonable price. This can occur, for example, when the market for a stock suddenly drops, or if trading is halted due to recent news events or unusual trading activity. The more volatile a stock is, the greater the likelihood that problems may be encountered in executing a transaction.

(7) In addition to normal market risks, you may experience losses due to system failures. The firm and its clearing broker rely upon sophisticated computer software and hardware to execute transactions, which are subject to failure due to a variety of factors. In addition, Nasdaq and the Alternative Trading Systems have computer systems that often malfunction. Among other events, you may experience losses due to: system crashes during both peak and low volume periods; the loss of orders on both

SOES and SelectNet; and, delayed, conflicting and inaccurate confirmations on orders or cancellations that you initiate.

(8) The use of any margin or leverage in an account can work against you as well as for you.

Leverage can lead to large losses as well as gains. You may sustain a total loss of the initial margin funds and any additional funds that you deposit with your broker to establish or maintain a position, and you may incur losses beyond your initial investment. If the market moves against your position, you may be called upon to deposit a substantial amount of additional margin funds, on short notice, in order to maintain your position. If you do not provide the required funds within the time required, your position may be liquidated at a loss, and you will be liable for any resulting deficit in your account.

(9) You should consult your broker concerning the nature of the protections available to safeguard funds or property deposited in your account.

All of the points noted above apply to Electronic Day Trading of domestic equity securities. If you are contemplating trading futures or options contracts, you should be aware that these instruments possess additional risks. The risk of Electronic Day Trading may be substantial. This brief statement cannot, of course, disclose all the risks and other aspects of Electronic Day Trading. Only risk capital should be used for such trading.

Neophyte day traders should expect to lose money for at least their first three to six months at a trading station, but they may also continue to lose for a year or two before they begin to trade profitably.

Day-trading brokerage firms typically require new traders to deposit between fifty thousand and a hundred thousand dollars in order to open an account. Trading on margin of two-to-one, presently the maximum margin legally allowed, means that the trader can buy two dollars of stock for every one dollar of equity in the account. This leverage effectively doubles the trader's potential return by doubling the money at risk. So, a trader who opens an account with $50,000 can lose $100,000, and many traders lose their entire investment well before they reach the end of the "learning curve."

Some advisers therefore recommend that people who open a day-trading account go in with the expectation that they will lose the entire sum. But confidence in one's ability to trade successfully is itself an important prerequisite to success at trading. People who go into day trading expecting to lose their entire investment will lose their entire investment.

Aspiring traders must be prepared to control losses. This means they should approach the business of day trading with the expectation of winning. It is possible to make a great deal of money at the Extreme Investing game, but making money takes discipline, and the most important discipline is the ability to take a small loss before it turns into a big loss. Traders should approach the business of day trading as they approach any individual trade and decide in advance on a stop-loss point at which they will force themselves to admit that day trading is not working, take their losses, and get out.

It is emotionally difficult to accept the loss of one's own money, but people who borrow from family or friends in order to day trade make this difficult challenge even tougher. Borrowed money is usually scared money, and scared money almost always loses. People who raise their trading stake with a help of a third-party backer, related or not, may also break the law. In 1998, the state of Texas shut down a day-trading firm that had lined up wealthy Colombian investors to back day traders. The day traders were fined approximately three thousand dollars each for acting as unregistered investment advisors or dealers.

Day trading is a very competitive, high-risk game. Day traders pit themselves against the best professionals on Wall Street and against each other. Winning is not easy. With sufficient preparation, discipline, and capital, it is just barely possible to make slightly more winning trades than losing trades. The Extreme Investing game is as tough as professional football, according to a former NFL linebacker-turned-day trader. But at least professional football was not penalized by the tax code. Extreme Investors must endure a long losing

period before they begin to win—and then their financial prospects are complicated by tax regulations that can require them to pay tax on their gains while forbidding them to deduct their losses. This point is often ignored or glossed over in training programs offered by day-trading brokerage firms, where day trading is usually described as a business and prospective traders are left with the impression that, as in any business, they will pay taxes only on their net earnings. In fact, the tax code contains provisions that may disallow or severely limit deductibility of day-trading losses. The tax issue is far too complex to be treated in detail here, but it is a knotty problem for many day traders and likely to get knottier as day trading grows in popularity. Prospective traders should consult a professional tax adviser and factor tax liabilities into their financial projections before they put capital at risk in the markets.

Besides capital and discipline, success at trading also requires some degree of skill with numbers, especially fractions. A prospective trader ought to be able to know without stopping to think whether ⅞ is bigger or smaller than ¹³⁄₁₆ or ²⁵⁄₃₂ or ¾.

It is an unpleasant fact of life that age makes a difference in this business. Older candidates are well advised to approach this game with caution. Actuarial statistics suggest that a fifty-five-year-old has less time to recover from a major financial loss than a twenty-five-year-old. Moreover, some people who take up the Extreme Investing game late in life seem to have more difficulty adapting to the fast pace than their younger colleagues.

Day traders must place their trades through brokerage firms with connections to the various exchanges and Electronic Communications Networks that comprise the market. At the better brokerages, prospective traders are typically required to take a training course. The training courses vary widely in quality, from month-long intensive programs that include weeks of paper trading to sessions of a few hours that barely introduce the basics of how to use the trading software. In most cases, traders who have completed the training program, usually at a cost ranging between $1,000 and $5,000, then move onto the trading floor, where the brokerage provides a computer, software, and sometimes lunch. Operating a trading room is a high-overhead way of doing business, and the brokerage has a keen **187** interest in commission revenue. No surprise, then, that most day-trading brokerages seem to promote a trading style that emphasizes fast, in-and-out action that maximizes commissions.

Although most day trading still takes place in trading rooms, Internet day trading is gaining ground fast, and there are sound economic reasons to expect Internet brokerages will supplant trading rooms as the major venue for day trading. The Internet broker has lower fixed costs—the customer of an Internet brokerage sits at his or her own desk and accesses the brokerage through his or her own computer. Since day-trading success depends on fast access to the market, it should go without saying that the trader must use the fastest computer and modem available. People who decide to trade remotely, either on the Internet or by dial-in access to a trading room, frequently find that they have to install a dedicated computer and high-speed telecommunications line or cable modem for this purpose.

Because the remote trader bears the cost of technology and telecommunications, the Internet brokerage has fewer fixed costs to cover than the trading room brokerage and is therefore under less pressure to generate commission revenues to cover its costs. But this does not mean that Internet brokerages encourage less activity.

Some traders prefer working in trading rooms because they like the opportunity to sit with and learn from more experienced traders. It is therefore worth mentioning that day-trading brokerage firms often give special terms to their more experienced, more successful traders, including not only reduced commissions but also a percentage of the commissions paid by new, less-experienced traders. Traders also receive financial incentives to bring new customers to the brokerage, so much of what they have to say about their success may not be the unvarnished truth.

Successful traders who keep trading and generating commissions are a rare and valuable asset to a day-trading brokerage—so rare and so valuable that some brokerage firms fight over them in court.

That fact is worth pondering.

A Day-Trading Primer

T his section will begin by outlining some general principles that apply in almost any traded market, including but not limited to the markets of most interest to day traders. After that general discussion, it will focus more narrowly on such issues as reading the action on Nasdaq Level II screens, following market makers, using ECNs, and other matters specifically of interest to day traders.

A. Principles of Successful Trading

1. STUDY

Study is the first discipline of trading. No one succeeds at trading without paying close attention to whatever market he or she plans to trade. Study implies close, sustained, thoughtful attention leading to the development of an idea, an understanding of what the important facts are and how they affect each other.

Beginning day traders are usually advised to follow a few stocks closely, understand them well, and trade them continuously so that they learn who the dominant market makers are and what they do; how the stocks trade relative to other stocks in their industry or group; how they react to changes in the S&P futures (SPooze), the Dow, the Nasdaq, and other major indices; and how fundamental news about earnings, regulatory approvals, interest rates, and the like translates into the stock price. By paying close attention to a few stocks, the new trader will learn much that is important about all stocks. In the interest of keeping risk relatively low during the learning period, novices should pick stocks that are less volatile but have good liquidity indicated by the presence of several market makers, narrow spreads, and a tendency for the stock to move in price increments, or levels, no more than an eighth to a quarter of a point at a time.

Two books that have stood the test of time and ought to be read by every aspiring trader:

Mackay, Charles, LL.D., *Extraordinary Popular Delusions and the Madness of Crowds* (New York: The Noonday Press, 1932).

Originally published in 1841, this compendium of crazes, manias, enthusiasms, hysterias, and frenzies is an excellent inoculation against the contagion of the lemming run. Bernard Baruch recommended it, apparently as an antidote to the dismal psychology that gripped the country in the thirties, saying, "I have always thought that if in 1929 we had all continuously repeated 'two and two still make four,' much of the evil might have been averted."

LeFèvre, Edwin, *Reminiscences of a Stock Operator* (New York: John Wiley & Sons, 1994).

First published as a series of magazine articles in *The Saturday Evening Post,* this is the thinly veiled, first-person account of legendary trader Jesse Livermore, as told to journalist LeFèvre. No other book so well captures the spirit of the trading life. But *Reminiscences* was written in the 1920s, at the peak of Livermore's fame and fortune, and is somehow incomplete without the context of the account of his suicide that appeared in the November 29, 1940, edition of *The New York Times*. That account was recapitulated earlier in Chapter 2.

2. Technical and Fundamental Analysis

Students of markets speak of two kinds of facts: fundamental and technical. Fundamental facts are those that underlie and eventually determine prices. They include supply, demand, economic conditions, competitiveness, etc. Technical facts are price movements, seen as an expression of market psychology. Technicians believe that market prices move in repetitive patterns, a belief that implies that the analyst who correctly identifies the pattern in which prices are moving can accurately predict the next move.

Both fundamental and technical facts are important to the day trader. Because most Extreme Investors are momentum traders who hope to make their money by riding price trends, technical facts dominate their view of the market. They tend to be more concerned with the fact that prices are moving and much less concerned with the fundamental reasons behind the move. Still, even though most day traders do not analyze financial statements and industry positions of companies they trade, it's a rare trading room where no television is tuned to CNBC and no copies of *The Wall Street Journal* or *Investors Business Daily* are scattered around. Price changes—technical facts—happen in a context of fundamental facts, and the astute trader pays close attention to both the prices and their context.

There are numerous books about various schools of technical and fundamental analysis. For a good insight into how various traders integrate the two, see *Market Wizards* and *The New Market Wizards*, both by Jack D. Schwager, the director of Futures Research and Trading Strategy at Prudential Securities, Inc. These books are compilations of interviews in which top traders of the 1970s and 1980s discuss various approaches to markets including commodities, currencies, debt, and equity. **191**

3. Useful Practices

a. Paper Trading.

Extreme Investors debate the merits of "paper trading," which bears the same relationship to live trading as training in a flight simulator bears to flying a plane. Opponents of paper trading say that because the paper trader is not risking real money, he or she does not learn to cope with the gut-wrenching fear of loss that makes live trading so challenging. Success at paper trading is no predictor of success at live trading. Yet failure at paper trading might reasonably be interpreted as a sign that one should not risk real money in the markets. For this reason, traders ought to spend a few weeks or months paper trading before they go live.

Some training programs provide paper traders with performance logs in which they note the time of each trade, the price at which they booked the trade, the price at which they exited, the number of shares bought or sold, the commission, and the net gain or loss. Without some such permanent record, it is almost impossible for a trader to make an unbiased assessment of paper-trading performance.

b. Defining Risk Tolerance.

The new trader should not take a single undisciplined step. One expert on commodity-trading strategy suggests risking no more than 3 percent of one's equity on any single trade, and for him, a single trade means a single trading idea—such as being long on a grain contract because a drought has been forecast. A similar discipline would prevent a day trader from loading up on Internet stocks on the basis of a favorable news report. Limiting risk means limiting potential gains—but it also means limiting potential losses, and for beginners, small gains are undoubtedly preferable to large losses.

c. Loss Control.

With only a small amount of capital at risk, the new trader should establish a stop-loss point on each trade and make no exceptions or excuses about getting out of every trade at that point. Consider the losses incurred to be something like a tuition payment to the market for training in the survival skill of loss control.

d. Schedule Homework.

Every trader should develop a daily schedule that allows at least an hour before the open or after the close of the market for concentrated study. This time should be spent reviewing previous trades, studying the news to see what fundamental or technical facts have changed, thinking about how the market will react, and developing some ideas for new trades.

e. Diary.

It is advisable to keep a trading diary, a personal performance record that includes general observations about the market, the thinking that led to each trade, an assessment of how each trade worked, whether or not it met expectations, why, and any conclusions that may be drawn from the way things worked out.

f. Managing Expectations.

All of this analysis and paperwork will take much of the thrill out of trading. This is for the best. Thrills come from encountering the unexpected, and success at trading depends on knowing what to expect.

For example, prices usually do not move smoothly and steadily up and down. Instead, they bounce around even as they move in a general direction. The art of trading consists largely in knowing which pullbacks are just bounces that will be followed by another move in the direction of the trend and which pullbacks are genuine changes in direction.

Even when they are confident about the stock's general direction, traders must learn to balance two somewhat contradictory principles. On the one hand, if they believe that a stock is heading up (or down), they should trade in that direction even if part of the move has already occurred. On the other hand, they must also learn to time their entry carefully so that they do not buy a rising stock just before a bounce down that may shake them out of the trade by taking the price below the stop-loss level.

So, successful traders must combine quick and decisive action with continuous reassessment of their positions. In fact, they must **193** learn to trade almost as if they had no positions at all. A good trader must be able to look at the market conditions and decide where prices are going without being influenced by hope or fear. Similarly, a trader who gets in to a trade expecting certain things to happen should get out of the trade if those things don't happen, whether the trade has turned into a loser or not. If there is no compelling reason to be in a trade, good traders get out. The fact that one is in a position is not a compelling reason to stay there.

g. Managing Profits.

Holding winners is almost as important as cutting losers. Stocks usually go up and down all day long. It makes more sense to take a small gain than to ride a stock up only to ride it down again. But if conditions still favor being long, it makes more sense to stay with the position until conditions justify selling than to make a small profit even smaller by the amount of a sales commission.

B. Extreme Investing: Market Information

1. NASDAQ SCREENS

Extreme Investing developed in the context of the Nasdaq markets, and Nasdaq stocks remain the day-trading favorites. Nasdaq offers several levels of detail about stock trading.

a. Level I.

Level I information includes the company's name, stock symbol, the direction of the last price move, how far the stock has moved during the day, the quantity of shares that changed hands at the last sale, the time of the last sale, the high and low for the day, the volume of shares traded at this point in the day, the current best bid and offer prices, and the previous day's closing price. Most Level I information can be accessed without any specialized software or equipment, in the newspaper, on television financial news shows, or at numerous sites on the Internet and the Web.

b. Level II.

Level II information is far more detailed than Level I, identifying every market maker and ECN presently in the market with a bid or offer for the stock. Each market maker or ECN is identified by an acronym, for example, *MSCO* for Morgan Stanley, *ISLD* for the ECN Island, etc. After the acronym comes that market maker's or ECN's bid or offer price, followed by an indication of the quantity desired or offered for sale.

Level II information usually appears in two vertical columns, with the bid prices on the left and the offer prices on the right. The most widely used software sets price levels off from each other by color. Thus, if a stock is 30 bid and 30⅛ offered, all of the market makers or ECNs bidding 30 would appear in the same color, on the left, and all of those offering 30⅛ would appear in a uniform color on the right. Underneath the 30-bid level, the trader sees a stack of other colored strata bracketing the market makers and ECNs at each progressively lower bid price. Similarly, under the 30⅛ best offer price, different-colored strata bracket the market makers and ECNs asking higher prices at each stratum.

Day traders call these price strata "levels." The thickness of these levels shows the strength of supply and demand for the stock. The amount by which the price changes from level to level is an important indication of the risk involved in trading the stock. A stock with only a few, widely separated bids and offers will probably be riskier to trade than a stock with a deep array of bids and offers separated from each other by only a sixteenth of a point or so.

Nasdaq Level II information is now widely available through day-trading brokerage firms and online financial information services. There are quality differences among information vendors; some are faster and fresher than others. Day-trading brokerage firms typically provide a package consisting of quote information and execution software. Billing arrangements for such packages differ from brokerage to brokerage: some charge a flat monthly fee; others do not charge for the software provided customers trade actively enough to cover the cost through commissions. **195**

2. ECNs

a. List.

The most important ECNs and their symbols are:

INCA	Instinet
ISLD	Island
BTRD	Bloomberg TradeBook
TNTO	Archipelago
REDI	Spear Leeds
BRUT	Brass
ATTN	All-Tech

b. Using ECNs.

ECNs, or electronic communications networks, are venues in which buyers and sellers of stock can meet and transact business. Instinet, the first ECN, was originally conceived as an alternative to the stock exchange. Its inventor intended it to be a tool to match trades for institutional investors with an interest in buying and selling stock without involving brokers, dealers, or specialists. Instinet's direction changed in the early 1980s, as brokers, dealers, and specialists joined, and it became a sort of wholesale version of the Nasdaq.

Island, still the biggest and most important ECN for day traders, was invented because Instinet refused to allow day-trading firms access to its network. Prior to the invention of Island, day traders had only two ways of getting their orders executed. The first was SOES, the Nasdaq's Small Order Execution System, which allowed for automatic execution of small orders, but imposed restrictions on when, how many, and how often. The second, SelectNet, was an electronic network to which traders could send orders for voluntary execution by market makers. Because market makers were under no obligation to execute SelectNet orders, many day traders found that their orders languished. Island allowed the day traders to buy and sell among themselves without the involvement of market makers.

Orders sent to ECNs are first matched internally. If there is no internal match, they typically go to the Nasdaq. Some ECNs will canvass the market electronically before sending the orders to the Nasdaq, in order to see whether any market maker or any other ECN has a match.

Customers of an ECN generally receive important additional information about the flow of orders through the ECN—information that is not available to noncustomers. For example, they see, for any given stock, not only the Nasdaq Level II information but also all of the bids and offers internally within the ECN. ECN orders that cannot be matched internally are posted on the public market. Others in the market can execute against those orders by "preferencing," a term that refers simply to sending an order to a specific destination for execution. ECN customers may be notified whenever a preference order from any other market maker or ECN is executed on the network. The notice typically includes the identity of the buyer or seller preferencing the order—an important clue indeed if the buyer is a major market maker in the stock.

3. SELECTNET

SelectNet is a voluntary execution system that traders may use to send orders to market makers, either by broadcast or by targeting a specific market maker with a confidential preference order. Market makers are under no obligation to execute these orders. Therefore, some day traders rely on SelectNet for a sort of barometric reading of the pressure of supply and demand for a stock among market makers. Prompt execution of a bid sent to SelectNet could indicate weakness in the stock, since a market maker is selling; difficulty buying on SelectNet, or ease in selling, would by the same reasoning point to underlying strength in the stock. Orders sent to SelectNet primarily in order to get such information are called "scouts."

C. Extreme Investing: Reading Market Makers

1. WHY WATCH MARKET MAKERS?

Market makers are firms that must stand ready to buy and sell securities in response to customer orders. Every market-making **197** firm posts a price at which it will buy and a price at which it will sell each stock in which it makes a market. Market makers are not equally willing to be on either side of any stock at all times. It is reasonable to assume that market makers should quote highly competitive bids when they are keenly interested in buying and highly competitive offer, or ask, prices when they have a keen desire to sell. That is sometimes true. But the market is like a game of cards in which all players, including market makers, use an arsenal of stratagems to bluff, bamboozle, and deceive the competition. So, Extreme Investors have turned the analysis and interpretation of market maker actions into a gnostic craft in which plain appearances must be distrusted, deconstructed, and reassembled before their real meaning can be discovered.

2. IDENTIFYING THE MARKET MAKERS

Some market makers operate only in a few small stocks. Others are active in a broad range. Some are hardly noticed by the day-trading community; others are watched closely, usually because they have a large institutional client base and are often supposed to be buying and selling in immense, market-moving size.

Among the most watchable market makers on the Nasdaq, listed here by alphabetical order of acronym, are:

Name	Acronym
Alex Brown	ABSB
First Boston	BBCO
Bear Stearns	BEST
Goldman Sachs	GSCO
Hambrecht Quist	HMQT
Lehman Brothers	LEHM
Merrill Lynch	MLCO
Montgomery Securities	MONT
Morgan Stanley–Dean Witter	MSCO
Nike Securities	NIKE
Paine Webber Inc.	PWJC

Robertson Stephens	RSSF
Smith Barney–Shearson	SBSH
Furman Selz, Inc.	SELZ
Volpe & Co.	VOLP
Weeden & Co.	WEED

3. THE AX

The ax is a market maker with an especially strong interest in the stock, possibly because it participated in the underwriting, or because its research department follows the group and company closely, or because it has a big retail business in the shares or a large ownership stake in the company, or for some other reason. In another industry, the ax would be called a "price leader," a company whose decisions on pricing tend to be followed by lesser forces in the business. Day traders try to identify the ax, figure out where the ax is trying to go with a stock, and get there first, a task made more difficult by the ability of the ax to work anonymously, when it chooses, through institutional ECNs.

4. MARKET MAKERS AND SOES

Market makers have an ambivalent relationship with SOES and with day traders, generally. Publicly, they have opposed SOES because it compels them to execute transactions automatically. SOES traders who knew what they were doing could presumably use SOES to force market makers to sell them stocks that were going up, and to buy from them stocks that were falling.

On the other hand, as more and more day traders have come into the market, it has become hard to deny that most of them do not know what they are doing. Therefore, astute market makers are believed to have found a silver lining in the SOES cloud. Instead of trading against a crowd of other professionals just as sophisticated as themselves, market makers have the opportunity to trade against a crowd of amateurs, neophytes, and wannabes, people whose record in general is not very impressive. Experienced day traders believe that market makers use their less-sophisticated **199** day-trading brethren to move stocks where the market makers want them to go.

For example, suppose that the ax in a stock receives a customer order. By flashing a public "bid," the ax can induce day traders to use the SOES system to buy stock from other market makers on the offer. (Market makers themselves cannot initiate trades on SOES.) Having induced the day traders to buy the stock, the ax then switches from a competitive bid to a competitive offer price, sending a false signal that it intends to sell. That false signal leads weak hands among the day traders to sell, probably bringing down the price of the stock several levels, at which point the ax may flip to the bid side again to pick up the stock at a more agreeable price.

5. WHEN MARKET MAKERS MOVE QUOTES

Day traders who attempt to follow market maker actions have identified several patterns of activity associated with market makers trying to push prices up, hold them steady, or bring them down.

a. From Bid to Offer.

The market maker who moves from bid to offer seems to have changed its mind and suddenly become a seller. But the market maker's real intention may be simply to push the stock price lower by creating a false impression that there is selling pressure. In fact, if the market maker suddenly switches from quoting the best bid to quoting the best offer price, it is such a public advertisement of intention to sell that it arouses suspicion among the most skeptical (and successful) day traders. They do not follow the market maker to the offer side, but wait for the market maker to return to the bid later. When it does, they climb on board with bids of their own in order to ride the market maker's wave back up.

b. From Offer to Bid.

Conversely, when the market maker (especially an ax) goes from quoting the best offer to quoting the best bid, it is a very strong signal of interest to buy—perhaps too strong a signal to be taken at face value. Day traders who have survived many such games and are long in the tooth wait, watch, and make their own move when the ax comes back to the offer. The move is likely to be to sell the stock short on the first good uptick after the ax returns to the sell side.

c. From Best Bid to Less Than Best Bid.

In this case, the market maker's acronym remains on the bid side of the screen but drops a level or two below the top. The market maker's remaining on the bid side probably indicates a serious but less aggressive interest in buying. The stock has support, temporarily at least, at the new level. In fact, a desire to support the stock price or at least slow its fall may also be part of the market maker's motivation for this move.

d. From Best Offer to Slightly Worse (Higher) Than Best Offer.

In this case, the market maker, after offering the best quote on the offer side, raises its quoted selling price only slightly. On the Level II screen, the market maker's acronym falls from the top of the offer side to one level below. The market maker is probably seriously interested in selling but has reason to believe that a better price can be gotten. This move may also signal a determination to slow a rise in the price of the stock.

e. Refreshing.

Market makers who refresh their quotes do not change them, but make a deliberate decision to maintain them at the same level. A decision to refresh the best bid or best offer is a strong indication that the market maker may be working a large buy or sell order, respectively, and is willing to accept automatic execution via SOES against its quoted bid or offer price.

6. TIME OF DAY

Experienced day traders tend to be wary of trading at the market's open. They reason that the market makers have in hand a stack of orders that came in overnight and therefore enjoy a critical information advantage during the first fifteen minutes to half-hour of trading.

Many of the more experienced hands at the day-trading game wait and watch until the first flurry of market activity begins to subside and some underlying direction begins to appear. Stocks that have gapped down or up at the open—that is, stocks that opened at prices sharply discontinuous with the price at the close—may be expected to attempt to close the gap at this time.

Reliable evidence of trends begins to appear at the open, but a reaction often sets in about twenty minutes later. Shortly before 10:00 A.M., stocks frequently move in the opposite direction to the trend. Many day traders attribute this reaction to the fact that market makers have been filling customer orders and need to recover or dispose of positions. For example, if customer demand for a stock has been strong, the market maker is likely to have sold short or sold from inventory and will want to cover the shorts or replace the inventory. Using techniques outlined in the previous section, the market maker will, it is thought, try to move the stock price down in order to buy at a more agreeable price. The converse occurs if customers have been selling in the morning and the market maker has bought unwanted inventory.

Many day traders look at this reaction period as a good opportunity to get on the same side as the market makers. They will watch patiently until the reaction has reached its limit. A possible signal: The ax who initiated the reaction, perhaps by a shift from the bid to the offer side, comes back aggressively to the bid. Another signal: The stock, having returned during the reaction to the trading range from which it broke out in the morning, begins to move out again. At that point, typically a half-hour or so after the reaction began, the trend resumes.

Extreme Investors watch the S&P futures (SPooze) index and the Nasdaq 100 (NDX) for clues to the overall market environment. Some work by a rough rule of thumb that says the mornings are for playing the long side and the afternoons, the short side. The morning ends, typically, about 11:30, when the market decelerates in preparation for the lunch hour. Most day traders counsel caution about trading during the lunch period because the market tends to be too slow to allow them to move nimbly in and out of positions.

The action picks up again around 2:00 P.M., and trading conditions generally remain favorable until about a half-hour before the close. Many day traders regard the last few minutes before the close of the trading day with the same cautious skepticism with which they greeted the first minutes after the open. They reason that market makers, who are judged by their clients on how their buys and sells compared to the day's average price in the stock, attempt to artificially influence the closing price. So, for example, a market maker who has been working a big order and has bought stock at an average price of 75, may have an interest in pushing the closing price up as far above 75 as reasonably possible in order to make that average purchase price look better by comparison. Day traders who buy in at the high closing levels may find no "greater fools" to take the shares off their hands.

D. The Trend Is Your Friend, and Other Truisms of the Day-Trading Life

1. THE TREND IS YOUR FRIEND

Higher highs and higher lows define an up trend; lower lows and lower highs define a down trend. Day traders seek to get into stocks on up trends when the prices pull back and get out when they approach new highs.

2. GET OUT WHEN YOU CAN, NOT WHEN YOU HAVE TO

Sell out of the long position, or buy back the short, when the opportunity still looks good enough that someone else is willing to take the side you are leaving. Don't wait until you see clearly that there is no money left to be made in the stock. You won't be the only one to notice that.

3. DON'T SWING FOR THE FENCES

Small, consistent profits add up faster than big, occasional ones.

4. THE TICKER IS YOUR MUSIC

Don't dance when the music isn't playing: don't try to trade when the market isn't moving.

5. KNOW WHERE THEY'VE BEEN TO KNOW WHERE THEY'RE GOING

Pay close attention to where stocks have been trading within the past five minutes, the past hour, the past day, week, month, six months. Know them cold.

6. THE MARKET ALWAYS TRIES TO CLOSE A GAP

Expect prices to move in the opposite direction, up when they've gapped down, down when they've gapped up.

7. BUY STOCKS THAT ARE STRONG IN A WEAK MARKET; SHORT STOCKS THAT ARE WEAK IN A STRONG MARKET

They'll be the first to move sharply when the market turns.

8. THE BEST PLACE TO BE A BUYER IS ON A LOW OR A PULLBACK

Even when stocks are going up, there will often be a chance to buy at a relatively good price.

9. FOLLOW THE PATH OF LEAST RESISTANCE

Don't buck the market.

10. TRADE THE TRUTH

Base trades on what is happening, not on what you wish or hope.

11. KNOW WHEN TO GET SMALL

When things are going badly, trade less volume and fewer positions.

12. EASE IN, AND EASE OUT

Going slowly and building positions gradually will naturally impose a discipline tending to keep you small when things are bad. Incidentally, beginners are probably best advised to learn a few stocks well and then expand their horizons. In the interest of keeping risk relatively low during the learning period, they should pick less volatile stocks, watch them attentively, and learn how the prices move. By paying close attention to a few stocks, the trader will learn much that is important about all stocks.

Section **III**

Taking Your Broker to Court

Extreme Investors make a lot of trades. Some win, some lose. But every time a trader makes a trade, the cash register rings for the day-trading brokerage. An active trader can generate several thousand dollars' worth of commissions a day. So Extreme Investing is a great business to make money in, if you happen to be a broker. There's only one big problem: most people who try this game will lose money and go broke or else drop out. Either way, they stop ringing the cash register.

Day-trading brokers deal with this hard fact of life in different ways, as related in the preceding text. Some require new customers to sign legal documents with carefully drafted noncompete clauses. These clauses forbid the trader to do business with any other day-trading firm, for years into the future. If the customer happens to beat the odds and succeed at the game, and then decides to leave and trade at another firm, the brokerage might sue for violation of the noncompete clause.

There aren't many businesses where the provider of a service can sue someone for deciding to get that service from a competi- **207** tor, but one of the biggest day-trading brokerage firms did exactly that to a group of its former customers. The good news for the customers is that such agreements are generally unenforceable; the suit against these customers was eventually dropped, but not until after they had taken a wad out of their market winnings to pay their own lawyers.

Because the day-trading business is quite new, the rules to govern it are literally still being written. For example, in the spring of 1999, the National Association of Securities Dealers (NASD) asked for public comment on a proposed new rule that would require day-trading brokerage firms to determine whether Extreme Investing is a suitable strategy for a customer before allowing the customer to start losing money at a trading station. This is not hyperbole—even the industry association for day-trading brokers acknowledges that most customers lose money for months before they (just some of them) begin to get the hang of day trading.

Lawyers who specialize in representing investors who've been scammed by sleazy brokers are looking forward to seeing such a rule established. Mark Maddox, president of the Public Investors Arbitration Bar Association (PIABA), says that he and his colleagues have been getting lots of calls from people who want to sue the day-trading firms where they learned the hard way why the word "Extreme" is in the phrase "Extreme Investing."

For the most part, the lawyers listen politely and hang up. They work on contingency, usually a third of any arbitration award, so they only get paid when they win, and it's hard to win cases where people traded their own money and lost it. Especially when there are no rules of the game that the lawyers can prove were broken. "If the chances of success don't look good, you're generally disinclined to accept a case," Maddox says.

But several day traders have managed to sue successfully, and at least one has made more money through the courts than his record suggests he could have made in a lifetime at a trading station. This was Kevin Burke of Dallas, Texas, the fascinating details of whose story will be found in Chapter 9. The gist of it is that **208** Burke sued a man who had loaned him money to support his day trading by covering his margin calls. A Texas judge decided that the interest rate met the legal definition of usury. Burke won approximately $3.5 million. As this book was going to press, Burke had another suit pending on similar grounds, seeking more than eleven million dollars from another group of lenders.

A rule requiring brokers to determine whether day trading is suitable for customers might boost the chances for success of so-called financial suicide actions against the brokerages. The reasoning behind these cases is similar to the logic of "dram shop" actions, in which a drunk, or the drunk's survivors, sue the bar where the drunk was knocking them back before the horrible car wreck. Bars and restaurants, and their deep-pocketed insurers, have been hit with big judgments on grounds that bartenders have a legal responsibility not to keep selling drinks to drunks. "A similar theory has been propounded in the securities context, with very limited success," Maddox says. "The concept is that at some point the house, the brokerage or day-trading house, has a duty to prevent you from committing financial suicide."

The odds of successfully suing a day-trading broker rise markedly when the person filing the action isn't the trader, but an investor who provided capital. Several such actions, described in Chapter 11, were pending against day-trading brokers in the spring of 1999. Heart-rending stories in which brokers lose the life savings of unsophisticated investors are the meat and potatoes of PIABA members. "The duties are much higher when the broker is making the investment than when the investor is making the calls himself," Maddox says.

People whose brush with the Extreme Investing scene has led to financial disaster, and people just thinking of trying to grab a piece of the Extreme Investing action, should keep the following points in mind:

1. Waivers and disclaimers may not be worth the paper they're written on: Some day-trading brokerage firms require new customers to sign waivers and disclaimers absolving the broker of any responsibility for the customers's losses. These waivers **209**

and disclaimers are filed and forgotten until the investor, having incurred losses, demands restitution, at which point the broker waves the disclaimer in the air as though fanning away a bad smell. The good news for the investor in this scene is that many disclaimers and waivers have no legal force at all. This is particularly true if the brokerage firm has committed fraud.

2. If you invested the money with a broker or with a trader introduced to you by a broker and he lost it, your chances of getting restitution are much better than if you traded through the brokerage and lost it yourself.

3. Because most securities arbitration lawyers typically work on contingency for a third of the eventual award, the investor's losses must be substantial before an attorney will deem the case worthwhile. Lose less than forty or fifty thousand and most lawyers won't be interested.

4. Keep records of everything you are told, promised, or assured of. Documentation can make all the difference in a courtroom or arbitration hearing.

5. An ounce of prevention is worth, etc.: It is better not to lose money in the first place than to lose and try to recover. Approach all brokers and investment opportunities with cautious skepticism. In particular:

   a. Beware of any promises or "guarantees" of success in any investment strategy—especially day trading. There's nothing riskier. The reason that the rewards from day trading can be astonishingly big is that the risks are astonishingly big. Regardless of what anyone says, represents, or claims, rewards in the market are never greater than risks.

   b. Beware of churning, the practice of trading an account frequently in order to generate commission revenues. Brokers earn commissions whether their customers win or lose. This is true in any kind of investing, but day trading is an extraordinarily commission-intensive business. Churning has been charged in almost every action filed so far by clients of day-trading brokerage firms.

c. Check out brokers before you do business with them. Every state has some sort of division of securities regulation that can help you get background information on brokers and investment advisers, free for the asking. If you don't know how to contact your state securities regulators, get in touch with the North American Securities Administrators Association (on the Web at http://www.nasaa.org). NASAA's website is a convenient first stop. In addition to providing contact information for regulators, it also offers a lot of useful information about securities scams and investor rights.

6. If you have had a bad experience with a day-trading brokerage, or any other kind of brokerage, contact an attorney. The Public Investors Arbitration Bar Association (PIABA) is a good way to identify a lawyer in your area who has experience with securities law and arbitration. Most disputes between investors and brokerages go to arbitration, not to court. PIABA members offer a free initial telephone consultation to help investors decide whether they have a case. Contact PIABA on the Web (http://www.piaba.org) or else through more traditional means at:

Public Investors Arbitration Bar Association
    1111 Wylie Road, No. 18
    Norman, OK 73069

    Toll Free: 1-888-621-7484
    Office: 1-405-360-8776
    Fax: 1-405-360-2063
    E-mail: piabalaw@aol.com

The Extreme Investor Lexicon

Active   Characterized by an extraordinary amount of buying and selling. Can describe stocks or traders.

Ask   The price that sellers demand for their stock; the price at which stock is offered for sale. Synonym: *offer.*

At the Market   Referring to execution of an order at the best price available when the order goes to the market. Distinguished from *limit order* (which see).

Ax   The dominant market maker in a stock; the market maker who leads price moves. There may be more than one ax in a stock.

Back Away   To refuse to transact at a quoted price. Usually applied to market makers.

Bear   One who expects prices to fall.   **213**

Bid   The price at which a buyer seeks to purchase a stock.

Bucket Shop   A venue for speculating on stock price moves without actually buying or selling stocks.

Bull   One who expects prices to rise.

Bull Trap/Bear Trap   Big price moves up or down that look likely to be sustained, but that are instead followed by sudden, sharp, and sustained reversals. These moves trap bulls or bears by seeming to confirm their underlying expectations, then reversing. See also *Sucker Rally*.

Close
(1) The end of the market day.
(2) To sell a stock one owns, or buy back a stock one has sold short, in order to terminate a trade.

Come In   Of a stock, to drop in price.

Crossed Market   A condition in which the bid is higher than the ask, or offer. In a crossed market, the most aggressive buyer bids more to buy a stock than the most aggressive seller demands to sell it.

Day trader   One who buys and sells stock within a single market day.

DAX   Deutsche Aktien Index. See *Index*.

Diverge   To move in opposite directions. Often applied to indices, as when the Nasdaq goes up and the S&P goes down. Divergence indicates that the market has favored one group of stocks and frowned on another, therefore cannot be described as uniformly bullish or bearish.

214 ***Dow***   The Dow Jones industrial average. See *Index*.

Downtick   A downward move in price.

Drop   To lower a bid. Usually applied to market makers.

ECN   Electronic communication network, an electronic venue in which buyers and sellers may transact stock trades. Examples: Instinet (INCA); Island (ISLD).

Electronic Day Trader   One who day trades via electronic linkages to exchanges and ECNs.

Entry point   The point at which a trader chooses to enter a trade by opening a long or a short position.

Equity   Shares of ownership, as opposed to debt. Also, the trader's own cash or collateral, as distinguished from funds borrowed from the brokerage to trade on *margin* (which see).

Exchange   A venue, physical or electronic, in which buyers and sellers may buy and sell. Examples: New York Stock Exchange; Nasdaq. In the United States, stock and other financial exchanges enjoy special legal status and responsibilities as self-regulatory organizations (SRO).

Extreme Investor   A trader who thrives on the pressure, risk, and intense action of day trading.

Fade   To trade in the opposite direction of another trader or a price move. For example, "The best traders fade the gap."

Fill   To execute an order.

Five-minute rule   A regulation restricting SOES traders to one 1,000-share trade in a stock within any five-minute period.

Flat   Having no position in the market. For example, "Don't **215**

carry overnight positions; it's too risky. Close everything out; go home flat."

Fundamental   Involving or influenced by such nontechnical factors as economic conditions, corporate earnings, competitiveness, etc. See also *Technical.*

Gap   A discontinuous move in stock prices, as when stocks open at a price sharply higher or lower than the previous day's closing price. Gaps may also occur intraday, usually as a result of a sudden shock to the market in general or the stock in particular.

Go   To open a position. Usually in conjunction with *long* or *short:* To "go long" is to buy a stock; to "go short" is to sell stock one does not own in expectation of buying it back later at a lower price.

Hit   To sell a stock to a bidder at the bid price.

Index   A measure of the composite performance of a stock or group of stocks. Indices are usually either price-weighted or capitalization-weighted. In price-weighted indices, the highest price stocks are most important, irrespective of the number of shares outstanding. In capitalization-weighted indices, the stocks with the greatest market capitalization are most important, irrespective of the price per share. Among the indices most closely watched by day traders are the following:

DAX: Deutsche Aktien index, a capitalization-weighted index of leading German stocks.

Dow: Dow Jones industrial average, a price-weighted average of thirty leading industrial stocks. The Dow is not a simple average but is calculated according to a specific, proprietary formula.

Footsie: FT-SE 100, a capitalization-weighted index of leading British stocks.

Nasdaq: Nasdaq composite index, a capitalization-weighted index of over more than 5,400 Nasdaq stocks.

NDX: Nasdaq 100, a capitalization-weighted index of the one hundred largest, nonfinancial Nasdaq stocks.

NIKKEI: The most widely watched index of Japanese stocks. Price-weighted.

SPooze: The index of futures on the S&P 500 index.

Inside Market   The best bid and the best offer prices for a stock. The best bid is the highest price the trader could receive by selling stock at the market; the best offer is the lowest price at which an investor could buy the stock at the market. Synonym: *National Best Bid and Offer.*

Level

(1) The increment by which a stock price moves. Some stocks trade up and down in increments of $\frac{1}{16}$, others by a full point or more. Not only do levels differ from stock to stock, but the levels for any given stock can change over time. Levels are determined purely by market supply-and-demand conditions for the stock.

(2) Of Nasdaq information, Level I and Level II refer to different degrees of detail. See The Extreme Investor's Manual Section II.

Lift   To raise the offer price. Usually applied to market makers.

Limit order   An order to buy or sell stock at a specific price, as distinguished from an order to buy or sell *at the market* (which see).

Listed

(1) Eligible for sale or purchase in a given market; for example, "Intel is listed on the Nasdaq; General Electric is listed on the New York Stock Exchange."

(2) Harking back to a time when the Nasdaq was called the over-the-counter (OTC) market, this anachronistic but still current expression applies to stocks traded on the New York Stock Exchange to distinguish them from stocks traded by Nasdaq market makers.

Load   Commission charge to buy or sell.

Locked market   A market in which the best price bid for a stock is exactly equal to the best offer or ask price.

Long   Referring to a position of ownership; for example, "I'm long Microsoft" means "I own Microsoft stock."

Margin   The amount of cash or collateral in a trader's account upon which credit is extended by the brokerage. Traders buying "on margin" put up only a portion (usually 50 percent) of the value of the stock they buy. They borrow the rest of the purchase price as a margin loan from the brokerage.

Margin Call   A notification that a trader has violated margin loan regulations, usually because the trader has bought more stock than legally allowed or because stock price declines have pushed the trader's equity below the legally mandated level.

Market Maker   One who buys and sells in response to orders from customers or clients. On the Nasdaq, a firm that uses its own capital to buy and maintain an inventory in a stock in order to sell when customers seek to buy and buy when customers seek to sell. Market makers must quote both bid and offer prices for every stock in which they are active.

Market Order   An order *at the market,* as distinguished from a *limit order* (which see).

218   **Momentum**   Price movement. Momentum traders buy stock because it is moving up and sell it because it is moving down, generally without analyzing the reasons behind the move.

Moving Average   A trend line calculated by taking the average of a stock price or index level over a specific period of time, usually the most recent 5, 30, 60, 90 or 120 days. The average "moves" because each passing day subtracts the oldest day's price and adds the newest to the series of addends.

Nasdaq
    (1) An electronic exchange listing approximately 5,400 stocks.
    (2) The composite index of these stocks. See *Index.*

National Best Bid and Offer   See *Inside Market.*

Offer   See *Ask.*

Open
    (1) The time at which stocks begin to trade.
    (2) To initiate a position in a stock.

OTC Market   Over-the-counter market. See *Listed.*

Overbought/Oversold   Describing a condition in which the stock or index price is too high or too low and therefore likely to move in the other direction; technical analytical terms. See *Technical.*

Play the Downside   To try to make money by selling stocks short.

Play Through   To buy stock at a price lower or sell at a price higher than the quotes on the *Inside Market* (which see).

Point   A dollar; as in "The stock moved up a full point." Synonym: *stick.*

Position Trader   One who enters stock positions with the intention of holding the position for several days and then exiting at a profit.

Preference   To send an order to a specific market maker or ECN.

Refresh   To decide to maintain a bid or offer quote. Applied to market makers.

Resistance   The presence of sellers at a given price, with the implication that the availability of supply at that price will prevent the stock from moving higher.

Running   Describes a stock whose price is going up fast. Synonym: *ripping*.

Saturation   The point at which demand and supply are equal; price equilibrium.

Short   To sell stock one does not own in expectation of a price decline. The trader sells borrowed shares and closes the position by purchasing new shares to make the lender whole again.

Short Squeeze   A sharp escalation in price intended to panic short sellers into closing their short positions. This phrase usually implies some degree of manipulation by parties with an interest in supporting the stock price or injuring the short-side traders.

SOES   Small Order Execution System, a Nasdaq electronic order routing and execution system that requires automatic execution by market makers at their advertised prices for orders of one thousand shares or less.

SOES Bandit   One who attempts to use the SOES to trade profitably; an *electronic day trader* (which see).

Speedometer   A specialized ticker set up by some traders as a guide to market momentum.

SPooze   The index of futures on the S&P 500. See *Index*.

Spread   The difference between the bid and the offer prices for any given stock. The profit margin for the market maker who buys and sells the stock.

Spread Cutting   Reducing the spread by offering at a slightly lower price and bidding at a slightly higher price.

Stay   To continue to display a bid or offer quote even after being executed against. Usually applied to market makers.

Stick   A dollar; a point. "It ran up two sticks" means the stock increased in price by two dollars per share.

Sucker Rally   A rise in prices that looks enough like the beginning of a solid upward trend to trap the unwary. See also *Bull Trap/Bear Trap*.

Support   The presence of buyers at a given price, with the implication that the demand at that price will prevent the stock from moving lower.

Take   To buy stock at the ask, or offer, price. Usually used in the phrase "took the offer."

Take Out   Of a stock, to move above the highest or drop below the lowest price at which it has traded, for example, "CSCO took out its high."

Technical   Involving or influenced by the analysis of stock price movements, as distinct from *fundamental* (which see).   **221**

Teeny   A sixteenth of a dollar, expressed as ¹⁄₁₆.

Tick   A movement in price. See also *Downtick* and *Uptick*.

Ticker   A monitor of stock price changes.

Uptick   An upward move in price.

Uptick Rule   Regulation that forbids traders from selling a stock short when its most recent price move has been downward.

Warrant   An option, usually issued for a period longer than a year, allowing the holder to buy or sell a stock at a specific price and time or at a series of prices and times specified in the warrant agreement. Favored by European day traders.

A Short List of Websites

The following list is intended not to be comprehensive, but to provide a basic set of links from which connections may be made to other links and resources. No recommendations pro or con are expressed or implied by inclusion or exclusion on this list. No brokerage Web pages are included, but several of the sites below do offer links to brokers.

Day Trader-U Online S&P Daytrading School
http://www.daytrader-u.com

Daytradingstocks
http://www.daytradingstocks.com

Electronic Traders Association
http://www.electronic-traders.org

National Association of Securities Dealers
http://www.nasd.com

North American Securities Administrators Association
http://www.nasaa.org

Public Investors Arbitration Bar Association
http://www.piaba.org

The Pristine Day Trader
http://www.pristine.com

The Rookie Day Trader
http://www.rookiedaytrader.com

Securities and Exchange Commission
http://www.sec.gov

Silicon Investor
http://www.techstocks.com

Acknowledgments

Thanks first to my wife, Martine, for constant encouragement, frequent advice, and unfailing patience, and to my children, who tolerated the absences that this project required, but complained enough to let me know that my presence matters. I am grateful to my agents, Glen Hartley and Lynn Chu, for their exemplary commitment and valuable counsel. Editor John Mahaney of Times Books recognized the potential in a short proposal, supported it in the competition for attention and resources, and demonstrated excellent editorial judgment when he received the completed manuscript, for all of which I am thankful. Ben Stanley and his colleagues in the reference department of the Plainfield, New Jersey, Public Library came through again and again, ferreting out urgently needed information, articles, and books, often on short notice or with only the sketchiest of hints about dates, names of authors, or titles—profuse thanks.

Many traders, brokers, academics, regulators, and software developers spent time with me in interviews and helped me develop a thorough understanding of the forces driving the growth of day **225** trading. They are too numerous to name here, and some spoke only on condition that they not be named. I am especially grateful to Harvey Houtkin of All-Tech Investment Group, Inc. and Marc Friedfertig of Broadway Trading, both of whom invited me to attend their training programs without seeking to impose any restrictions or limitations on what I might write; to James Lee, president of the Electronic Traders Association, and to his communications director, William Lauderback, who provided several helpful introductions and considerable background on the industry; to Bill Lupien, architect of Instinet and coinventor of Optimark, who made room in a very busy schedule for several hours of interviews about the development of the new electronic markets; to William Christie, Paul Schultz, and David Whitcomb, scholars all, who helped me see both the market forest and the econometric trees. Erik Tonley of The Northern Trust provided a rare view of the markets from behind the trading desk of a major money-management institution, and I appreciate his candor and his courage in speaking on the record. Stuart and MarrGwen Townsend graciously invited me to the headquarters of Townsend Analytic Systems in Chicago, and very generously answered my many questions about the development of day-trading technology. Josh Levine of Island never failed to respond in frank detail to my e-mail. Gerald Putnam of Archipelago; Christopher Doubek of Terra Nova; Holt Hackney, Communications Manager of CyBer-Corp; and Robin Dayne, a trading coach based in New Hampshire, all provided important information for which I am grateful. Neil Gibbons and Daniel Huber of First Quote; Hugo Assi, formerly of the Bank of Italy; Dr. Gerald Sandler of Berliner Effektenbank; and Robert Prior of Interactive Brokers helped me to get a sharp picture of the fast-breaking developments in Europe. Frank Hornig, a colleague in journalism, has kept *Der Spiegel* far ahead of the European pack with his excellent and timely articles about trading, and went a long way beyond the call of duty to share what he knew with me. State securities regulators, particularly Denise Crawford and Mike Gunst in Texas, Matt Nestor in Massachusetts, William Reilly in Florida, Doug Willburn in Missouri, and Phil Feigin, currently executive director of the North American Securities Administrators Association in Washington, gave me a new appreciation of the challenge of policing the borderless electronic market. The assistance of court clerks and file-room personnel in Dallas and Houston was invaluable—thank you. Finally, I would like to acknowledge my good friend William Falloon, and my brother, James Millman, whose hospitality in Chicago and in Houston, respectively, made traveling to those cities a pleasure I hope to enjoy again.

Notes

Chapter 1

3 *Harvey Houtkin sits:* Harvey Houtkin, interview by author, Montvale, NJ, 21 October 1998.

4 *The regulators were in bed:* See *Report Pursuant to Section 21(a) of the Securities Exchange Act of 1934 Regarding the NASD and the Nasdaq Market,* Securities Exchange Act of 1934 Release No. 34-37542, U.S. Securities and Exchange Commission, 8 August 1996.

4 *as he did for* Fortune *magazine:* Houtkin has this photo and article mounted on a plaque in his office. He has also claimed the "Bandit" title in his two books: *The SOES Bandits' Guide: Day Trading in the 21st Century* (privately published by Houtkin in 1995) and *Secrets of the SOES Bandit* (New York: McGraw-Hill, 1999).

4 *He's the reason why thousands:* Houtkin's paternity of SOES Bandit day trading is undisputed. See, for example, the story by David Barboza, "Golden Boy," in *The New York Times,* 10 May

1998, sec. 3, p. 1, which in discussing SOES says, "Harvey J. Houtkin, the founder of the All-Tech Investment Group in Montvale, N.J., found a way to exploit this system."

5 *owe their existence to Harvey's victories:* This is true most especially of the 1993 Timpinaro case. See John A. Byrne, "The Power and the Politics of SOES," *Traders Magazine,* April 1997, p. 36, for a discussion of the importance of this case to the day-trading industry.

7 *Harvey modestly claims:* Houtkin, interview, 21 October 1998.

8 *impossible to get trades executed on the Nasdaq:* This was widely reported. For authoritative confirmation, see SEC, *Report Pursuant to Section 21(a),* Appendix, pp. 68–69.

9 *scandalous culture of collusion:* See SEC, *Report Pursuant to Section 21(a).*

10 *In September 1998:* Descriptions of people and events at Broadway Trading are based on the author's several visits to the firm during August and September 1998, interviews with co-founders Marc Friedfertig and George West, interviews with employees, interviews with traders, and attendance at sessions of training seminars. All interviewees were advised that the author was a journalist working on a book about day trading. All interviews were on the record. However, as a courtesy to interviewees, most are referred to only by their first names, except those who have already been widely publicized, such as Friedfertig, West, and Serge Milman, the subject of an April 1998 cover story in *Forbes.*

10 *a band of waterfront hustlers:* Marshall E. Blume, Jeremy J. Siegel, and Dan Rottenberg, *Revolution on Wall Street: The Rise and Decline of the New York Stock Exchange* (New York: W. W. Norton, 1993) pp. 21–24.

13 *many old rules no longer apply:* Traders accustomed to historical price levels were baffled by stock prices in the late 1990s. **229**

13 *Milman became the pinup boy:* For background on Serge Milman, including his birth in Russia, fondness for video games, and turndowns by Wall Street banks and brokerage houses, see Matthew Schifrin and Scott McCormack, "Free Enterprise Comes to Wall Street," *Forbes,* 6 April 1998, p. 114.

14 *It took extraordinary measures to make a trader out of Noah:* Noah, interview by author, 15 September 1998.

15 *Jay is Marc Friedfertig's brother-in-law:* Background on Jay comes from several interviews with Marc Friedfertig and Jay conducted by the author during August and September of 1998.

15 *a relationship to which he owes his presence in the firm:* interview, Marc Friedfertig, 14 August 1998.

15 *puckish online pranks:* Jay, answering a question in a training seminar session, 14 September 1998.

15 *Jay entertains an elevator full of students:* Witnessed by the author, 14 September 1998.

16 *"It's addictive. . . . two.":* Jay, answering a question in a training seminar session, 14 September 1998.

17 *Later, Marc Friedfertig comes into the room:* Witnessed by author, 14 September 1998.

17 *even Serge had done badly:* Comment by Marc Friedfertig in a training session, 14 September 1998.

19 *The VWAP:* For more detail, see Marc Friedfertig and George West, *The Electronic Day Trader* (New York: McGraw-Hill, 1998) p. 117.

20 *Serge Milman and his buddy Landon:* Witnessed by the author, 15 September 1998.

21 *His roommate:* Information on Landon's background was provided by Mara Kustra in an interview conducted by the author, 14 September 1998.

22 *Greg D. took the introductory course:* Greg D. spoke to the author in several interviews conducted in person during August and September 1998 and by phone in October 1998. The interviews were on the record, and he did not request that his identity be masked, but since he spoke frankly, this author uses his first name only, as a courtesy.

27 *A race car driver:* The account of this suicide is based on the author's interviews with Marc Friedfertig, Robin Dayne (a trading coach formerly affiliated with Broadway Trading), and Greg D. The interviews were conducted in August, September, and October 1998.

27 *After that happened:* Marc Friedfertig and Dr. Frederic Wolverton both gave the same account of the beginning of their relationship.

27 *Why a specialist in addictions?* Dr. Frederic Wolverton, interview by the author, 9 October 1998.

30 *They call him "Dr. Mark" here:* Dr. Mark was interviewed several times, on the record, in August and September 1998. He did not request that his identity be masked. But since he spoke frankly about personal matters, this author uses his first name only, as a courtesy. His trading record was confirmed by Marc Friedfertig in interviews conducted in August and September 1998; the fact that he was a patient of Dr. Wolverton's was confirmed by the doctor in an interview.

33 *former manager of a Harley-Davidson dealership:* Andrew Lias, interview by the author, 21 October 1998.

33 *A self-test for trading aptitude:* See Harvey Houtkin, *Secrets of the SOES Bandit* (New York: McGraw-Hill, 1999) p. 35.

33 *He was a waiter:* Marc Friedfertig and Greg D., interviews by the author, August and September 1998.

34 *But market regulators worry:* Phil Feigin, executive director **231**

of the North American Securities Administrators Association, interview by the author, 23 October 1998.

34   *the flamboyant founders of Block Trading:* See Steve Fishman, "Brokers Wild," *Details,* October 1997, and Edward Welles, "Bad Boys of Wall St.," *Inc.,* January 1997. Reprints of these articles were sent to the author by Block Trading.

34   *cold-calling stock pushers:* See Jenalia Moreno, "For Those Who Want to Be Players," *Houston Chronicle,* 18 October 1998, sec. C, p. 1.

34   *several hundred phone numbers:* The work habits of Chris Block and Jeff Burke, including push-ups and dancing on desktops, were reported by Steve Fishman in *Details,* cited above.

34   *One day, Harvey Houtkin's name turned up on the cold-call list:* Reported in articles in the *Houston Chronicle, Details, Inc.,* all cited above. Confirmed by Houtkin, in an interview with this author, 21 October 1998.

35   *they allied themselves with the little guy:* Publicity flyer, Block Trading.

36   *Marc Friedfertig, cofounder of New York's Broadway Trading, had exulted in print:* See Friedfertig and West, *The Electronic Day Trader,* op. cit., pp. 4–6.

36   *In fact, he strongly recommended:* Ibid. The recommendation also appears on a list of recommended reading given to candidates for the training seminar and is reinforced by George West in the Broadway Trading videotape "Interviews with Successful Traders."

Chapter 2

39   *talked articulately to a good reporter:* Edwin LeFèvre's *Reminiscences of a Stock Operator* (New York: John Wiley, 1994) was first published as a series of articles in *The Saturday Evening Post* during the early 1920s.

41 *the market cataclysm that forced President Teddy "the Trust Buster" Roosevelt to ask:* See Robert Sobel, *Panic on Wall Street* (New York: Truman Talley Books, 1988), pp. 297–322.

41 *"which he watched . . . statisticians":* "Jesse Livermore Ends Life in Hotel," *New York Times*, 29 November 1940, p. 22.

42 *Most got their taste of market action in these quasi brokerages:* See Ann Fabian, *Card Sharps, Dream Books & Bucket Shops: Gambling in 19th Century America* (Ithaca: Cornell Univ. Press, 1990), pp. 188–200.

43 *The first time his name appeared in the papers:* See "Jesse Livermore Ends Life in Hotel," p. 1.

44 *In 1906, on vacation in Atlantic City:* LeFèvre, *Reminiscences*, p. 73.

45 *While he was fishing:* For this account and the ensuing story of Livermore's Anaconda coup, LeFèvre, *Reminiscences*, pp. 103–109.

46 *"It sounds very easy . . . human nature.":* Ibid., p. 124.

46 *In 1908, he lost almost a million dollars:* The summary of Livermore's career ups and downs and the account of his suicide draws on "Jesse Livermore Ends Life in Hotel," op. cit.

47 *"For my services . . . sustained life.":* LeFèvre, *Reminiscences*, p. 173.

47 *On November 28, 1940:* See "Jesse Livermore Ends Life in Hotel."

Chapter 3

49 *Bill Lupien, a specialist:* Information about Lupien's career comes from the author's interviews conducted with Lupien at Optimark's offices in New York on 5 November 1998 and 12 November 1998.

51 *Instinet's inventor:* Lupien, interviews, 1998.

56 *When, in 1991, two young college professors:* William Christie, interview by author, 20 January 1999, and Paul Schultz, interview by author, 1 June 1999.

57 *it doesn't really matter whether corporations raise capital by issuing stock or by borrowing:* See quote from Miller in Peter L. Bernstein, *Capital Ideas: The Improbable Origins of Modern Wall Street* (New York: Free Press, 1992), p. 178. Bernstein's discussion of the theory is one of the most accessible to the financial nonprofessional.

58 *They decided to start their collaboration:* Christie and Schultz, interviews, 1999.

60 *The Paltrow article:* Scott J. Paltrow, "Study Suggests Collusion among Brokerage Firms," *Los Angeles Times,* 26 May 1994, p. D1.

61 *In October, a spokesman for the Justice Department:* Jeffrey Taylor and Warren Getler, "U.S. Examines Alleged Price Fixing on Nasdaq," *Wall Street Journal,* 20 October 1994, p. C1.

61 *in November, the SEC launched:* Richard S. Taylor and Warren Getler, "Nasdaq Dealers Are Being Investigated in a Separate Probe Launched by SEC," *Wall Street Journal,* 15 November 1994, p. A4.

61 *Apparently, they had a little trouble:* Warren Getler and William Power, "Street Insiders Set to Review Nasdaq Market," *Wall Street Journal,* 21 November 1994, p. C1.

61 *they hired Merton Miller:* Molly Baker, "Nasdaq Fights Back on Pricing Allegations," *Wall Street Journal,* 6 April 1995, p. C1.

62 *"It is . . . happens spontaneously.":* Ibid.

62 *the Justice Department stumbled on another cluster:* Deborah Lohse, "NASD Knew of Trading Spread Issue As Early As 1990, U.S. Documents Say," *Wall Street Journal,* 19 July 1996, p. C1.

62 *And the SEC found a cluster of tapes:* Jeffrey Taylor and Deborah Lohse, "SEC Report on Nasdaq Is Full of Tough Talk," *Wall Street Journal,* 9 August 1996, p. C1.

62 *market makers cut in half the spreads:* William G. Christie, Jeffrey H. Harris, and Paul H. Schultz, "Why Did Market Makers Stop Avoiding Odd-Eighth Quotes?" *The Journal of Finance,* vol. 69, no. 5 (December 1994) p. 1841.

62 *Thanks to Instinet:* See ibid. See also Michael Schroeder, "Leveling Nasdaq's Playing Field," *Business Week,* 2 September 1996, p. 70: "With new electronic markets such as Instinet Corp., owned by Reuters Holdings PLC, the ability of brokers to strike favorable deals at prices better than the spread has become prevalent."

63 *The SEC decided to treat the Nasdaq's disorder:* Ibid. Schroeder. See also Anita Raghavan, and Jeffrey Taylor, "Will NASD Accord Transform Nasdaq Market?" *Wall Street Journal,* 28 August 1996, p. C1, and SEC, *Report Pursuant to Section 21(a),* op. cit.

63 *of which lawyers for the plaintiffs got:* Diana B. Henriques, "Lawyers Are Awarded $144 Million from Class Action Stock Suit," *New York Times,* 10 November 1998, p. C1.

Chapter 4

65 *investigators from the Manhattan district attorney's office and the Securities and Exchange Commission had dug deep:* David Barboza, "Golden Boy? He's Dazzled Wall Street, but the Ghosts of His Company May Haunt His Future," *New York Times,* 10 May 1998, sec. 3, p. 1. See also David Barboza, "Some Clouds Dim a Star of On-Line Trading," *New York Times,* 10 July 1998, first business page.

65 *"Under him, Datek . . . industry,":* Ibid. "Golden Boy." Harvey Houtkin voiced similar sentiments about Maschler in an interview with the author, 21 October 1998.

65 *People still talk about the press conference:* Professor David Whitcomb, interview by the author, 19 October 1998. Also see Barboza, "Golden Boy?" op. cit.

65 *Maschler kept company with Robert Brennan:* Barboza, "Golden Boy?" op. cit.

65 *a record wide enough to embrace both stock fraud and drug dealing:* Ibid.

65 *Before he was twenty, Jeffrey would be a millionaire:* Ibid. See also Matthew Schifrin and Scott McCormack, "Free Enterprise Comes to Wall Street," *Forbes,* 6 April 1998, p. 114.

65–66 *A lot of the credit for that sudden prosperity goes to a high school dropout named Joshua Levine:* Levine outlined in detail in e-mail correspondence with the author the genesis of Island. Parts of the story were also told in David Barboza's "Golden Boy?" article and in Schifrin and McCormack's "Free Enterprise Comes to Wall Street" article cited above.

66 *He split the wires:* Barboza, "Golden Boy," op cit.

66 *The Monster Key:* Schifrin and McCormack, "Free Enterprise," op. cit.

66 *He modestly deflects credit:* E-mail correspondence between Joshua Levine and the author. All direct quotes from Joshua Levine come from that correspondence.

67 *Instinet had pulled its terminals:* Houtkin, interview, 21 October 1998, and comments by instructors in the All-Tech training program in October–November 1998.

67 *"They sent two . . . and left.":* E-mail correspondence from Joshua Levine to author.

68 *David Whitcomb, professor of finance:* Whitcomb, interview, 19 October 1998.

69 *"Propelled by . . . in the world,":* See Bill Burnham, *Online Trading Quarterly, 4th Quarter 1998,* 28 January 1999, pp. 4–5.

69 *An initial public offering:* David Barboza, "Some Clouds Dim a Star of On-Line Trading," op. cit.

69 *Although it was only:* See Bill Burnham, *Online Trading Quarterly,* op cit., and see also Gretchen Morgenson, "Sailing into Murky Waters," *New York Times,* 28 February 1999, sec. 3, p. 1.

70 *One February afternoon:* The author visited the offices of Townsend Analytic Systems, Archipelago, and Terra Nova for two days, 11–12 February 1999.

70 *a team from Zion Bank:* Charlie McQuinn, interview by the author, 12 February 1999, and follow-up on 19 March 1999.

Chapter 5

75 *A dark green Lexus:* Telephone interviews with Hugo Assi were conducted by the author on 18 and 22 February 1999 and supplemented with e-mail correspondence.

78 *In Berlin, Dr. Guido Sandler:* Telephone interview with Dr. Guido Sandler conducted by the author, 17 March 1999. Sandler is the German equivalent of president and CEO of Berliner Effekten-bank AG, the investment banking (corporate finance and private banking) member firm (40 percent holding) within the Berliner Freiverkehr (Aktien) AG group. The group planned a name change to Berliner Effektengesellschaft AG in June 1999. Sandler was also a board member of Berliner Freiverkehr (Aktien) AG.

78 *A costly mistake:* Sandler, interview, 17 March 1999. Account of traders arbitraging the Xetra system was confirmed by Frank Hartmann, press officer of the Deutsche Börse in Frankfurt, on 17 May 1999, who said that Xetra may have started with eight hundred listings, but carried two thousand at the time the arbitrage took place. "The arbitrage took place at the end of last year and the beginning of this year," Hartmann elaborated, "due to the fact that there was more liquidity in the traditional floor trading on the eight local exchanges."

82 *First Quote, a venture:* Information about First Quote sourced from the author's several interviews with Neil Gibbons, president and CEO, and Daniel Huber, vice president and COO, of Virtual Telecom, supplemented by e-mail correspondence from Gibbons.

84 *a German entrepreneur opened a day-trading room:* See Frank Hornig, "Töbende Dummköpfe," *Der Spiegel,* August 1999, p. 102.

84 *Interactive Brokers, a member of:* Robert Prior, interview by the author, 30 April 1999, and a visit to www.interactivebrokers .com.

85 *the Nasdaq was likely to extend trading hours:* Greg Ip and Bill Spindle, "Nasdaq Plans to Set Up a New Stock Market in Japan; Softbank to Invest in Proposed Project," *Wall Street Journal,* 16 June 1999, p. A19.

Chapter 6

86 *the story of a little, Chicago-based husband-and-wife software shop:* MarrGwen and Stuart Townsend, interviews by the author, 11 and 12 February 1999.

92 *One evening, over dinner:* Gerald Putnam, interview by the author, 11 February 1999. Putnam's account was confirmed by Stuart and MarrGwen Townsend in separate interviews, 11 and 12 February 1999. See also Morgenson, "Sailing into Murky Waters," op. cit.

95 *Christopher Doubek, who had managed:* Christopher Doubek, interview by the author, 12 February 1999.

97 *Called Bloomberg TradeBook:* Kevin Foley, manager of Bloomberg TradeBook initiative, interview by author, 5 February 1999. Supplemented with publicity and promotional materials provided by Bloomberg's corporate communications staff.

99 *Said E*Trade spokesman Lisa Nash:* Lisa Nash, interview by the author, 4 March 1999.

Chapter 7

101 *Erik Tonley, vice president and senior equity trader of the Northern Trust Company:* Erik Tonley was interviewed by the author by telephone on several occasions in January and February 1999 and in his office in Chicago on 12 February 1999.

107 *And according to one database:* Clemons and Weber wrote that "66% of the orders for stocks in one U.S. database are greater than 50% of average daily trading volume in those stocks, suggesting that order flow has become extremely lumpy." Eric K. Clemons and Bruce W. Weber, "Restructuring Institutional Block Trading: An Overview of the Optimark System," Proceedings, HICSS-31, vol. 6, Hawaiian International Conference on Systems Science, January 1998, p. 301. Contact clemons@wharton.upenn.edu or bweber@stern.nyu.edu for more information about this paper.

108 *After selling his stock in Instinet:* Bill Lupien, interviews by the author, 5 and 12 November 1998.

108 *"After giving . . . price and size?":* "Optimark: Launching a Virtual Securities Market," Harvard Business School, Case no. 9-399-005, p. 9.

110 *among the first brokers to sign up for access to Optimark's liquidity:* Bill Lupien, interview, 12 November 1998.

Chapter 8

113–153 The author attended phases one, two, and three of the training program at All-Tech Investment Group's Montvale, New Jersey, headquarters in October and November 1998 at the invitation of Harvey Houtkin. All-Tech's general counsel, Linda Lerner, and president, Mark Shefts, also met with the author prior to his participation in the program and reinforced Houtkin's invitation. At no time did anyone request any agreement or commitment of any sort by the author to any restriction, limit, or prior review of anything he might observe or write. The author advised the instructors and all fellow students that he was attending the pro- **239**

gram in the capacity of a journalist working on a book about day trading and would be writing about what he saw and heard. He took notes and used a tape recorder in class. He also interviewed students and faculty members outside of class hours. Although the entire training program was therefore on the record for journalistic purposes, the author has used first names only, as a courtesy to students and instructors in the class sessions who might prefer to maintain a low public profile.

Chapter 9

158   *the case of Kevin Burke against Dr. Gene Burke:* Kevin and Kristi Burke v. Gene Burke, No. DV98-534-D, in the District Court of Dallas County, Texas, 95th Judicial District.

158   *Kevin Burke had another lawsuit in the works:* Kevin M. Burke, Plaintiff, v. Russell Grigsby, Ed Naylor, Kira Stadele, David Burch, and David Jamail, Defendants, No. 97-11397-G, in the District Court of Dallas County, Texas, 134th Judicial District.

158   Inc. *magazine and even made the pages of* Details: See note 34, above.

158   *Dr. Gene Burke was nowhere near as high-profile as his famous son:* In Kevin and Kristi Burke v. Gene Burke, No. DV98-534-D, see Oral Deposition of Dr. Gene Burke; Affidavit of Kevin Burke; Plaintiff's Motion for Summary Judgment; Defendant Gene Burke's Response to Plaintiff's Motion for Summary Judgment and Defendant's Motion for Leave; and Final Judgment and Order on Summary Judgment.

159   *According to Massachusetts state securities regulators:* In Docket No. R-98-53, Notice of Adjudicatory Proceeding.

159   *Texas Regulators say:* Denise Voigt Crawford, interviews by the author, 8 and 13 April 1999.

159   *When he received his daily fax from Block:* See Oral Deposition of Dr. Gene Burke, and Plaintiff's Motion for Summary Judgment in Case No. DV98-534-D cited above.

160 *"By doing business this way . . . loan sharking.":* Kevin and Kristi Burke v. Gene Burke, No. DV98-534-D, op. cit., Plaintiff's Motion for Summary Judgment, p. 11.

160 *He traded so heavily that:* Kevin M. Burke v. Russell Grigsby et al., No. 97-11397-G, op. cit. See Affidavit of Kevin Burke, p. 7.

161 *Burke blames his lack of success at trading on everything but a lack of skill:* Ibid., pp. 2–3, 6.

161 *Relatively more successful traders helped relatively less successful traders with margin loans:* The source for this description of margin lending practices at Cornerstone is from the file of No. 97-11397-G, op. cit., especially Plaintiff's First Amended Original Petition; Plaintiff's Motion for Summary Judgment; Defendants Burch, Jamail, and Grigsby's Response to Plaintiff's Motion for Summary Judgment; Affidavit of Russell Grigsby; and In The Court of Appeals Fifth District of Texas at Dallas, No. 05-98-01236-CV In Re Kevin Burke, Relator Motion for Rehearing.

162 *Among the attorneys of record on Hamilton's motion for summary judgment appears the name of John A. Lee:* Case No. 97-11397-G, Plaintiff's Motion for Summary Judgment, Certificate of Service, states that

> a true and correct copy of the foregoing was forwarded to all attorneys of record herein. . . . The item was addressed as follows:

> Andrews & Kurth
> John A. Lee, James L. Truitt, Rocky Robinson
> 1717 Main Street
> Suite 3700
> Dallas, TX 75201
> (214) 659-4401

162 *John Lee is the lead attorney for Momentum Securities in another lawsuit against Cornerstone:* Momentum Securities, Inc., Momentum Securities Management Co., Momentum Securities Partners, L.P., and CSLNET, Incl, Plaintiffs v. Cornerstone Se- **241**

curities Corporation; Cornerstone Houston, L.P.; Cornerstone Securities Management, L.L.C.; Cornerstone Securities Holdings, L.L.C.; Cornerstone Securities Partners, L.P.; Lithos Investments, L.L.C.; ABBDM Gropu, L.L.P.; Bid/Ask Investments, Inc.; David R. Burch, Individually; Russell A. Grigsby, Individually; David G. Jamail, Individually; Andrew S. Kershner, Individually; Luis G. Gonzalez, Individually; Richard A. Engle, Individually; Ken Johnson, Individually; Currin Van Eman, Individually; Mike Arnold, Individually; and Julian DeAyala, Individually, Case No. 98-05914, in the District Court of Harris County, Texas, 234th Judicial District.

162 *He's also the brother of James H. Lee:* Relationship and role in suit confirmed by James H. Lee in a telephone interview with the author, 27 April 1999.

162 *James H. Lee got to know the day-trading business by backing a trader:* James H. Lee, interview with the author, 27 April 1999.

162 *This was Extreme Investing indeed:* Case No. 98-05914, op. cit. Second Amended Petition pp. 7–8 provided the description of the business and Momentum's commission earnings.

163 *James Lee located his headquarters in the posh Galleria district of Houston:* The author visited Momentum's headquarters and trading room on 14 April 1999 at the invitation of James H. Lee, who unaccountably did not keep the appointment, though he was in the office at the same time as the author. A public relations spokesman met with the author and declined to discuss the litigation.

164 *According to court records, at least some customers used to make quite bit of money trading here:* Case No. 98-05914, op. cit., Plaintiff's Second Amended Petition, p. 12.

164 *"clandestine" meetings with Cornerstone:* Ibid.

164–165 *"What happened next . . . leave Momentum.":* Ibid., p. 13.

165 *The attorney for Cornerstone and the traders being sued responded:* In Case No. 98-05914, op. cit., see Defendants' Original Answer, p. 2, for the source for the information and quote in this paragraph.

165 *"With the push of a button . . . source of the trade, ":* Ibid., p. 4.

165 *when James Lee of Momentum apparently managed to develop a "mole":* In Case No. 98-05914, op. cit., see Original Application to Court Orders Ancillary to Arbitration Proceedings, para. 10, p. 6. This document indicates that the word "mole" was first used by an attorney for Momentum.

165–166 *According to documents filed in court records of yet another suit:* Cornerstone Securities Corporation, Plaintiff, v. Susan Harrison, Defendant, Case No. 98-57473 in the District Court of Harris County, Texas, 61st Judicial District, see Plaintiff's Original Petition. See also Before the National Association of Securities Dealers, Inc., Cornerstone Securities Corporation, Claimant v. Momentum Securities Inc., James H. Lee, Jack E. Earnest, Jr., and Keith Sultemeier, Respondents, Consolidated No. 98-00848, which quotes from testimony given in a deposition by James H. Lee.

166 *Momentum's attorneys wrote the following:* Quote from Case No. 98-05914, op. cit., Plaintiffs' Second Amended Petition, para. 45, p. 14.

167 *When a visitor reads that passage to Texas securities commissioner Denise Voigt Crawford:* The author read that passage to the commissioner on 8 April 1999.

Chapter 10

168–170 *Denise Voigt Crawford is:* Background on and all quotes attributed to Crawford come from interviews conducted by the author on 8 and 13 April 1999, at her office in Austin, Texas.

171–173 *In May 1998, the Texas Securities Board shut down:* Information about Infinitum drawn from State Office of Administrative Hearings, Shelia Bailey Taylor, chief administrative law judge, 4 May 1998 Proposal for Decision, Re: Docket No. 312-97-0760; Infinitum Capital Management Inc. (Infinitum Capital), Juan Carlos Nieto (Nieto), Juan Carlos Nieto dba Infinitum, Infinitum Management Company, Inc. (IMC), Infinitum Management Inc., Kelly Buck, Roberto Moral Garcia, Marcus Kallman, David Knoll, Scott McGuirt, Ann Quioga, Thomas Roy, Roger Kim Speir.

172 *Instead, Infinitum was shut down:* The State of Texas State Securities Board, SOAH Docket No. 312-97-0760 (SSB Docket No. 97-011) Order No. CDO/FIN-1329, Order to Cease and Desist and Assessing Administrative Fines.

173 *a checklist of salesmanship tips given to employees of Harvey Houtkin's All-Tech:* The checklist is Exhibit B in The Commonwealth of Massachusetts Secretary of the Commonwealth Securities Division Docket No. R-98-77 in the Matter of All-Tech Investment Group, Inc., Mark D. Shefts, Harvey I. Houtkin, Fred A. Zayas, Isaac Belbel, John Powell, Respondents.

173 *Fred Sharp, a Maytag man:* Sharp's complaint before the National Association of Securities Dealers provides the details, some of which were previously reported by *The Wall Street Journal.* See Rebecca Buckman and Aaron Luchetti, "Day Trading Faces Rivalry and Increasing Scrutiny," *Wall Street Journal,* 8 October 1998, p. C1.

173 *Brenda Richardson, a single mother in her fifties:* See Ianthe Jeanne Dugan, "In Bull Market, the Urge to Gamble Is Rising," *Washington Post,* 2 February 1999, p. A01. See also National Association of Securities Dealers, Inc., Division of Arbitration, Case No. 98-02900, Brenda S. Richardson and Erica R. Richardson, Claimants v. Gro Corporation, Go Trading, Inc., Pension Financial Services, Inc., Huan Cao, Hahna Global Securities Trading, Tae Goo Moon, Hahna Global Capital Management, Inc., and Prov-

idential Securities, Inc., Respondents, Second Amended Statement of Claim. On 17 March 1999 the author also interviewed, not
for attribution, a party familiar with details of the case.

174 *"aggressively seeking to date her, making direct propositions of an intimate relationship,":* Original Statement of Claim
before the National Association of Securities Dealers, Inc., Arbitration Division, given to the author with agreement that the identity
of the claimant would not be revealed.

174 *An attorney who specializes:* Interview by the author, not
for attribution, 16 March 1999.

Conclusion

177 The quote from Phil Feigin of the North American Securities
Administrators Association comes from an interview conducted by
the author at NASAA's offices in Washington on 23 October 1998.

177 *whether any of All-Tech's customers:* See The Commonwealth of Massachusetts Office of the Secretary of the Commonwealth Securities Division, Docket No. R-98-77, "Stipulated Order"
dated 3 May 1999 and "Offer of Settlement" dated 3 May 1999.
Supplemented by author's interview with source in Division, 5 July
1999.

178 *"bandits do not have . . . Nasdaq market maker":* Jeffrey
H. Harris and Paul H. Schultz, "The trading profits of SOES bandits," *Journal of Financial Economics* 50 (1998), p. 61.

Extreme Investor's Manual

183 *the Electronic Traders Association posted on its website:*
See http://www.electronic-traders.org for form.

208–209 *Mark Maddox, president of the Public Investors Arbitration Bar Association (PIABA):* All comments by Maddox
sourced in an interview conducted by the author, 27 April 1999.

Index

About the Author

GREGORY J. MILLMAN has written for many publications, including *Fortune, Forbes, Worth, The Wall Street Journal,* and *The Washington Post.* His previous book, *The Vandal's Crown: How Rebel Currency Traders Overthrew the World's Central Banks,* was a *Business Week* bestseller and has been translated into nine languages.